THE PRACTICE OF
PUBLIC RELATIONS

the practice of
public relations

L. ROY BLUMENTHAL

the macmillan company, new york

collier-macmillan limited, london

The Macmillan Company
866 Third Avenue, New York, New York 10022

Collier-Macmillan Canada, Ltd.,
Toronto, Ontario

Library of Congress catalog card number: 70-161430

Printing   Year

1 2 3 4 5 6 7 8   2 3 4 5 6 7 8

*I dedicate this book to my father,
who taught me how and when to laugh.*

foreword:
fifty years to perfection

The last fifty years have witnessed almost incredible advances in medicine and science. Matching these great leaps forward has been the development in fields of communications. Radio is no longer a crystal set with earphones. It has hundreds of millions of outlets in homes, factories and automobiles throughout the world. Television, only dreamed of fifty years ago, is in the world's castles, apartments, shanties and even the mud huts in the African Congo. With this instant communication of ideas, events, products and services the role of public relations and advertising has grown from that of peddler to professional.

Today it is a very dull president of a corporation who does not give first priority to presenting his services, products and even himself to the vast public by way of professionals in communications. The good product truthfully presented by the professionals will outsell the good product that ignores public relations. The developing new nation that wisely uses professional public relations guidance will be on the best path to economic, political and cultural advancements. Political leaders, as well as governments of nations advanced or not so advanced, must, to succeed, tell their stories truthfully and hopefully to the millions of great and humble peoples of the world.

Roy Blumenthal describes the many areas of public relations with a thoroughness and humor that make good study and unforgettable understanding. With this book, an authoritative text for college students and an articulate guide for executives, he has performed a great public service.

The late Secretary of State Dean Acheson named his latest book on the development of American foreign policy "Present at the Creation." Roy Blumenthal can claim his presence at the creation of modern public relations. For thirty-five years he has played a leading part in making communication the success that it is today.

foreword

Today, as president and chief executive officer of Roy Blumenthal International Associates, Inc., he guides the public relations of the West German Government.

Frank L. Howley, Brig. Gen., Ret.

Former Vice Chancellor of
New York University

Public relations is a recent arrival on the academic scene, following a meteoric expansion of its use in the complicated organization of our community. Its boundaries are still nebulous, and are likely to remain so for several generations to come.

For the last forty years I have been actively engaged in the practice of public relations, with a record of having been retained by more than 200 clients—corporate, institutional and governmental. During this time I have guided more than a hundred young apprentices through their formative period. Often I wished for a text that I might place in their hands which would be interesting enough to hold their attention through the rudiments of the work out of which they had to mold a career. The book would at one time have to combine theory, practice and a sense of utility to the community without being pedantic or unnecessarily technical, and reflect a lifetime that the author found exciting.

I also thought that the text should contain an introduction to, and an exploration of, each of the principal areas in which a public relations firm might be engaged in the normal pursuit of its business. These are included in the first seven chapters of the present volume, and in each case I have sought to make the student, or embryo practitioner, sufficiently familiar with the problems most likely to be met, and the tools with which to approach them to be professionally effective.

Because there are twilight zones in which all of these areas meet, I have also attempted a clinical approach addressed to the general subject of communications so that the young practitioner might at least be equipped with a compass as he verges on the maze of Madison Avenue. If I may labor a metaphor, the sextant is only acquired by years of experience.

I hope I will be forgiven for the few personal anecdotes that I have included. If I could have thought of anything that would make the points clearer, I would have used other means, but in each case I found the anecdote more suitable than the expounding of ivory-towered theory. They are true stories, but very well disguised.

The text will, I feel, stir a student's imagination or open a new perspective to the person already engaged in public relations. This wish prompted the writing of the book and in writing it I discovered, as most others do, a new dimension in myself—that I had always had a subconscious desire to teach.

Because public relations is a comparatively new but lusty part of our way of life, it will continue to demand an ever-growing academic facility. Eventually I believe there will be graduate schools in important universities entirely devoted to the teaching of communications in all its various areas. Major among these will be public relations.

L. R. B.

acknowledgments

It is with deep gratitude that I acknowledge the invaluable aid given to me by Professor Otto Lerbinger, Chairman, Division of Public Relations, School of Public Communication at Boston University, whose counsel adjusted my perspective to academic priorities.

I am also grateful to Dr. Franz Pick, world's foremost currency authority, whose guidance on matters of international trade was invaluable to me in the writing of the financial and commercial chapters.

contents

Foreword: Fifty Years to Perfection by Frank L. Howley   vii

Preface   ix

1   INTRODUCTION TO THE PRACTICE OF PUBLIC RELATIONS   1

Defining public relations   1
Growth of communications systems   1
Functions of public relations campaigns   2
Public relations-advertising relationship   3
Exercises   4
Suggested supplemental reading   5

2   ROLE OF THE PRACTITIONER   7

The newspaper medium   7
Press appraisal   8
Satisfying editorial requirements   17
Elements of release writing   19
Structure of feature articles   20
Placing a story   20
Press conferences and parties   21
News syndicates   22
Magazines   23
Trade press   24
Radio and television   25
Choosing your media   26
Exercises   26
Suggested supplemental reading   27

contents

3 FINANCIAL AND INDUSTRIAL PUBLIC RELATIONS 29

What is financial public relations? 29
Publicizing a new issue 31
The corporate financial personality 33
Interim and annual reports 34
Stockholders' meetings 37
Corporate industrial personality 38
Establishment of corporate character 38
Management-labor friction 39
Industrial films 40
Exercises 41
Suggested supplemental reading 42

4 COMMERCIAL PUBLIC RELATIONS 45

Defining commercial public relations 45
Publicizing a product 45
Introducing a new product 49
Sales conventions 50
Utility and service companies 51
Bank and insurance companies 53
Real estate publicity 55
Tourism 56
Fashion 59
Exercises 61
Suggested supplemental reading 62

5 INSTITUTIONAL PUBLIC RELATIONS 65

Funds for health, welfare and education 65
Corporate donors 68
The role of foundations 70
The individual donor 71
Mass fund-raising drives 73
Exercises 78
Suggested supplemental reading 79

6 GOVERNMENTAL PUBLIC RELATIONS 81

Information versus propaganda 81
Public relations for foreign tourism 82

Foreign Agents Registration Act   85
Techniques of foreign information programs   86
Supervising visiting dignitaries from foreign governments   89
Requisite publications   91
Radio and television publicity   93
Exercises   93
Suggested supplemental reading   94

7   IMPACT OF TELEVISION ON PUBLIC RELATIONS PRACTICE   95

The power of the medium   95
Function of television networks   97
Television's role in politics   97
Human credulity   101
Exercises   104
Suggested supplemental reading   104

8   THE ART OF GETTING, HOLDING AND LOSING CLIENTS   105

Who needs public relations   105
Pinpointing the problem   105
Necessary objectivity   106
Proper presentation   108
A case in point   110
Staffing the account   113
Exporting public relations   114
Exercises   117
Suggested supplemental reading   117

9   ETHICS OF PUBLIC RELATIONS   119

The concept of the "Image"   119
Practitioner's responsibility for client claims   120
Evaluating a prospective client   122
Public relations and lobbying   123
Formula for fees   124
Client-practitioner relationship   125
The practitioner image   126
Exercises   128
Suggested supplemental reading   128

contents

APPENDIXES   129

    A: Case Exercises   131

    B: An Annual Report   181

    C: News for Release (Introducing a New Product)   187

    D: Public Relations Program for German Wines in the United States   193

    E: A Public Relations Program for an Appliance Corporation 199

    F: Department of Justice "Foreign Agents Registration Act of 1938 as Amended"   209

    G: Prospectus for a Foreign Tourism Account   219

    H: Securities and Exchange Commission Statement of Policy   241

INDEX   271

"Oh wad some power the giftie gie us
To see oursels as others see us!"

Robert Burns

introduction to the practice of public relations

DEFINING PUBLIC RELATIONS

No matter how primitively, nor on what level of sophistication, every human being practices some form of public relations from the moment he becomes conscious of other people appraising his personality assets and liabilities.

The art of building one's own personality up to a level where one is able to meet and deal with the exigencies of everyday living falls into the realm of psychology. The art of performing the same task for businesses, institutions, governments and all manner of other profit and nonprofit groupings is public relations.

The practice of public relations itself has as wide a gamut of operations as the practitioner's imagination. To define its effect on the general population, it might be termed *mass conditioning*. Although in most cases this would be an overstatement, in some it is a very conservative appraisal of how continuous campaigns over long periods of years have made an indelible impact on our population.

GROWTH OF COMMUNICATIONS SYSTEMS

What we are setting out to study here is the public relations industry's tools and methods. The tools are our present hugely complicated communications system, which, in a short span of fifty years, has advanced from a slow postal system and a provincially oriented newspaper network to today's gargantuan radio and television networks, highly developed and far-flung press wire syndications and all the other modern news and feature vending apparatuses that have become an accepted part of our daily lives.

American public relations goes back as far as Thomas Paine. He was the man who wrote the pamphlets that carried the message of the American Revolution to the general public. At that time only 30% of the American public was literate and people used to read his pamphlets aloud in public houses and in general stores. Certainly, Paine was the press secretary of the American Continental Congress.

Public relations for American corporations, up until about 1885, was a European operation. American railroads were financed in Europe; also American industry. It was not until the emergence of American banks that European backing was no longer necessary. Our first financial public relations was in Europe—to get them to finance us.

Today we live in a world in which the latest toothpaste commercial gets an infinitely wider coverage than the Gettysburg Address received in the twenty years after it was made. Add to this mechanical omnipotence the fact that our nation, as well as many other nations, has enjoyed within the same period of time a dramatic rise in literacy and a subsequent sharply heightened interest and understanding of the world around it.

Living standards have kept apace of this literacy explosion so that the ability to afford to buy the printed and spoken word, as a picture in one's own living room, has given the *word* as much, or more, power than the deed.

If we take the word and consider it a product that the public relations industry produces, the purpose for which the word is conceived is in a pure sense the objective of public relations. Its dissemination is the technique of publicity. Public relations is the formulation of policy in the use of communication, whereas the business of publicity is its widest possible circulation.

FUNCTIONS OF PUBLIC RELATIONS CAMPAIGNS

A public relations campaign is a continuous extensive effort to create and maintain a mental environment conducive to the acceptance of a product, an idea or ideology, or a personality, individual or corporate. Usually, campaigns are conducted in four principal categories: industrial and financial, commercial, institutional and governmental.

Industrial and financial public relations embrace all efforts made toward establishing a favorable public concept of a business enterprise. The areas of particular concentration following the all-inclusive general public are the financial or banking community, the stockholders and potential stockholders, the particular section of the public or trade that uses the product or services offered, employees and potential employees, the community or communities in which offices and factories are located, and if a large volume of business is transacted with governmental agencies, an attempt should be made to develop a favorable news climate in the Capital.

Commercial public relations usually is concerned with furthering the public acceptance of a product or a service. Because an entire chapter will be devoted to this, as well as to the other categories, it is important to note that, in this particular instance, publicity as a technique of public relations plays a dominant role.

Institutional public relations is concerned mostly with nonprofit organizations whose subsistence depends on public subvention through fund raising. This classification, because it includes all nonprofit social, political, health and welfare, as well as educational institutions in our country, is vital to the maintenance of a free society. It is the voluntary nature of their support that makes the impact of good public relations in their behalf give shape to the pattern of our community life.

Governmental public relations, in its most generous concept, is the representation and counseling of foreign governments as well as totally, or partially, owned commercial subsidiaries of foreign governments. These include tourism organizations, transport facilities, national banks and development corporations designed to encourage American investment abroad.

PUBLIC RELATIONS-ADVERTISING RELATIONSHIP

Perhaps it would be valuable, at this point, to clarify the twilight zone that chronically obfuscates the difference between advertising and public relations.

Advertising is the use of paid space or time for the presentation of a sales message.

Public relations rarely uses paid space. Instead, the practice of public relations is the use of all communications media for the promotion and furtherance, subtle and overt, of a commercial property or a cause without the use of paid space.

Although these two uses of communications media are closely related and very often overlap each other in broad campaigns, their techniques are vastly different. Each has its own method of producing maximum pervasiveness. In their general use, they are, more often than not, combined for maximum saturational effect. However, the student must understand that motivationally advertising and public relations stem from the same root, and that very often one or the other can be chosen to bear the main burden of a campaign. The choice, however, as to which one would be the most effective in each case, is public relations in its truest sense.

EXERCISES

1 Prepare a feature article about 1000 words in length describing the general use of public relations as an integral part of the framework of modern communications.
2 Describe briefly the use of public relations in the building of historical recollections of
   a. people
   b. nations
   c. commercial properties
3 Prepare a 2000 word READER'S DIGEST stylized article on public relations as a factor in accelerating the popularity of one of the following choices:
   a. a consumer product
   b. a charity
   c. a president
   d. war or peace
4 Which one of the following personalities identified with the Revolutionary War do you consider primarily a publicist:
   a. George Washington
   b. Benjamin Franklin
   c. John Hancock
   d. Alexander Hamilton
   e. Patrick Henry
   Give the reasons for your choice and explain how you restrict the area of function.
5 If a new toothpaste were introduced to the American market by
   a. A full-page ad in LIFE magazine
   b. An article in the news section of THE NEW YORK TIMES
   c. A television commercial
   all three extolling therapeutic benefits to be derived from the use of the product, discuss your personal reaction to the three, explaining why one would be more effective in influencing immediate individual trial use of the product.
   Expand by giving your opinion of the effectiveness of each one of the three and why all three should be used, or which, economically, could be eliminated.
6 Prepare a budget inclusive of TV and advertising costs.
7 Pertinent Case Exercises (See Appendix A)
   These are basic situations keyed to various facets of public relations discussed in the previous and ensuing chapters of this book. They

1 / introduction to the practice of public relations

have been devised to give the student or practitioner actual experience in solving problems he might encounter in the future pursuit of his profession.

a. BOOKED FOR TAKE-OVER
b. PRACTICAL PHYSICIAN
c. DOLLARS AND SCENTS
d. PLANT FOR PINA

SUGGESTED SUPPLEMENTAL READING

Budd, John F. *An Executive Primer on Public Relations.* Philadelphia: Chilton Book Company, 1969

Canfield, Bertrand. *Public Relations.* (5th ed.). Homewood, Ill.: Richard D. Irwin, Inc., 1968

Cutlip, Scott M. *A Public Relations Bibliography.* Madison: University of Wisconsin Press, 1957

Cutlip, Scott, and Allen Center. *Effective Public Relations.* (3rd ed.). Englewood Cliffs, N.J.: Prentice–Hall, Inc., 1964

Darrow, Richard W., Dan J. Forrestal, and Aubrey O. Cookman. *Public Relations Handbook.* (2nd ed.). Chicago: Dartnell Publishing Company, 1967

Harlow, Rex F. *Social Science in Public Relations.* New York: Harper & Brothers, 1957

Marston, John E. *The Nature of Public Relations.* New York: McGraw–Hill Book Company, Inc., 1963

Pimlott, J. A. R. *Public Relations and American Democracy.* Princeton: Princeton University Press, 1951

Raucher, Alan R. *Public Relations and Business, 1900–1929.* Baltimore: Johns Hopkins Press, 1968

Riesman, David, in collaboration with Neuel Benney and Nathan Glazer. *The Lonely Crowd.* New Haven: Yale University Press, 1950

Steinberg, Charles S. *The Mass Communications: Public Relations, Public Opinion and Mass Media.* New York: Harper Brothers, 1958

Zollo, Burt. *The Dollars and Sense of Public Relations.* New York: McGraw–Hill Book Company, Inc., 1963

role of the practitioner

2

THE NEWSPAPER MEDIUM

Despite a trend toward amalgamation and several outstanding casualties, there remained in 1971 some 1750 daily newspapers in the United States. Because the printed word is more salvageable for reuse than the word not recorded—as in radio and television—the newspaper has survived the onslaught of more modern media better than might have been predicted. Press notices in the dominant regional newspapers remain the basic currency of publicity.

The United States is blessed with one of the few essentially honest newspaper systems left in the world. As yet, it does not suffer the blight of government control and it has remained, for the most part, free of industrial and unscrupulous political influences. Our newspapers have many faults. But they stand so far above the standards set by most other countries, that any comparisons tend to become invidious.

However, because at least 50% of the public relations practitioner's time normally is pointed toward making his client worthy of press notice, a working familiarity with the American network of newspapers is mandatory.

Although literacy is almost universal in the United States, the volition, not to speak of the ability, to read intelligently, is not. The volition of an adult to read a good newspaper is almost directly proportionate to the individual's curiosity about the world around him.

PRESS APPRAISAL

Unfortunately for Mr. and Mrs. Average American, the world consists of their town, village or small city. National interest intrudes on their consciousness during periods of great tension, such as wars, national elections and occasional catastrophes.

This insular attitude shapes our press. The press very rarely, if ever, expands this attitude. It has proved far too expensive financially. Therefore, it is not unusual to have a medium-sized city's major newspaper feature a local fire or traffic accident rather than the European Common Market's decision to eliminate a tariff on wheat. The most diminutive local event never yields precedence to a major national event. International news, even in many newspapers that honestly endeavor to include adequate coverage, is usually reduced to wire service slugs and relegated to inside pages.

The philosophy behind this conformity is very simply that it sells newspapers and that national weeklies and other supplementary reading supply the subscriber who demands more.

This condition, in some part, has been partially remedied by the regular purchase of syndicated columns, which supply an editorial or viewpoint coverage rather than publication of spot news.

For the most part, the student should know that the majority of the newspapers in the United States are interested in printing what their readers demand—good coverage of the local scene, socially, politically and culturally.

However, juxtaposed against this general situation, our country can boast of the finest newspapers in the world. These dailies, through their own correspondents, literally cover every corner of the world and follow a tradition of accurate reporting that leaves very little more to be desired for the individual who wants to keep abreast of current affairs.

And then there is the group of newspapers that falls between the categories of full coverage and local coverage. They tend to one side or the other with the fluctuations of events. Therefore, we recommend that the student divide the American newspaper network into three main categories:

A Top circulation papers carrying full coverage on international, national and local news.
B Newspapers that publish mainly local news, with a good larding of syndicated editorial material along with spot coverage of the most important nonlocal items.
C Newspapers that concentrate on intense local treatment of the news.

The following two lists of newspapers are those considered by this writer to be of primary importance for news dissemination.

(A) List Daily Newspapers
(Circulation: 100,000 and over)

Alabama	Birmingham	News (e & S) *
Arizona	Phoenix	Republic (m & S)
Arkansas	Little Rock	Gazette (m & S)
California	Fresno	Bee (e & S)
	Long Beach	Press-Telegram (e & S)
	Los Angeles	Herald-Examiner (e & S)
		Times (m & S)
	Oakland	Tribune (e, Sat. m & S)
	Sacramento	Bee (e & S)
	San Diego	Union (m & S)
		Tribune (e)
	San Francisco	Chronicle (m)
		Examiner (e)
		Sunday Examiner & Chronicle (S)
		Wall St. Journal (m)—Pacific Coast Edition
	San Jose	Mercury (m)
		Mercury-News (S)
Colorado	Denver	Post (e & S)
		Rocky Mountain News (m & S)
Connecticut	Hartford	Courant (m & S)
		Times (e & S)
	New Haven	Register (e & S)
District of Columbia	Washington	News (e)
		Post (m & S)
		Star (e & S)
Florida	Jacksonville	Times-Union (m & S)
	Miami	Herald (m & S)
	St. Petersburg	Times (m & S)
	Tampa	Tribune (m & S)
Georgia	Atlanta	Constitution (m & S)
		Journal (e)
Hawaii	Honolulu	Star-Bulletin (e)

* m: morning edition; e: evening edition; S: Sunday edition.

(A) List Daily Newspapers
(Circulation: 100,000 and over)

Illinois	Chicago	News (e)
		Sun-Times (m & S)
		Tribune (m & S)
		Wall St. Journal (m)—Mid-West Edition
Indiana	Indianapolis	Star (m & S)
		News (e)
	South Bend-Mishawaka	Tribune (e & S)
Iowa	Des Moines	Register (m & S)
		Tribune (e)
Kansas	Wichita	Eagle (m)
		Beacon (e)
		Eagle & Beacon (S)
Kentucky	Louisville	Courier-Journal (m & S)
		Times (e)
Louisiana	New Orleans	Times-Picayune (m & S)
		States-Item (e)
Maryland	Baltimore	News-American (e & S)
		Sun (m, e & S)
Massachusetts	Boston	Christian Science Monitor (m)
		Globe (m, e & S)
		Herald Traveler (m & S)
		Record American (m)
Michigan	Detroit	Free Press (m & S)
		News (e & S)
	Flint	Journal (e & S)
	Grand Rapids	Press (e & S)
Minnesota	Minneapolis	Tribune (m & S)
		Star (e)
	St. Paul	Pioneer Press (m & S)
		Dispatch (e)
Missouri	Kansas City	Times (m)
		Star (e & S)
	St. Louis	Globe Democrat (m ex. Sat.)
		Post-Dispatch (e & S)

* m: morning edition; e: evening edition; S: Sunday edition.

(A) List Daily Newspapers
(Circulation: 100,000 and over)

Nebraska	Omaha	World-Herald (m, e & S)
New Jersey	Hackensack	Record (e ex. Sat.)
		Sunday Record Call
	Newark	News (e & S)
		Star-Ledger (m & S)
New York	Buffalo	Courier-Express (m & S)
		News (e)
	Garden City	Newsday (e)
	Jamaica	Long Island Press (e & S)
	New York City	News (m & S)
		Post (e & S)
		Times (m & S)
		Wall St. Journal (m)—Eastern Edition
	Rochester	Democrat & Chronicle (m & S)
		Times-Union (e)
	Syracuse	Herald-Journal (e)
North Carolina	Charlotte	Observer (m & S)
		News (e)
	Raleigh	News & Observer (m & S)
		Times (e)
Ohio	Akron	Beacon Journal (e & S)
	Cincinnati	Enquirer (m & S)
		Post & Times-Star (e)
	Cleveland	Plain Dealer (m & S)
		Press (e)
	Columbus	Citizen-Journal (m)
		Dispatch (e & S)
	Dayton	Journal Herald (m)
		News (e & S)
	Toledo	Times (m ex. Sat.)
		Blade (e & S)
Oklahoma	Oklahoma City	Oklahoman (m & S)
		Times (e)
	Tulsa	World (m & S)
		Tribune (e)
Oregon	Portland	Oregonian (m & S)
		Oregon Journal (e)

* m: morning edition; e: evening edition; S: Sunday edition.

(A) List Daily Newspapers
(Circulation: 100,000 and over)

Pennsylvania	Philadelphia	Bulletin (e & S)
		Inquirer (m & S)
		News (e)
	Pittsburgh	Post-Gazette (m)
		Press (e & S)
Rhode Island	Providence	Bulletin (e)
Tennessee	Knoxville	News-Sentinel (e & S)
	Memphis	Commercial Appeal (m & S)
		Press-Scimitar (e)
	Nashville	Tennessean (m & S)
Texas	Dallas	News (m & S)
		Times Herald (e & S)
	Ft. Worth	Star-Telegram (m, e & S)
	Houston	Chronicle (e & S)
		Post (m & S)
	San Antonio	Light (e & S)
Utah	Salt Lake City	Tribune (m & S)
Virginia	Norfolk,	Ledger-Star (e)
	Portsmouth,	Virginian-Pilot (m & S)
	Virginia Beach	
	& Chesapeake	
	Richmond	Times-Dispatch (m & S)
		News Leader (e)
Washington	Seattle	Times (e & S)
		Post-Intelligencer (m & S)
	Tacoma	News-Tribune (e)
		Tribune & Ledger (S)
Wisconsin	Milwaukee	Journal (e & S)
		Sentinel (m)

* m: morning edition; e: evening edition; S: Sunday edition.

(B) Daily Newspapers
(Circulation: 50,000 to 100,000)

Alabama	Birmingham	Post-Herald (m) *
	Huntsville	Times (e & S)
	Montgomery	Advertiser (m & S)
Arizona	Phoenix	Gazette (e)
Arkansas	Little Rock	Democrat (e & S)
California	Long Beach	Independent (m)
	Sacramento	Union (m & S)
	San Bernardino	Sun (m & S)
	San Gabriel	Tribune (e & S)
	San Jose	News (e)
	Santa Ana	Register (m & S)
	Stockton	Record (e & S)
Connecticut	Bridgeport	Post (e & S)
Delaware	Wilmington	Journal (e)
Florida	Fort Lauderdale	News (e & S)
	Jacksonville	Journal (e)
	Miami	News (e)
	Pensacola	Journal (m & S)
	West Palm Beach	Palm Beach Post (m & S)
Georgia	Macon	Telegraph (m & S)
	Savannah	News (m & S)
Hawaii	Honolulu	Advertiser (m & S)
Illinois	Rockford	Star (m & S)
	Springfield	State Journal (m & S)
Indiana	Evansville	Courier (m & S)
	Fort Wayne	Journal-Gazette (m & S)
		News-Sentinel (e)
	Gary	Post-Tribune (e & S)
	Hammond-East Chicago	Times (e & S)
Iowa	Cedar Rapids-Marion	Gazette (e & S)
	Davenport-Bettendorf	Times-Democrat (all day & S)
	Sioux City	Journal (all day & S)
	Waterloo-Cedar Falls-Evansdale	Courier (e & S ex. Sat.)

* m: morning edition; e: evening edition; S: Sunday edition.

(B) Daily Newspapers
(Circulation: 50,000 to 100,000)

Kansas	Topeka	Capital (m)
		State Journal (e)
		Capital-Journal (S)
Kentucky	Covington	Post & Times Star (e)
	Lexington	Herald (m)
		Leader (e)
		Herald-Leader (S)
Louisiana	Baton Rouge	Advocate (m & S)
		State Times (e)
	Shreveport	Times (m & S)
Maine	Bangor	News (m)
	Portland	Press Herald (m)
		Sunday Telegram (S)
		Express (e)
Massachusetts	New Bedford	Standard-Times (e & S)
	Quincy	Patriot-Ledger (e)
	Springfield	Union (m)
		News (e)
		Republican (S)
	Worcester	Telegram (m & S)
		Gazette (e)
Michigan	Kalamazoo	Gazette (e & S)
	Lansing	State Journal (e & S)
	Pontiac	Press (e)
	Royal Oak	Tribune (e)
	Saginaw	News (e & S)
Minnesota	Duluth	News Tribune (m & S)
		Herald (ex. Sat.)
Mississippi	Jackson	Clarion-Ledger (m & S)
		News (e)
New Hampshire	Manchester	Union Leader (all day)

* m: morning edition; e: evening edition; S: Sunday edition.

(B) Daily Newspapers
(Circulation: 50,000 to 100,000)

New Jersey	Atlantic City	Press (m & S)
	Camden	Courier-Post (e)
	Elizabeth	Journal (e)
	Jersey City	Journal (e)
	New Brunswick	Home News (e & S)
	Passaic-Clifton	Herald-News (e)
	Paterson	News (m & e)
	Trenton	Times (e ex. Sat.)
	Union City	Hudson Dispatch (m)
New Mexico	Albuquerque	Journal (m & S)
		Tribune (e)
New York	Albany	Times-Union (m & S)
		Knickerbocker News–Union-Star (e)
	Binghamton	Press (e & S)
	Schenectady	Gazette (m)
	Staten Island	Advance (e & S)
	Syracuse	Post Standard (m & S)
North Carolina	Greensboro	News (m & S)
		Record (e)
	Winston-Salem	Journal (m & S)
		Twin City Sentinel (e)
Ohio	Canton	Repository (e & S)
	Youngstown	Vindicator (e & S)
Oklahoma	Oklahoma City	Journal (m & S)
Pennsylvania	Allentown	Call (m & S)
	Erie	Times (e & S)
	Harrisburg	News (e & S)
	Johnstown	Tribune-Democrat (all day)
	Lancaster	New Era (e)
	Scranton	Times (e & S)
	Wilkes-Barre	Times-Leader, News (e)
Rhode Island	Providence	Journal (m & S)
South Carolina	Anderson	Independent (m & S)
	Charleston	News & Courier (m & S)
	Columbia	State (m & S)
	Greenville	News (m & S)

* m: morning edition; e: evening edition; S: Sunday edition.

(B) Daily Newspapers
(Circulation: 50,000 to 100,000)

South Dakota	Sioux Falls	Argus-Leader (e & S)
Tennessee	Chattanooga	Times (m & S) News-Free Press (e & S)
	Knoxville	Journal (m)
	Nashville	Banner (e)
Texas	Beaumount	Enterprise (m & S)
	Corpus Christi	Caller (m & S)
	Dallas	Wall St. Journal (m ex. Sat.)-- Southwest Ed.
	El Paso	Times (m & S)
	Fort Worth	Press (e & S ex. Sat.)
	Lubbock	Avalanche-Journal (m, e & S)
	San Antonio	Express (m. ex. Sat.) News (e ex. Sat.) Express-News (Sat. & S)
Utah	Salt Lake City	Deseret News (e)
Virginia	Roanoke	Times (m & S)
Washington	Spokane	Spokesman-Review (m & S) Chronicle (e)
West Virginia	Charleston	Gazette (m & S) Mail (e)
Wisconsin	Madison	Wisconsin State Journal (m & S)

* m: morning edition; e: evening edition; S: Sunday edition.

SATISFYING EDITORIAL REQUIREMENTS

The student of public relations should be a constant reader of a generous sampling of all three newspaper categories listed. Not only the range of coverage is important. Editing style, departmental emphasis and actual copy requirements are of equal importance to practitioners.

It will be noted quickly that, in each case, the handling of stories is as varied as the number of editors responsible for approving them before they are set in type. Each editor exercises his discretion even on wire service stories: expanding, contracting or using them verbatim, according to his interpretation of his publishing policy.

As a general rule, a national release of a news or feature story by a public relations agency should be fitted to at least the three broad classifications of newspapers that are its targets. In every case, the editor makes the ultimate decision on the use of a release and this decision is made on the basis of its ability to fulfill the general philosophy of his paper.

A general release purporting to contain news of sufficient public interest, to deserve space, should first be of general public interest— that is, its content must include knowledge of an event about which the greater number of America's newspaper readers will have a normal curiosity. It need not affect the course of their daily lives, but it should have a sufficient quotient of importance to stimulate interest.

If the release quotes an individual, or contains the statements of a group, the status and validity of the source must be made clear at the outset.

The ideal release, from any editor's viewpoint, is one having a lead that can be printed alone and tell the whole story. To come up to the subject matter circuitously or verbosely reduces its chances of appearing in print. The most successful release is the one that prompts the editor to call the source for more material.

Literally thousands of releases arrive on editors' desks from hopeful aspirants for publication that are tossed into the wastebasket. It needs little more than a glance to discard them. Many of these releases simply contain no news. If couched as feature stories and directed to newspapers devoting space to feature pieces, they might have a chance. The difference lies mainly in the knowledge of the anatomy of the individual newspaper.

The (A) list contains newspapers that are thoroughly departmentalized. Each one of these departments has an editor who supervises a department of his own for which he bears complete responsibility. These departments generally are

Advertising	Home Furnishings
Aviation	Music
Book	News
Business-Financial	Radio, TV
Columnists	Real Estate
Dance	Religion
Editor for the Arts	Science
Fashion	Society
Film and Theatre	Sports
Food	Sunday Magazine
Garden	Travel

A release sent to the proper departmental head has a far greater chance of publication than a release addressed to the editor or city editor.

It is also well to remember that within the past twenty years a profitable newspaper has been the exception rather than the rule. Staffs have, in many cases, been reduced dramatically. There is, therefore, a far greater dependence on public relations practitioners as a source of legitimate copy.

It would be very helpful to research several daily papers for the extent of their use of material from public relations sources. This scanning of the daily press would reveal quickly that, aside from crime and accidents, the preponderant number of stories are re-writes of finished releases supplied by accredited public relations representatives.

One of the most interesting public relations campaigns, and certainly recent history has proved it prophetic, was the use of the press to make the governing trustees of Columbia University amenable to dropping the quota system in choosing undergraduate students. This writer was assigned to the task by a number of social agencies representing dominant ethnic groups.

Possibly the great lesson to be learned from the experience was that a radical change in the policy of the vested interests of the university could be accomplished without a single broken window or any violence of any kind, not even a whispered expletive.

The method used was very simple. In the name of the agencies involved, a petition, that could truthfully be said to represent a majority of the people of the State of New York, was brought before the Board of Estimate to remove Columbia University from its tax-exempt status. A hearing was held in City Hall at which a succession of more than two hundred witnesses took the stand testifying to the use of the quota system and its effects on students seeking a college degree from a university enjoying tax exemption on properties approaching a value of almost one billion dollars. Taxes that might have been collected on this property might have been sufficient to support another school that would not use a quota system in choosing students.

The daily testimonies were front-page news for a week. That week also signalled the end of Columbia's quota system.

ELEMENTS OF RELEASE WRITING

Although this is not a course in journalism, it might be well at this point to review the rudimentary elements of release writing. Aside from the value of a good lead, which we discussed previously in this chapter, the writer of a good release should exercise extreme economy of words. Supplementary material should not be contained in the main body of the releases, but should be attached in the form of notes along with line drawings, photographs, charts, financial statements or any other pertinent material. Facts should be clearly stated, unobfuscated by descriptive verbiage. If the release contains quotes from a statement, a speech or a manuscript, the supplementary material should contain the complete text of the source of the quote. Other possible corroborative sources should be parenthetically added to the foot of the release.

The release should be marked "For Immediate Release" or bear a clear release date. Pictures attached to the release should be clearly captioned, also dated, with credits either rubber stamped or written in. The release should be proofread for correct grammar, as well as facts. There is nothing as pathetic as a grammatical error or awkward syntax.

These are rules generally applicable to all categories of releases. However, a discussion of specific releases for different types of public relations activities will be handled in future chapters.

If the client representation is new, or if the subject matter has never sought publication before, a note to the editor explaining the relevance of the material, as well as the public relations representative's continuing relationship with it, should be attached. It should not be forgotten that an editor's principal concern is with the responsibility and reliability of the source. It is true that he cannot be fooled twice, but more often than not, he cannot be fooled once.

Do not sensationalize news. Remember your release must fit into the slipstream of all the newsworthy events occurring on that day in the world. If the news your release bears has exaggerated its true importance, it cannot fit into a printed page. Try to understate and allow ample margin for the editor to play his own role.

STRUCTURE OF FEATURE ARTICLES

Even though these fundamental principles should be exercised in the writing of a news release, quite the opposite holds true in the composing of a good feature article. Here all the stops on the organ can be pulled out in the knowledge that human interest dominates the theme of a good feature story. Write as lengthily as the subject matter will bear. There is a difference between coloring and exaggeration. The feature editor will forgive flamboyance if it is in consonance with the subject being handled. Exaggeration is simply toying with truth and this is never forgivable.

A feature article need not be news, but the farther it strays from news, the more intense must be its human quality.

In the release of a feature article, some degree of exclusivity must be guaranteed the editor to whom it is sent. Usually this exclusivity need not be guaranteed for more than a single paper in any single location. This detail should be clearly stated at the top of the lead page with a deadline for automatic rejection included.

PLACING A STORY

One of the most abused areas in the practice of public relations is what has come to be known as "planting" a story. Coming face to face with an editor in an office, or at lunch, or even less effectively at a cocktail bar, not only tests the knowledge and skill of a practitioner, but also lifts or lowers the ethical level of this entire industry of communications in which public relations plays such an important part. This procedure mainly involves the planting of feature articles because in the handling of news releases, personal contact with the press is maneuvered most conveniently by means of a press conference.

The discussion in a meeting of this kind, aside from the amenities of conversation, should be confined to the properties of a story in relation to the requirements of the newspaper. Irrelevant, tangential reasons for placement are not only wasted minutes, but are usually distasteful to a hard-working practical editor to whom the appointment meant the introduction to a productive use of space.

The practitioner should·be armed with two weapons: a well-written article with a range of interest suitable to the publication he has contacted and sufficient knowledge of the publication to discuss usage on the editor's terms.

PRESS CONFERENCES AND PARTIES

The same differences separating news releases from feature releases also establish the dichotomy between press conferences and press parties. A press conference is used only when the material presented is clearly and unmistakably an occasion for the announcement of a news event so important that the principals involved are required for direct interrogation by members of the press.

Press parties can be organized for a variety of reasons, all of which should, in a direct way, relate to the presentation of background material for future feature stories.

Press parties are most useful in the introduction of new products so large, or so expensive, that they cannot be transported to and from more intimate interviews in offices. Of course, the focal point of these parties should be the product or, as it is more often called, the show. The press party usually involves a luncheon, less often a dinner, built around a product, or the use of a product, that requires a tangible demonstration to press personnel.

In a press conference, proper public relations procedure requires notification of editorial desks at least a week in advance of a chosen date. Notification should be accompanied by a fact sheet that clearly sets forth the nature of the news to be handled, principals who will be present and time and place chosen. It should include a note to the photography desk, if photographic subjects are going to be present. On the morning of the date for the conference, an advance release should arrive by messenger on each invited editorial desk containing the essentials of the material to be covered at the conference.

During the press conference itself, from the moment the gathering is called to order, good protocol requires that the public relations representative be as unobtrusive as it is possible to be. Free discourse between press personnel and the principals of the conference should always be maintained. If an off-the-record interview is required by the nature of the material handled, the on-the-record, off-the-record announcements should be made by a well-coached principal. Do not allow the conference the appearance of being overprofessionalized. To be valuable, questions and answers must retain a free give-and-take spirit, which develops confidence and an aura of reliability. Before terminating a press conference, make sure that all possibilities of interrogation

21

are exhausted. To cut questioning short is an almost certain guarantee of press negativity.

The same advance release, hand delivered to editorial desks in the morning, should be handed out to the press at the conference. Arrangements for photography should be made as convenient as possible for the newspapers sending photographers.

The ideal time for a press conference in communities having both morning and evening newspapers is between the hours of 2:30 and 4:30 P.M. This allows for a last edition of the afternoon press and all editions of the morning press to cover.

In the organization of a press party, social convention rather than press convention becomes dominant in protocol. Invitations should be formal, printed if the budget allows. Seating should be prearranged and clearly designated. The atmosphere should be considerably more relaxed than at a press conference. However, each invitee, on entering, should be recorded by name and publication and should be handed a press kit containing a collection of material pertinent to the product being introduced. This material should be complete with specifics and details so that feature writing can be made easier by virtue of the research and fact gathering contained.

NEWS SYNDICATES

We have omitted mentioning, in the greater portion of our discussion of newspapers as a medium, the special function of news syndicates. For the practitioner, news syndicates, such as Associated Press (AP) and United Press International (UPI), should be serviced in exactly the same manner as major local newspapers.

Feature syndicates should be serviced according to the material in the release or in the feature story. Some of them are highly specialized, particularly those who feature by-line columns, whose purpose is o substitute for departmental personnel on individual papers. Research of the material handled by each of these major syndications is usually very rewarding for placement.

A complete list of wire syndicates and feature syndicates is available in the EDITOR & PUBLISHER YEAR BOOK.

MAGAZINES

TIME, NEWSWEEK and U.S. NEWS & WORLD REPORT represent a new direction in news media. Although they are weekly publications, because of their superb editing and wide coverage, they fulfill the function of a complete newspaper and yet have the national circulation of a highly popular magazine with all the advantages this quality readership represents to national advertisers. In their departmentalization, they run about parallel to the major big-city dailies. But their quality of reporting generally can be considered to be more selective and more probing, which results in more depth and perhaps carries copy laden with a higher editorial opinion quotient than the average major newspaper.

To the public relations practitioner, these special-purpose news magazines should be serviced with both news and feature releases in exactly the same manner as the newspapers in the (A) list. It should be remembered, however, that all three are so highly stylized in their handling of copy that fact sheets, along with relevant supplemental material, will be far more effective than completed stories to their departmental editors.

Consumer magazines are both numerous and varied in their focal points of interest. Feature placement in the more prominent of these magazines is most valuable to public relations campaigns because of the residual benefits resulting from the merchandising of reprints. Many of these magazines enjoy high reader fidelity, not to mention credulity, which gives their material substantial impact.

Because most of these magazines (incidentally, they are called books in the trade) frequently buy completed articles from free-lance writers and photographers—some of whom enjoy excellent relationships with the editors—some names are actually associated in the readers' minds with the magazines. With this condition existing more often than not in this situation, placement can be done either through an editor or through a contributing free-lancer. Either channel is valid and is usually as effective as the material permits.

In this group, it may be a good idea for the student to separate LIFE and READER'S DIGEST from the rest. The circulation of these magazines is prodigious, and their story impact on the population is powerful. The practitioner must acquaint himself with the editorial routine of these magazines so that the material he introduces does not try editorial patience. Outlines submitted must be concise; picture possibilities, especially in the case of LIFE, should be amply described, and in each case, human-interest values should be unmistakably obvious.

TRADE PRESS

The list with the greatest number of publications—of which there are thousands in existence—is what has come to be known as the trade press. Some of these have unassailable reputations and have functioned for more than a century. Others have grown up like mushrooms as industries have burgeoned forth in the long postwar period of prosperity. Because as a group they lack definition and, in many cases, circulation spills over into consumer areas, they are most aptly described as magazines and newspapers servicing closed business communities.

Some of them, such as the WALL STREET JOURNAL, VARIETY and WOMEN'S WEAR DAILY, are read and quoted widely because their editorial policies allow for coverage that relates to, but is not bounded by, the business segments they service. Magazines such as FORTUNE, BUSINESS WEEK, NATION'S BUSINESS and a few others also enjoy circulations beyond the confines of the business community.

Commercial clients require the establishment and maintenance of status within their own and related industries. News about their business activities, future plans and personnel changes, ordinarily meriting a line in a consumer paper, earn full pages in the trade journals of their own industries. Good relationships must be sought with the journals important to the client and a regular information service should be kept in continuous action. Even though the WALL STREET JOURNAL is a financial newspaper and should be serviced with news relating to a financial side, it is recommended, because of the special nature of this national newspaper, that it be serviced with consumer releases as well, in exactly the same manner as the general press. FORTUNE and BUSINESS WEEK should also be serviced as both consumer magazines and trade publications.

A perusal of the trade journals (excepting those already identified by name) will show that most of the copywriting is in the vernacular of the particular trade in which they specialize. Their editorial success usually depends on not only ample news coverage, but also generous space allowance to personalities.

Although the servicing of this group by the practitioner offers no special difficulties, to neglect them separates the client from the mainstream of his industry.

Subsequent chapters will discuss in detail the technique required for the maintenance of a good relationship with the trade papers in each of the specialized fields of public relations.

RADIO AND TELEVISION

The communications media throughout the world, and possibly especially in the United States, have been in a state of revolutionary change since the advent of voice broadcasting in the early 1920s. With the introduction of television, this process of change became far more swift and radical in its effect on the new conditioning of the world's population to the channels of mass communication. Just as motion pictures changed habit patterns in the early part of the century, the twenty years following the Second World War have witnessed the creation of a new dimension to our way of life. The full impact of it will not be measurable for several decades, for it is obvious now that every phase of daily living has been altered, and there is no longer any doubt that television reigns supreme as the leading communications medium in our country.

Beginning with the removal of the traditional newsboy's cry of "EXTRA!" in city streets until the present, our broadcasting networks of television and radio have employed news staffs far beyond the supportive ability of the great majority of the press. The fact is that spot news is broadcast and telecast long before it can be set in type. There has been a gradual relegation of the printed word to a supplemental status, which it is more or less gracefully fulfilling.

The daily number of viewers and listeners is astronomical and their dependence on the medium of broadcasting is virtually complete. This condition must direct the thinking of all public relations practitioners. The saturational pervasiveness of any campaign requires the fullest exploitation of the possibilities inherent in radio and TV. For the practitioner, this is perhaps a fortunate development because words are spoken and pictures exhibited at a speed that outdistances reading to the extent that the appetite for radio and TV material is prodigious.

New material is in constant demand by the networks and individual stations and entertainment values compete much more successfully on the air than they ever did in the national press. There is no program on the air that does not offer an opportunity for constructive infiltration by public relations practitioners. Only when the subconscious aspects of the saturation of public consciousness peculiar to this medium are understood, can they be properly evaluated. Every piece of furniture, every seemingly unimportant accessory in a dramatic presentation, is absorbed almost as readily as the dialogue—in some cases, more readily. Whether a popular actor smokes or abstains affects the habit formations of millions. How a soap opera heroine wears her hair and whether she changes the style often enough can cause turmoil in the beauty parlor industry. The instances and effects are countless to such a degree that habits, fads and conditioning results of all kinds evolve and recede at a terrifying tempo. To the advertising business, it was the dawn of a new and very profitable world. To public relations, it has given new perspective to horizontal boundaries that take a good amount of courage to exploit effectively.

CHOOSING YOUR MEDIA

In assessing all of the foregoing media in relation to any given set of a client's problems, the areas of the most effective application should become apparent. Each campaign's objectives, after they are clearly understood, should reveal the obstacles in the way of their attainment. To a public relations practitioner these obstacles are usually overcome by the process of changing a public attitude, or antipathy or even apathy to positive acceptance.

Because the public it is necessary to reach in any single campaign is seldom the complete population, certain segments of the population become the natural target areas. The choice of the proper medium, or media, as the case may be, of communications is part of the public relations application toward solution.

EXERCISES

1 With a limited budget that could not afford a nationwide clipping service, list the twenty newspapers you would choose to show the broadest coverage in
  a. a commercial product
  b. a resort
  c. a financial statement
  d. the discovery of a new drug
2 Write a five hundred-word feature article with a contrived news peg that tells which newspaper is your favorite and why you are a faithful reader.
3 Discuss thoroughly in essay style the growing use of syndicated feature columns and how they have become effective in molding sections of public opinion.
4 Write a lead sentence on a political event in the style of TIME, NEWSWEEK, and U.S. NEWS & WORLD REPORT.
5 Using the news section of THE NEW YORK TIMES, identify
  a. feature material emanating from public relations sources
  b. news articles that are rewrites of public relations releases

   c. news articles covered by on-the-spot reporting
   d. photographs distributed by a public relations source
   e. photographs taken by a staff photographer
   Discuss briefly in each case how the identification was made.

6 Describe each stage of the formation of a press conference, detailing all techniques and give reasons for their use.

7 Write an outline planned to stimulate magazine publication of a profile of the president of a client corporation.

8 The product is a mechanical device to prevent air pollution from diesel exhausts. Write a note to a TV network producer with the intention of stimulating interest in building a feature program around the product and its uses.

9 Describe a program that would give the product maximum exposure without detracting public interest.

10 Pertinent Case Exercises (See Appendix A)
   a. FREE WHEELING
   b. ARTISTIC ENDEAVOR
   c. SURPRISE PARTY
   d. BRUSH UP

SUGGESTED SUPPLEMENTAL READING

Angel, Juvenal L. *Where to Look for Employment in the Field of Public Relations.* New York: World Trade Assembly Press, 1956

Bacon's Publicity Checker. (17th ed.). Chicago: Bacon's Clipping Bureau, 1969

Barnouw, Erik. *Mass Communications: Television, Radio, Film, Press; The Media and Their Practice in the United States of America.* New York: Rinehart and Company, 1956

Editor & Publisher International Year Book. (51st ed.). New York: Editor & Publisher Company, Inc., 1971

Jacobs, Herbert Austin. *Practical Publicity: A Handbook for Public and Private Workers.* New York: McGraw–Hill Book Company, Inc., 1964

McLuhan, Herbert Marshall. *Understanding Media: The Extensions of Man.* New York: McGraw–Hill Book Company, Inc., 1964

Schoenfeld, Clarence Albert. *Publicity Media and Methods: Their Role in Modern Public Relations.* New York: The Macmillan Company, 1963

Stephenson, Howard. (ed.). *Handbook of Public Relations.* New York: McGraw–Hill Book Company, Inc., 1960

Warneryd, Karl-Erik and Nowak. *Mass Communication and Advertising.* New York: International Advertising Association, 1969

financial and industrial public relations 3

WHAT IS FINANCIAL PUBLIC RELATIONS?

It is not generally well known that American business has operated under a state and federal legal system since the beginning of the twentieth century ordaining by law that all companies having shares publicly held shall maintain a policy of full disclosure. Incidentally, the United States is the only country in the world in which the shareholder and the investing public enjoy the legal provision that they be fully informed. Other countries have, by comparison, rather vague regulations, but the standard of their requirements is far less rigid and as a result, far less revealing.

Although at first business interests fought bitterly against these acts, known generally as Blue Sky laws, and then again fought the regulations of the Securities Exchange Commission (SEC) at the time of its advent during the Great Depression of the 1930s, today business executives recognize that the ensuing publicity has given them an accrual of benefits immeasurable in terms of status, prestige and, most important, earnings. Important financial and industrial interests traditionally used to seek the protection of seclusion from the public eye. Today, through their public relations operations, they compete for notice and they actually contest with each other for space and time.

The public response has given industrial management or proprietorship and the general public common cause in the maintenance of a healthy economy. It has caused the investing community of America to grow into a structure that has rejected any form of collectivism in a world that has half accepted it. By the same token, a healthy business has nothing to hide from the business or general community in which it prospers. The machinery of disclosure is industrial and financial public relations.

There are two general areas, each subdivided into many segments, at which financial publicity is aimed. The first is the financial community itself, which includes banks, private banks, underwriting banks, stock and bond brokerage firms, the financial press, mutual funds, closed investment trusts, financial research publishers, stock market analysts and investment counsel firms.

The second, because it involves the consumer public, organized labor, stockholders and potential investors, must be considered to be within the less defined general media area. This audience is becoming more diffuse as time goes on because the labor market is developing shortages and the stockholder population is climbing sharply.

To operate as a public relations functionary within this complicated field, at least a superficial knowledge of the workings of the financial community is necessary.

The roster of publicly owned companies in the United States is very long and continually growing. The conversion process from private ownership to public ownership of American concerns was accelerated sharply by the capital gains provision of the income tax laws. This made it possible for a majority interest to sell out through a financial underwriting to multiple interests with a comparatively minor penalty of a 25% capital gains tax. In most cases, control was still maintained by the seller because a sufficiently entrenched minority interest could still control corporate activities.

The legal process prior to sale, although tediously complicated, consists of the procedure of a financial firm acting in the role of a securities underwriter, estimating the public demand for the shares of a company, as well as a price per share that would not be high enough to inhibit the demand, and bidding this amount, minus an underwriting commission, to the owner or owners of the shares. Under the Securities Exchange Commission Regulations Act these underwritings, if they exceed a minimal amount, receive Commission scrutiny and require approval before sale is permitted.

While SEC permission for underwriting is in abeyance, no public relations or publicity on the issue is permitted by law. Once registration under the act is granted, all the attributes, advantages, income and growth potentials may be publicized within the limits of the Commission's opinion of the validity of the claims. If the issue has applied for privileges through listing on a major stock exchange, the rules and regulations of the particular stock exchange regarding the publicizing of reports on the company in question must also be followed implicitly. (See "SEC Statement of Policy," Appendix H.) The methods of the practitioner are in this case fairly well defined.

PUBLICIZING A NEW ISSUE

Although methods of publicizing a new issue vary greatly, the variance lies mostly in the adornments that can be added to the fundamentals. The basic piece of publication in the launching of a new issue is very rarely, if ever, prepared by a public relations representative; it is the registration announcement, the legal requirement of full disclosure for the SEC. This printed form is invariably prepared by the attorneys for the registrant. It is required to contain all pertinent information about the company: the reason for financing, the principals involved, a complete statement of the company's financial condition, a description of the company's business, a listing of subsidiary and affiliate companies (as well as the exposure of major stockholders), legal and public relations fees, underwriter's commission and option agreements for participation in the offering below and above the stipulated sale price of the stock.

From this document, the public relations operation ensues. First a fact sheet containing a condensation of all the pertinent information is prepared for attachment to a release that concisely tells the story of the offering in journalese rather than legal terminology. This should be sent as soon as possible to the following: financial press, financial editor of the consumer press, financial research publishers, analysts and stock market statistical executives. If the stock is to be listed on an exchange, all releases should also be sent to the designated department of that exchange.

The foregoing is the fundamental operation, but the follow-up activities make the difference between the mundane and the exciting. The company's management personnel, the products manufactured or services rendered, and the range and quality of consumer demand all have to be probed for feature material. This examination should develop many legitimate feature story potentials that should be written, or at least outlined, in the styles of the publications for which they are intended.

In an operation of this kind, it might be well for the practitioner to bear in mind at least one salient fact underlying the public relations value of a story. It holds as well for the financial community as for any other community of interest. In the public relations view, all working adults are first members of the general community and then members of a business or professional community. As important as the financial trade press is in the shaping of opinions and attitudes, no trade press, even the financial press, shapes these attitudes as finitely as the most influential consumer press. That is, when a business executive reads about the public financing of a new company in his favorite trade paper, he knows that publication depended on the relationship of that company to his industry. When the same executive reads it in THE NEW YORK TIMES, or in another paper of that quality, he knows that this particular piece of financial news was considered as meriting the attention of the world. The impact on his own attitude thereby becomes many times more forceful. By the same token, a company undergoing public financing that manufactures a new drug is of course of interest to drug manufacturers. Perhaps it is of a little more interest to the doctors who might prescribe it. Neither the news about the financing in a financial paper, nor the news about the drug in a medical paper would ever have as much effect on both manufacturers and doctors as a well chosen 1500-word story in READER'S DIGEST on the favorable effects or curative powers of the drug. Strangely enough, it will also expand public acceptance of the financing.

Therefore, in the flotation of a new issue, the financial press must be thoroughly serviced with news and feature stories. But never neglect the consumer press, because it may hold the key to a successful operation.

The reason for starting this chapter with a description of the rudiments of a new issues campaign is that this particular phase of public relations began with the plethora of new issues underwritten between the years 1958 and 1962. Until this unprecedented new issues market, financial public relations was an integral part of general industrial practice.

In 1958, with new issues doubling and tripling their value almost overnight in a wild over-the-counter speculative market, a new specialization in publicity was created. Because of the fevered nature of this part of the general market in securities, the publicity attending it became almost as embroidered as theatrical press agentry. Many new public relations firms sprang up overnight with the sole purpose of giving glamour to new issues

After the collapse of May, 1962, during which many of these new issues disappeared entirely from active trading, the SEC, as well as responsible media, began to look askance at the publicity operations serving new flotations. Unfortunately, the barn doors were locked too late. Underwriting became more conservative, SEC scrutiny more rigid and over-the-counter trading more cautious, at least for the survivors. To separate industrial from financial public relations is a mutilation of the informational process of business and it is to be hoped that the aberrations of that period will never be repeated.

What is important for the student to consider is the relationship between investors and the channels of investment in publicly held companies. If one considers that the ability of the government to borrow is dependent on the ability of the government to tax the revenues of the nation's business, it becomes clear that the process of investment is the backbone of the American economy. Stock markets are the reflection of the health or sickness of the economy at any given time. But the constant balance between buyers and sellers, as recorded by each day's tabulation of prices, measures most accurately the collective confidence or lack of confidence existent in the investment community. To a great degree, trust or fear of the daily valuations springs from what this community reads and hears about the elements affecting each segment of the nation's industries.

THE CORPORATE FINANCIAL PERSONALITY

The legal derivation of a corporation has its genesis in the creation of a commercial entity devoid of a personal, that is, an individual's, liability under the law. The creation of this invulnerable quality is the purpose—the only purpose—of an incorporation. The age of doing business as an individual, or a group of individuals in a partnership, is almost extinct.

However, we buy from, sell to, and work for corporations that, because of our individual emotions, we invest with personalities. They have good or bad reputations; they are either trustworthy and reliable or deceitful and dishonest according to each individual's experience with them. The lack of this experience does not inhibit our judgment of them. We read about them or hear about them in one context or another and, in so doing, judgment is fixed. They develop personalities very much as individuals do and, big or small, they prosper or die by the success or failure of their relating to the masses.

The public relations practitioner has the responsibility for the environment in which this appraisal takes place. The management of this relationship is a huge and complicated variable that differs in almost every case. To apply a fixed set of rules is an injustice to the corporation, as well as to the public. Also, with the radical change of conditions we discussed at the outset of this chapter, corporate public relations is no longer a matter either of instinct or ivory tower inspiration. Corporate personalities are no longer redeemed by well-publicized philanthropy. Management, boards of directors and policy are subject to lively debate by tens of thousands of stockholders in open areas covered by the national press. Bookkeeping is subject to constant scrutiny and every public corporation has come to know and respect the cumulative weight of negative proxies.

Keeping in view the fact that public corporations lead public lives, in this chapter we are not concerned with these lives as they are lived through the advertising and publicizing of their products or services, but merely with the maintenance of their status as industrial entities. The personality characteristics of a corporation lie in its history, its generations of management, the precipitateness or gentle graduation of its curve of success, its relationship with its competitors in its own field, its banking sponsorship and the continuity of respect it receives from the investment community.

If it is a listed corporation on a large stock exchange, its price behavior, as reflected by a decade or more of its daily fluctuations, will give a very strong indication not only of earnings but of status projection as well. The important point here is that the valuation of a stock is made up of many hidden ingredients besides the obvious price-earnings ratio. Growth potential, comparative status in the industry and management qualifications are only three of the most important in this regard.

All of these elements lend the practitioner ample latitude for story development. However, the routine requirements, and some of them are made necessary by law, are just as important. Corporations listed on the New York Stock Exchange and the American Stock Exchange (these number more than 4000 of America's leading corporations) are required to make quarterly-earnings reports each year. In addition, the consolidated annual-earnings statements must be published along with a certified public accountant's audit.

INTERIM AND ANNUAL REPORTS

The interim statements are usually printed in one-fold single-sheet reports. They generally include, in addition to the financial data, a brief letter from the company's president. This letter usually contains a clarification of new developments, an explanation of new products or plans and a generalized prediction of the earnings trend. (See Appendix B.)

For the public relations representative, these occasions rarely demand more than the editing of the letter and a typographical composition of the accountant's report forming a well-designed leaflet for the printer, and thence mailing to stockholders.

However, at the end of every fiscal year an annual report must be prepared that, since the days of the Great Depression, corporations have made into a major production effort. Some of these exquisite products of the printer's art have become so lavish that stockholders have come to complain that their curtailment might mean greater dividends. Nevertheless, the indications are that they will become even more ornate and that this medium will remain for some time the status symbol for public companies.

It would not be remiss for the public relations man to remember that graphic splendor never really substitutes for content. A good annual report should contain the annual message by the company's president to the stockholders, a statement of the annual operations and the annual audit, a general history of the company, a description of its products and services, an explanatory listing of all subsidiaries and ancillary operations, a roster of board members and a photographic and chart treatment of all these elements if they have photogenic qualities.

Since the annual report is used as a year-round mailing piece to new stockholders as an introduction to the company's character, it should have a built-in reflection of its size and importance in its particular industry. There is a tendency, which the practitioner should resist, to go overboard in the design and printing of annual reports. After a certain point, which is mainly a matter of good taste, elaborateness could have an adverse effect and evoke negative comments.

With both the interim reports and the annual report, full-scale press coverage must be secured. Because publication in these cases constitutes a legal record, as well as a service to readers, good public relations treatment should elicit more than minimum space allotments.

At this point it might be well to discuss a media group peculiar solely to the financial community. For good or evil, the analytic section of Wall Street is the most articulate and verbose part of that community. This articulation finds its way into print with the result that every good-sized brokerage house, banking house and analytical investment counselor publishes daily, weekly, fortnightly, monthly and annual analyses ranging in subject matter the entire gamut of investment markets. All of this is in addition to individually mailed responses to inquiries. Because this profusion of material has the inherent purpose of generating purchases and sales, every issue discussed is concluded with a recommendation for the appropriate action by the reader.

Thus, in addition to the media of the annual report and interim reports, the practitioner is confronted with a third group of media having a weighty effect on his charge. It has become custom for corporation executives to confront these analysts periodically and to review for them the salient facts of their corporations' development. The analysts are also, when the occasion demands, brought to the companies' plants for on-the-spot inspections of these developments, or merely for general tours. It is a natural consequence that all published material and releases should be sent to this group of analysts and a working relationship with them must be maintained.

Publicity that leads to increasing the family of investors in any particular corporation has the two-fold purpose of increasing the demand for the stock—so that it commands as high a price-earnings ratio as its investment prestige merits—and maintaining a high credit quotient. This credit quotient reflects itself in the corporation's ease of obtaining new financing and, more important, heightens the ability to acquire the ownership of lesser corporations by an adroit maneuvering of payment in stock for those acquisitions rather than in cash. The higher the value of the stock the greater the ease in the process of acquisitions. Some of the largest corporate complexes are accumulated by payments in shares without affecting cash balances.

But it is mandatory for the practitioner to remember that no matter what the environment or circumstances of the assignment, his function is never that of a stock tout. Causing significant fluctuations in the price of a stock is not public relations in any sense. It is not only illegal, but it is also bound to result in a general disqualification from legitimate practice. Financial public relations is based primarily on arithmetical facts. Although a conservative extrapolation of these facts is sometimes permitted, the facts must be in consonance with statistical projections and capable of safe exposure to the hard light of sophisticated scrutiny.

In the last chapter, we briefly discussed trade media. In industrial public relations the relationship of any corporate unit to its competitors, or with wholesale sources of raw materials, as well as with industrial consumers, is maintained through the trade press. The only other important connecting link is usually found in trade associations. These associations exist in almost every industry. They are rigidly controlled by the major factions of each industry. Sometimes the associations maintain a press of their own, usually the sole means of keeping up the appearance of intraindustrial harmony. It is extremely important for the practitioner to know in this regard that intraindustrial collusion in such areas as price fixing, wage fixing and allocations of sales territories is illegal by federal and state statutes and any public relations done on this level—that is, the intraindustrial level—should only be attempted under the rigid control of the client's attorneys.

The greatest single facet in the investment power structure is the mutual funds, which has been gaining momentum during the past twenty-five years. Because of its easy availability in terms of price (some are even sold on an installment basis), it has become the favorite investment channel for the larger part of the lower-income group. Diversification, sagacious investment policy and other advantages that the small investor could not avail himself of if he chose to manage his own portfolio are some of the reasons for the popularity of these open-end trusts. Because mutual funds are usually buyers of large blocs of stock and because they are rarely short-term investors, the number of shares they hold in a corporation influences considerably the general prestige of the company in which they invest.

The public relations operation for an industrial client should recognize this situation and service the analysts of the major mutual funds with factual material and financial statements whenever they are available for release. This service should be augmented by occasional invitations to individual analysts for interviews with company executives. Some of these funds specialize in particular industrial groupings, so that it should become a regular practice to follow the published investment trusts. Those not operated on a mutual basis tend to have more set investment policies, but nevertheless their programs should be acutely examined for their possible interest in the practitioner's client.

STOCKHOLDERS' MEETINGS

For the most part, the successful public relations program for an industrial client can be gauged by whether or not the stockholders are happy. If they are, it is a good indication that the company is making continued financial progress, that its reputation in its particular industry is rising and that its roster of investors is increasing. There is nothing that represents less of a problem than an annual meeting of stockholders who are content with the policies and results of the incumbent management. Usually these meetings are very poorly attended and when very few appear, it is a sure sign that the main body desires nothing more than a continuance of the status quo. At these meetings, the public relations practitioner's responsibility usually consists of inviting the financial press to hear first-hand the company president's remarks and to record the answers to the more pertinent questions of the stockholders.

However, when the situation is unhappy, the problems multiply. Unhappy stockholders can organize a dissident group that, if enlisted to sufficient strength in the number of shares represented, can threaten the control of management and policy. Usually this struggle takes the form of a proxy battle, with each side soliciting the support of the registered stockholders. Some of these battles are heated and of long duration. Public relations counsel usually is sought by both the in and out groups and both sides attempt to amass the facts in a manner favorable to their side's viewpoint.

CORPORATE INDUSTRIAL PERSONALITY

Leaving the financial area, the industrial side presents many challenges to effective public relations practice. The broad opportunities offered by the consumer press and magazines to corporate items give ample latitude for the placement of continuous news and feature material.

Building the corporate industrial personality requires a careful analysis of all the elements in each individual case that can be publicized. Strength, solidity and growth are the three dominant octaves in which the tune must be played. Good research by the practitioner usually results in good copy. The corporate operations should be treated as a problem in anatomy, and a good dissection job should result in the exposure of the story with the best features for publicity. These elements should then be outlined and checked in every detail with the management.

Manufacturing and servicing processes should be studied to the extent that an intimate knowledge is acquired and distributional outlets to the ultimate consumer should be charted even if the corporation does not fully control its own final sales apparatus.

ESTABLISHMENT OF CORPORATE CHARACTER

In the last analysis, it is always the company's relationship to the national economy that determines, for the greater part, editorial space allotment. Always seek to prove, either subtly or directly, that the company is making a distinctive contribution to the living standards of the general population. Companies remote from the people are the most vulnerable to competitive pressure. To establish this closeness, start with the home site, or sites, as the case may be, of the company's factories. In all likelihood, it will prove to be the dominant economic factor in the limited boundaries of its own location. How it handles this responsibility and its relationship to the health and welfare agencies of its own community always makes for productive story material. As the circumference of the company's influence spreads, the national picture becomes the more important one and, if it is large enough to exert discernible impact on the nation's economy, story opportunities proliferate.

The practitioner's file on a corporate charge should include complete biographies of the principal executives composing the management. More often than not, a corporation's executives are more exciting story material than the company or its products. A good rule to follow in this connection is never to allow publicity on a corporate executive to drift far from the business of his company. If it does, an industrial public relations client can be lost by letting it retrogress to a press agent's assignment. Relate the executive to his company and, furthermore, relate him to his colleagues so that internecine envy does not work injury.

Manufacturing processes very often lend themselves to interesting photographic treatment. Industrial photography has become a most important factor in graphic arts. Make more than adequate use of photography and always keep a spare list of unused photographic opportunities to interest photography editors.

If overseas operations exist, explore their story possibilities. The operations of an American company in some of the more exotic locations abroad is most enticing to editors.

If overseas activities include participation in the more prominent trade fairs, European publicity in conjunction with these fairs should be scheduled. If the practitioner has no European correspondents or branch offices in Europe, effective contacts can usually be made with wire services maintaining outlets in the desired countries. If not, a reliable public relations firm having branches should be assigned.

MANAGEMENT-LABOR FRICTION

Even though industrial public relations does not embrace the highly specialized field of labor relations, its operations certainly impinge on employee affairs. This is especially the case when labor/management friction reaches the point of a strike. When labor relations counsel or legal counsel are involved with negotiations to prevent or settle a situation already exposed in the press, the responsibility for informing the public about the position of the company in the dispute falls into the public relations area.

In any strikes involving large numbers of employees, especially those in which the duration inflicts a hardship on the public, the company position should be made clear by executive statements. All public relations nuances surrounding the position of management in the strike dispute should be taken into consideration, and after the final draft is written, it should be thoroughly checked by legal counsel. These statements should strive for fairness and forthrightness in the presentation of the issues rather than appeal for public sympathy. The day is past when either management or labor wins public enthusiasm for its cause by emotional appeals. The public is more interested in the ratio of average wage in any plant to average living cost in the community in which the plant is located than in either side trying to adopt the attitude of beneficence.

Every measure possible should be taken to prevent violence or the threat of violence. The best technique developed in the past decade for keeping public feelings at temperate levels has been continuous (day and night) arbitration. Public officials can be involved in these sessions. They provide an ideal picture of management's willingness to abide by the results of fair negotiations. It is encumbent on the practitioner to release a statement on company attitude daily. Angry or vituperative phrases should be omitted in deference to calm dispassionate statements in which there is daily hope of a fast settlement. Any appearance of a lockout technique being used by the company for its own advantages is to be assiduously avoided, and the feeling that the strike is harmful to all concerned should be implicit in every paragraph. Sometimes it is of benefit to publish these statements as paid advertisements. A good note in this regard is that the company's paid advertisements should never be larger than the union's, if the union is indulging in such a campaign. If there is no competition for attention in paid space, avoid excessive page areas. Try always to include, when these tense periods end, a photograph of the strike antagonists in a harmonious handshake as soon as settlement has been achieved. Try to dispel in all other ways any suspicion of residual acrimony.

INDUSTRIAL FILMS

Every practitioner involved in industrial public relations is at some point confronted with the question of whether or not an industrial motion picture program should be considered. These industrial documentaries are expensive by-products of over-all campaigns, and because they budget a financial cost disproportionate to conservative information operations, their purposes should be rigidly researched. Almost no large corporation in America is without a vault full of obsolete, or otherwise unusable, films that were made at great expense. Commercial films, when they are outright documentaries extolling their company's virtues, are very rarely, if ever, acceptable for theater or unpaid television programming. Before such a picture is ordered to be made, the potential audience for the production should be carefully computed. This audience must not only be the audience you want but, to some extent, it must be captive. Never in the history of picture exhibition has there ever been an industrial film that enticed volunteer viewers in impressive numbers. The one unanimous demand of the American public is that their film fare be entertainment. An obvious attempt in film either to sell or lift the prestige of a commercial property is not only ignored, but resented to a point where it might work an injury rather than a benefit.

However, this is not to say that industrial films do not serve some important purposes. First, in large companies they fill an important historical purpose, giving a visual record of progress and growth. Secondly, they are excellent selling vehicles, especially for the portrayal of heavy industrial installations that cannot possibly be transported for demonstration purposes. Films are also of great use at fairs and at exhibitions where continuous rear-screen projection affords an eye-catching mechanism superior to most other techniques.

Perhaps the most valuable of all industrial films are those devoted to teaching sales methods to prospective and veteran sales personnel and teaching intricate manufacturing processes to engineering and skilled-worker personnel. These films are usually timesaving and far superior to wordy lectures or technical pamphlets. They should be encouraged whenever budget allows.

EXERCISES

1 (a) By observation of the financial sections of the daily press for a period of one week, correlate by actual examples stock market fluctuations with news events.
(b) Do the same for individual stocks.

2 (a) From a single issue of the WALL STREET JOURNAL, analyze the reasons for the editor's choice of which earnings reports are given front-page features, which are confined to a paragraph, and which are given merely a single line of copy.
(b) List the determinant factors in what might be considered their order of importance.

3 (a) Using a fictitious corporate name, list the various public relations techniques necessary for the introduction of a new issue to the public.
(b) Using this outline as a base, project a full year's campaign for maximum coverage of the financial community.

4 (a) Describe the organization of an analysts meeting in which the client, who is the president of a corporation, would be the sole speaker.
(b) What literature should be distributed at this meeting?

5 Choose any corporation listed on the New York Stock Exchange and, after sufficient research, outline an annual report.

6 (a) Write a release announcing a half per cent rise in interest rates on savings accounts for a large bank.
(b) Write an institutional ad for the same bank to cover a half page.

7 (a) A hypothetical corporation has suffered a serious decline in sales because of rising labor costs. A six-month report is about to be issued. Write an interim letter to the stockholders explaining the earnings decline.

(b) Convert this letter into a newspaper release.

8 Write a pamphlet intended to extol the virtues of a newly formed mutual fund that specializes in "growth" stocks.

9 Plan a stockholders meeting of a public utility company in which there has been stockholder friction with management. A proxy fight is threatening. The practitioner is counsel to the company. What recommendations should be made to management in preparation for the meeting?

10 Execute a corporate fact sheet, using any of the authentic statistical services for distribution, to financial analysts and editors.

11 Using a news story of an industrial strike, write an ad for insertion in paid space explaining and winning sympathy for management position.

12 Pertinent Case Exercises (See Appendix A)
a. HHV IN JEOPARDY
b. XERXES COMPLEX
c. CLOCK RUN-DOWN
d. CLIPPED WINGS

SUGGESTED SUPPLEMENTAL READING

Anders, Curtis L. "The New Guidelines for Corporate Information." *Public Relations Journal.* New York: Public Relations Society of America, Inc. (Jan. 1969)

Beveridge, Oscar M. *Financial Public Relations: Tested Techniques for Communicating with Financial Publics.* New York: McGraw–Hill Book Company, Inc., 1963

Brayman, Harold. *Corporate Management in a World of Politics.* New York: McGraw–Hill Book Company, Inc., 1967

Brooks, John. *Once in Golconda, A True Drama of Wall Street, 1920–1938.* New York: Harper & Row Publishers, Inc., 1970

Cheney, Richard E. "Tender Fights: Strategy and Tactics." *Public Relations Journal.* New York: Public Relations Society of America, Inc. (April 1968)

Dowell, Edwin E. "Our Longest Strike." *Public Relations Journal.* New York: Public Relations Society of America, Inc. (Oct. 1968)

Engle, Nathanael Howard. *Public Relations in Selected Large Corporations.* Seattle: Bureau of Business Research, College of Business Administration, University of Washington, 1955

Farley, William E. *Practical Public Relations for the Business Man.* New York: Frederick Fell, Inc., 1968

Ford, Henry II. "The Revolution in Public Relations." *Public Relations Journal*. New York: Public Relations Society of America, Inc. (Oct. 1970)

Henderer, Frederic Rhodes. *A Comparative Study of Public Relations Practices in Six Industrial Corporations*. Pittsburgh: University of Pittsburgh Press, 1956

Henderson, Carter F., and Albert C. Lasker. *20 Million Careless Capitalists*. Garden City, N.Y.: Doubleday & Company, 1967

Hughes, Anthony D. "Trends in Financial Relations." *Public Relations Journal*. New York: Public Relations Society of America, Inc. (Oct. 1970)

McCarty, John T. *Community Relations for Business*. Washington, D. C.: BNA, Inc., 1956

Zausner, Martin. *Corporate Management and the Investment Community*. New York: Ronald Press Company, 1968

commercial public relations 4

DEFINING COMMERCIAL PUBLIC RELATIONS

Commercial public relations can generally be defined as the publicizing of products and services. In this sphere, it assumes a role secondary to advertising. The main selling aid of consumer goods and consumer services is usually assigned to advertising agencies whose responsibility is the proper use of paid space and paid time.

As a general rule, but certainly not true in every case, the advertising budgets of large corporations selling directly to the public average approximately 12% of the gross sales. Of this budget, allotments to specific public relations activity extend from half of 1% to a maximum of 2%. These allotments are usually assigned to one of three potential practicing units: public relations departments within the advertising and promotion section of the corporation; the public relations department of the corporation's advertising agency; or individual public relations agencies. Surveys show that the three categories share about equally the total number of assignments. Very often they may be called on to supplement each other in different aspects of the same campaign

PUBLICIZING A PRODUCT

The public relations objectives for the successful publicizing of a product are initially to invest that product with an identity so marked that it almost develops a personality and, secondly, to make the product synonymous with its utility. That is, if it is a tire, its brand mark must be identified in the consumer mind so well that the word *tire* is synonymous with the brand. This kind of saturational objectives has actually been reached after protracted campaigns with many products so that its attainment is based on these elements: first and foremost, the product must be good; secondly, the advertising and public relations budgets must be ample, and of course, the practitioner must be able.

The technique of publicizing a product that either already has, or possesses the potential of, a nationwide market, is a "hard-work" routine. Ivory tower methods have very limited application to this particular field of public relations. A good formula is to begin with a complete research job on the product itself—how it is made; how it is marketed; who uses it and for what. This is the research assignment, but it is also the framework of the campaign. From each of these areas a complete story line can be developed.

Because a good many products have seasonal rises and declines of demand, good practice requires the seasonal placing of feature material, whereas other aspects less directly related to consumer marketing should be placed in the off-season months.

A good many products have maximum sales periods during a few short weeks, such as the Christmas and Easter seasons, and therefore require placement for maximum effect during the thirty days preceding these periods. Seasonal demands for any product or group of products can be charted and it is highly advisable to use an accurate sales chart before planning a continuous campaign. These charts usually are available from the sales manager of the plant, and when not available should be executed by the practitioner. It is a good rule not to seek for anything in these charts but sales volume; the principal concern remains maximum coverage, which is a secondary aid to sales. The major influence on sales is salesmanship, which is not within the purview of public relations.

Public relations requires virtuoso thinking, particularly when a client corporation makes an acquisition of a business totally unrelated to the company doing the acquiring.

One such example is a case with a company mainly involved with home appliances for use in connection with foods. The electric blender this company made had been publicized to the point where it had become the leader in sales in the industry.

When this company acquired a firm that made tools—that is, work tools—planning a campaign was a difficult assignment, mostly because there is perhaps nothing as mundane as a hacksaw or screwdriver. However, realizing that the "move to the suburbs" was steadily gaining momentum, literature was produced extolling the advantages of a workshop of splendid tools in every American basement.

This fast developed into a do-it-yourself movement that swept the country and created for the client a meteoric rise in sales.

In publicizing a product, the widest range of media should be used. The problem is how to obtain maximum exposure. Although it is true that basic exposure must be maintained in the consumer press and magazines in every department offering the possible use of the product material, the ancillary channels of exposure assume at least an equal, if not more productive, importance.

Some of this exposure range normally falls to the advertising agency. This would include all point-of-sales items and displays, counter and window space, and special exploitation in combination with paid advertising.

However, in more subtle areas, publicity techniques resume a major role. Here the fields of radio and television offer opportunities for the discreet placement of material that can have a vital sales effect. The practitioner should be aware that production executives of the radio and TV networks are most sophisticated in their consideration of blatant commercial placement. Therefore, it is wise not to be blatant. Do not seek to publicize a label. Publicize a product that is unlabeled, provided that it is identifiable by use, appearance, or even contour or faint reference. Very often a potential consumer in the audience will prove more suggestible to subtlety than to an easily resented commercial intrusion into his favorite program.

Very few of the popular private eye series on TV are produced without the hero getting into a resplendent new convertible with the top down as he chases after the villain. The camera never closes up on the name plate of the car, but the impact is powerful. It becomes mandatory for the effective practitioner to scan studiously all possible radio and television programs that might possibly lend themselves to the exposure of the product handled.

More fundamental is the myriad number of stories that can be developed for the various departments in the daily press. Placement with the press depends most on continuity of effort. For the average consumer product biweekly releases, amounting to an aggregate number of twenty-five a year, is what is meant by continuity of effort.

In publicizing a product that has been on the market for a number of years, it is very difficult to develop a news angle that will impress an editor. The practitioner must bear in mind that he should provide editors throughout the country with a continuous series of feature stories, both long and short. Even though the number of newspapers each week printing client release material may not be impressive, coverage computed over a period of years will show a substantial exposure not otherwise obtainable.

Many large dailies maintain departments specifically devoted to publicizing consumer articles for their readers. Advertising in the fields of fashion, household accessories, decoration, giftware, photography, automobiles and boating are highly profitable sources of revenue to the press. Therefore, the press has developed editorial sections that daily publish news items and feature articles about these products, which—in the large metropolitan dailies—are not necessarily related in any way to the space bought by large advertisers. The press must maintain a market place with a prodigious appetite for well-written copy that is a prime outlet for the practitioner.

Although the technique of merchandising has expanded its stratagems and tactics, in a strange reverse process the struggle to obtain sufficient space to place a product within sight or handy reach of a consumer has become a severe problem for the distributor of consumer products. This battle for the shelf or the counter became increasingly hectic when supermarkets replaced the corner grocery stores and when department stores in central locations replaced the neighborhood dry-goods stores in our age of automotive shopping.

Because the sale of the product in the final analysis depends on actual availability of the product to the customer, and because the retailer makes this availability possible in ratio to the manufacturer's advertising and publicity output, the conclusion to be drawn is obvious: The supermarket is loath to display a brand not sufficiently publicized or advertised.

To the public relations practitioner this fight for space takes place in the media he services. His success or failure is directly related to the aggregate number of feet of shelf space his product will be granted.

In the preparation of material for press dissemination, lavish use of photographs should be made. The product in use by an attractive model will be appreciated by the editor even if it does not merit publication because it will, in all likelihood, clarify the text of the release. If it is a household product, it will be placed in the file of that category of products, and if a round-up picture story is planned the photo will be given space along with its competing products. Even though this is not as rewarding as a story exclusively constructed around the client's product, it is far better than being omitted entirely.

If the product bears a retail price with reason, and if it is not perishable or too fragile to mail, it should be loaned to the proper departmental editors of large dailies for demonstration purposes. It should not be sent as a gift, but if the editor would like one for his own use, a normal discount from the retail price should be granted. The giving of gifts by public relations firms to editors is not an ethical practice and is frowned on by nearly all managing editors of good newspapers.

INTRODUCING A NEW PRODUCT

The introduction of a new product is usually highlighted by the kind of press party described in the preceding chapter. If the budget permits, the ideal press party is a luncheon at which an officer of sufficient stature in the company introducing the product greets the editors and other press representatives and explains, or even demonstrates, the product.

Because it is difficult to maintain a consistently increasing amount of publicity for an old product, many practitioners make the blunder of trying to capture the attention of the press by dressing up the old product with a new publicity line. The word *new* stamped on a package very often fools the public, and it has become a favorite device on television. However, it will not work with the press. Do not try it. By the title, *New Product,* the press understands that it is an improvement on the old to the extent that it makes the old obsolete.

A good practitioner will research by actual personal contact the knowledge of retail personnel selling his client's product and their method of selling it. Very often sales personnel in retail stores have only the vaguest background information about the product and are insufficiently oriented to answer a customer's most elementary inquiries

The best-organized publicity campaign can break down at this point, thereby giving competitors tremendous advantage. Sales personnel of this category, especially those handling products marketed in supermarkets or in large department stores, are notoriously resistant to educative material. Therefore, it is recommended that in at least one instance in the case of new products, as well as old, retail sales personnel be treated as a part of the media. The initial action upon the assumption of a publicity assignment for a product should be the composition of an explicit fact sheet containing all the necessary particulars about the product. This fact sheet, when it is distributed to the press, should be marked for file use and should include the name, address and phone number of the practitioner for the servicing of inquiries. The same fact sheet should be distributed in bulk to department store or supermarket buyers for redistribution to the sales personnel involved with the product. Sales people or buyers should be contacted by the practitioner only in this case or when specific projects are instituted by the client.

SALES CONVENTIONS

One of the major annual assignments demanding elaborate preparation by the practitioner is the event known as the sales convention. It is usually held in an attractive metropolitan area hotel or in a resort area having adequate facilities. There are wide differences of opinion on the effectiveness of these conventions, or even on their advisability, and for a great many corporations they have grown into annual junkets that are more social than business in emphasis. In large companies with sales and executive personnel numbering well into the thousands, the social objective is quite justified, mainly because it is the only feasible means of a huge spirited get-together on the theory that if people actually know one another, their working together will be more effective. There is also a holiday spirit about these conventions that makes the event somewhat of an incentive, or almost a bonus for the participants. Of course, the high-priority purpose is the generation of enthusiasm to a pitch that it is hoped will be contagious enough to infuse all with the drive to do better.

Usually the practitioner receives the assignment of programming the convention in coordination with the ranking executives in charge. It has become good form to invite a national personality to speak on a highly charged political level so that a maximum national press will be assured. Senators holding controversial views usually make the front page and guarantee maximum press attendance at the session. The arrangements for handling the assignment to obtain the personality chosen are usually done by the practitioner, who also arranges the honorarium to be paid.

The convention itself generally breaks down to work sessions in small groups with common interests and large sessions for addresses by the company's president, sales officers, plant managers and district sales managers. The plenary sessions usually continue throughout the day; large sessions usually are held at night. This balance is not mandatory and variations are to be encouraged. A program that tends to make the procession of events routine or dull should be avoided. There is usually a lavish use of charts and visual displays and if any industrial movies have been made during the year on the company's activities, the convention offers ideal audience potential.

Among the larger companies, there seems to be a rising tendency to make the sales convention entertaining. Songwriters are engaged to write uplifting tunes and lyrics and beautiful showgirls are employed to dance and sing them. These productions become more opulent each year so that a gay atmosphere can prevail. Like annual reports and other corporate luxuries, these affairs are products of the Internal Revenue Department rather than executive theatrical ambitions.

For the practitioner there are two important press releases: one covering the guest speaker and the other covering the president's message, which should contain a pressworthy prognostication of the company's business. Both should be serviced from the point of the convention and contain a paragraph giving the over-all attendance figure and duration of the convention.

UTILITY AND SERVICE COMPANIES

Service industries, which are industries having no saleable product, must be publicized on the basis of their continued utility. Convenience, economy, safety, excitement and dependability, along with many other features, are all productive publicity lines. Companies in the service industry fall into well-defined categories, such as utilities, transportation carriers, banks and insurance companies, leasers of equipment such as IBM and Xerox and many other similar businesses wherein no actual product is sold.

To the practitioner, the most important of these categories is the utility company, which services wide areas without competition. Conducting a business for profit that the people of the community must use in order to conduct their daily lives presents a public relations problem, as well as a political problem, that occasionally transcends ordinary business considerations. To the practitioner it means a continuous effort to prove that the client company always has a perpetual responsibility that places service to the community above financial gain.

The objective of such campaigns has developed a monotonous sameness during the twentieth century, which is the adoption of an institutional or quasi-governmental façade for the company. The intention is to soften what is, in most cases, a genuine monopoly, to the point that the citizenry comes to feel that a utility company yields as graciously to majority pressures as do elected representatives.

Although this objective has become fairly static, public relations methods vary considerably. The institutional approach through public spirited advertising and publicity, deep-level participation in community charities and the lending of a willing hand to civic improvement are tried and true methods that the practitioner should recommend and use.

However, in recent years there has been an increasing tendency to build around the "fair return" theme. The rise in the popularity of using a bolder admission of the profit motive stems mainly from the increased number of utility stockholders in the average American community. That this roster of stockholders also includes labor unions and pension funds helps materially.

To depend to too great an .extent on this line invites a substantial risk element that is usually difficult to detect, except during business recessions. It is always wise to remember that American stockholders in utility companies have a minority status and probably will have for many years to come. As soon as a business recession causes a swelling relief role, the utility companies offer too obvious a target to expose unnecessarily. A good middle-of-the-road course is to use publicity channels to prove that the utility company in your public relations charge is using an extraordinary proportion of its profits for expansion, which is usually the most effective element contributing to the community's growth.

Transportation carriers are almost in the same general category as the utilities and should be handled in practically the same way except that they usually are not monopolies and therefore do not have the same political nuances.

The great risk element ever present in carrier public relations is the accident, which very often in modern air and other high-speed transportation results in fatalities of catastrophic proportions. As a general rule, the practitioner should make absolutely no effort, overt or covert, to reduce the news coverage of an accident. Any effort on the company's part to conceal any element that might have contributed to the accident is almost sure proof of negligence or culpability. As long as there are human and mechanical frailties, high-speed transportation casualties will occur. The fullest disclosure of the causes of an accident is recognized by the public as a means of preventing the next one.

Good public relations requires that the fullest company cooperation with investigational authorities be evident. A good practitioner should be on the scene, if it is at all possible, as quickly as the press arrives. Interviews with survivors or the injured should be supervised so that false innuendos or hysterical exaggerations can be set right. The other important immediate action is to limit the statements of responsible company officials to expressions of sympathy with the victims. The scene of a catastrophe is the poorest possible location for an interview with an officer of the company. Make an effort to avoid it.

BANK AND INSURANCE COMPANIES

Probably the largest service industry in the United States is the banking business, and it continues to grow. Because this country can boast the world's most productive and prosperous middle class, and because this middle class is noteworthy for its quotient of confidence—which impels it to buy beyond its means—supplying credit made American banking the great service industry.

Credit accommodation has a multiplicity of forms, and its servicing has remained complex despite the installation of computers. It is only one hundred years ago that the banking business consisted of granting business loans and mortgages on prime real estate. Today our installment economy requires that a bank finance the purchase of a meal, a refrigerator, an automobile, a vacation or even an education. Fewer than fifty years ago only a person of substantial means could afford the luxury of a checking account. Today one of the principal sources of bank income is the ten-cent check and the account that requires no balance.

All this metamorphosis has made banks larger, and at the same time made them less austere. Instead of doing business with a privileged few, banks now compete in the open market to do business with the mass, or operations become unprofitable.

Of course, for the practitioner, the first requirement is to remember that the bank is one of the pillars of the community and that the banker heading it is among the community's foremost citizens. The austere façade and the aura of dignity must be converted into an easily entered place of business (and very personal business at that). The loss of austerity should be transferred into feelings of substance and respect.

Publicity for a bank must literally operate on both sides of the street. On one side, it must invite depositors with all the enticements that depositors require, and on the other, it must invite borrowers with quite another set of inducements.

Although most of these assignments have fallen to the lot of advertising firms, more banks use public relations practitioners today than ever before. The publication of literature explaining modern banking's multiple services is within the area of the practitioner and every innovation of banking service finds its way into the daily press. As most of these innovations develop new sources of credit, they have direct bearing on the business level of the community. Stories about them are invariably stories involving other businesses, as well as particularized sections of the population. The involvements are disparate, and the range is grist for the publicist's mill when the client is a bank. There should be virtually no stoppage in the legitimate news flow.

One of the most agonizing, if not terrifying sights, is a run on a bank. Anyone who has ever seen one will never forget the stamp of panic on the individual faces in line and the actual smell of anxiety of people in fear of losing their life's savings by the shutting of a door.

Very early in my career, I was called by the attorney for a rather large bank in an industrial city a short distance from New York. At the attorney's office, I met the bank president and they told me quickly that a run had developed a half hour before that day's closing and word was around that the bank would not survive. They asked if I could do anything to stem the panic in the community.

I took the problem home with me. I did not attempt to sleep that night because the solution had to be forthcoming before 9 o'clock the next morning. I realized that my first action, in an attempt to cope intelligently with a situation that explosive, must be to purge my own mind of panic.

At 10 o'clock that evening I drove to the city in which the bank was located, parked the car opposite the bank and sat and thought. As people passed, I noticed that their conversation was mainly in Polish and Italian. Sparked by this observation I started to drive through the streets seeking a large Catholic Church. At 11 o'clock at night I knocked on the pastor's door. I was cordially asked in and to three very tired priests I told my story.

The next morning the senior pastor, on the top of a car parked outside the main office of the bank, addressed the line of frightened depositors in Polish. I never saw a cloud of panic lift so quickly or faith restored so spontaneously to people whose own fears were about to ruin them. The bank is open today and is one of the largest institutions in the state.

To a lesser extent the insurance company, particularly the life insurance company, offers the same wealth of source material. However, in this case you have the added very volatile human interest in health and life extension. Most insurance companies conduct highly organized research programs whose findings, more often than not, are made public in print. Any story involving statistics of longevity, health, accidents, fires, floods, hurricanes and too many others to record invites continuing editor interest.

In the insurance field, too, there is a demand for inventiveness for new forms of protection and selling. These require the preparation of descriptive literature, which falls directly within the purview of the practitioner.

REAL ESTATE PUBLICITY

One of the most interesting categories in the wide gamut of public relations assignments is land development publicity. Because this fits neither the product nor service categories, sizeable real estate ventures require a promotional technique peculiar to themselves.

This field has grown tremendously over the last century to the extent that every state in the union and nearly every municipal government of any size maintains information departments whose main tasks are to produce come-hither publicity and literature. This particular field of public relations has enjoyed further expansion with the advent of urban redevelopment on a gigantic scale now in progress throughout the country.

Whether the problem presented to the practitioner is rural, suburban or urban development, the objectives are resolute inasmuch as huge segments of the population must be attracted to a way of life and habitation other than what they previously enjoyed. Climate, living facilities, transportation convenience, easy and economical shopping and nearby growth industries are the dominant chords.

Surveys have proved that the American population, unlike its European counterpart, has always been itinerant, at least in theory if not in practice. The October lease expiration date in our larger cities has taken on the aspect of a mass-migration day. The average American seems to have no fidelity to his home site. Newspapers are keenly aware of the American longing to move and they extend an inordinate share of space to real estate development and architectural progress.

The principal medium for good public relations in this field is the Sunday paper. This section is avidly read by all members of the family and very often the Sunday automobile trip is planned around a visit to the publicized sites. Most valuable to remember is the use of photographs and, still better, impressive architectural renderings.

It might be a very good idea for practitioners particularly interested in the real estate field to examine the urban renewal law governing activity of this type in his community or in his state and also to acquaint himself with zoning laws and other restrictive covenants. Interesting in this regard is the fact that most urban renewal projects are required by law to expend a set percentage of projected rentals for public relations and advertising purposes. Actually, the theory behind this ruling is official recognition of public relations as a channel through which an entire community may take pride in the development of only a part.

The purpose of urban redevelopment is to make entire cities more viable, and not simply a convenience for a small segment of the whole operation. In publicizing smaller projects, such as a new apartment house, or a new industrial plant, or a shopping center, the viewpoint for the practitioner to pursue must be what his client's project is doing for all, rather than merely for the prospective tenant. New concepts of architecture give our cities a constantly changing skyline, affecting the civic pride of all residents. To mobilize this feeling of pride in a real estate campaign gives meaning to the campaign and, most often, success to the client.

TOURISM

Very closely related to the publicizing of real property and territorial industrial promotion is the field of tourism, which has enjoyed a huge expansion over the last several years. First the automobile and then commercial aircraft have given the American public a concept of location accessibility that has made tourism a multibillion dollar industry.

From a public relations viewpoint, the practitioner must understand the multifaceted nature of the business because the handling of any facet is closely related to the others. For instance, publicizing a hotel in Arizona might depend for its success or failure on an airline schedule, which, in turn, may be determined ultimately by the popularity of the hotels in the district serviced. Therefore, the approach would have to be dual—that is, the airline campaign, for best effect, would have to be correlated, if not actually coordinated with the thematic elements of the hotel's advertising. Resort areas enjoy waves of popularity and, by the same token, suffer seemingly unexplainable sporadic desertions. To stimulate or regulate the traffic flow should be the highest priority among the objectives of a well-conceived campaign.

The far-seeing practitioner should not forget the railroads, which are about to enjoy a refurbishing of equipment and a scheduling system far more conducive to travel. There is no question that the deplorable traffic conditions on American highways and the high accident toll taken by holiday travel will give American railroads a renaissance in short- and medium-distance travel. It is a field well worth exploring.

The most important new impetus to American tourism has been the motel movement, which has multiplied accommodation facilities to the extent that the tourist is no longer dependent on expensive reserved-status housing on his travels. Many motels today, by advance design and construction, have themselves become resorts with an attractive character of their own and rate levels scaled to the financial ability of the family on vacation.

Another important consideration is the ever-increasing population of sun followers who migrate from north to south, and from east to southwest, and back, each year for the purpose of enjoying continuous summer. At one time, this was the privilege only of the rich, but it now includes huge numbers of the retired and semi-retired of moderate means and, incidentally, an increasing number each year of itinerant workers and marginal businessmen.

No single category of public relations material in original unexpurgated form has greater access to the press than travel and resort copy. The revenue from advertising from this source is expanding daily and what used to be a purely seasonal flow has become a four-season torrent.

Good editing requires the buttressing of paid advertising with attractively written editorial coverage. The range of this coverage makes individual reporting virtually impossible, so that the dependence on publicity copy is almost complete. All major dailies have appointed department heads to edit this flow of copy and the result has been the creation of sections attracting a huge readership.

Different from any other department of the paper, editorial policy in these sections is considerably more relaxed and a tendency toward flamboyance in copy receives sanction. Photography is vital to resort publicity and should be lavishly used. Many newspapers are not using color photographs and this fact should control photography assignments to a great extent.

The growth of tourism has had a great effect on magazine policy. One magazine, HOLIDAY, owed its genesis to this growth. Others, such as ESQUIRE, PLAYBOY and even LIFE, devote great allotments of space to resort features and welcome story suggestions specifically targeted for their readership.

Before very long every practitioner in the resort field is confronted with the junket problem. The junket is a free trip and short stay without charge for a group of newspaper and magazine writers (occasionally free-lance writers) whose exposure to the resort is calculated to stimulate laudatory copy. Although the percentage of actual return on the substantial investment in a junket is usually low, the temptation to organize one for the new or failing resort owner is very high. In the case of a new multimillion dollar venture, such as a lush hotel, a new airline, or a new ocean liner, it probably pays because the copy has a high normal demand and the authenticity of the staff writer carries weight. But the practitioner should know that those newspapers having the highest journalistic integrity insist on paying a reporter's expenses for a resort assignment, just as they would on any other legitimate assignment. Unfortunately, we are speaking of the exception, not the rule, but it is well to know the code of the publication with which you are working.

There are many cases in public relations in which the easy way proves to be the best way.

One of this writer's past projects was deeply beset with difficulties and a history of continued failure in attempts to solve them. The problem concerned a resort area in New York State in which tens of millions of dollars had been invested. This area, by accident or design (it hardly mattered), had acquired a national reputation for catering to a single ethnic group. Because the second and third generations of this group had no particular desire to identify exclusively with their antecedents, a plague of empty hotel rooms ensued and a wave of bankruptcies threatened. The process of deterioration was made even more painful because the district had great natural beauty with physical assets that many successful resorts envied.

To the Association representing hotel management, solutions always lay in the area of surgically removing, by the roots if necessary, all vestiges of ethnic identification. After considerable research, it was easily ascertainable that not even the use of nuclear weaponry could perform this task. One hundred years of public recognition in depth of its ethnic patronage so profoundly marked this district, that the name of the county in which it was located became idiomatic in the public consciousness. It would have taken at least fifty years to make an erasure effective, and fifty years was entirely too long to wait.

Our decision was to use the problem as a remedy; to make the exposure of the best and most attractive characteristics of a group a profitable method of enticing the tourist and vacationer to a resort area that was indeed unique. The public relations method was comparatively simple: We gave full exploitation to the elements that distinguished the group in their fun-loving proclivities, their exaggerated sense of entertainment, their insistence on the best in food and service, and their impatience with any routine leading to boredom. For many years these attributes had all been played down, if not hidden, by the various hotel managements. The results were almost immediate. The resort area became a convention mecca and attracted tourists from all parts of the country and every segment of the population.

Another adjunct of resort publicity is the ancillary or tangential tie-ins with unrelated products. A fashion feature of a new line of bathing suits for a fashion magazine must be photographed in the best setting possible. Resort publicists compete for this kind of tie-in and obtain maximum cooperation from their clients for the caption that identifies the resort represented. This is only one of a myriad of cases where resorts tie in as the location of photogenic events that accrue to the benefit of all concerned.

Since the day the steamships replaced sails in the Atlantic trade, European travel has become the inspired hope of financially able tourists. The early steamers, which brought tens of millions of immigrants to the United States in their steerage holds, returned to Europe with America's wealthy for what became the traditional voyage abroad. First, larger ocean liners with comparatively sumptuous tourist accommodations, and then the bargain-rate airliner, brought travel to Europe within reach of those with moderate incomes, who responded by the millions to the lure of the Old World. Today, European tourism is a bicontinental industry with an annual gross income of almost three billion dollars. If you add to this the traffic to South America, the Caribbean, the Near East, Far East and some of the burgeoning resort areas in Mexico and in the Pacific, the aggregate sum expended is astronomical. All of these areas, and the carriers servicing them, are dependent on the public appeal stimulated by the promotion activities at advertising and public relations agencies.

Although, for the practitioner, the approaches to overseas and out-of-the-country publicity are very similar to the methods used in publicizing domestic sights, there is one difference. In most cases the traveler to foreign lands is more prone to use a travel agency than one seeking local accommodations. Therefore it is incumbent to the formulation of a good campaign to work in close coordination with the routine practices of travel agencies. These practices are, to a great extent, uniform because of their well-organized status.

In both domestic and foreign travel publicity, the production of colorful literature is a prime necessity for effective promotion. Opulent brochures, colorful pamphlets and travel agency rack literature must be provided with glowing descriptions of steamships, hotels, resort areas, motels, restaurant and beach accommodations. The skillful composition of these pieces of literature demands the almost impossible task of transferring an attractive resort environment to paper. This can be done by combining color and creative copy which promise instant transition from the mundane to the fantastic. Severe editing sharply reduces effectiveness.

FASHION

Another realm of public relations in which the required methodology for the practitioner enjoys wide latitude in application and copy is fashion. Fashion publicity deservedly occupies a domain of its own that, for the most part, is unchallenged or avoided by those practitioners who have chosen not to specialize in this field. It perhaps encourages a closer client relationship than in any other category of public relations. This is the result of the character of the fashion industry itself, which is so promotional, so dependent on public whim, that its promotional aspects very often become the tail that wags the dog.

Even more than in other important industries, fashion has developed a nomenclature and a patter, if not a general behavior, peculiar to its own environment. For the practitioner specializing in this field, a familiarity with the conduct of the business itself must be acquired.

The twin cities of fashion are Paris and New York. They have developed a mutual dependency, either harmful or beneficial, according to any given season's fluctuation in trend.

The two fashion magazines, VOGUE and HARPER'S BAZAAR, enjoy bible status and the practitioner should approach them on this level. They are both prime advertising media for the most important business components of the industry and, because of their standing, exert a national influence on the feverishly oscillating determination by women of what they wear.

The outstanding trade paper is WOMEN'S WEAR DAILY, which also exerts a prodigious influence on the national garment industry. Incidentally, WOMEN'S WEAR DAILY is probably the possessor of a circulation composed of the most devout readers, possibly more devout than any other trade paper in the United States has yet succeeded in developing.

However, the most important factor in fashion media is the daily press. There is hardly a daily or weekly newspaper published in this country that does not try to hold its feminine audience by devoting space to fashion. They either have fashion editors of their own, or they buy syndicated columns that serve the same purpose. Around these features, the full-page dress ads, which characterize all of our successful newspapers, are deployed. The servicing of news and feature releases, as well as photographs, to these editors and syndicated columns is the first priority for the practitioner in the handling of a fashion account.

In fashion, photography takes on a new meaning. Fashion photography has become a highly specialized area of operation and the photographer himself a highly cognizant publicity practitioner in his own right. Peculiarly enough, fashion models have become stars and feature players in very much the Hollywood tradition and often the use of a well-known model exerts great editorial influence.

These are merely some of the underlying reasons why fashion publicity has become an entity almost separate from general practice

However, the major elements are worthy of study because there are very few product accounts whose campaigns do not at some time or another impinge on the province of fashion. A good example is the textile industry, natural or synthetic, in which a whole product line must be sold to the manufacturers of garments. In this type of account, the aim of a good campaign would be to enhance the value of a garment to the consumer if it is processed in the fabric represented. In this example one is confronted by a product relationship, but in the general mores of our time, no matter what the product, a pretty girl helps to sell it and a pretty girl is the natural exponent of fashion. If she happens to be photographed eating a cereal or shampooing her hair, or daubing herself with perfume, make sure the brand names represent your clients' products.*

EXERCISES

1 Write a prospectus soliciting the account of an actual corporation based on what is known about the corporation and emphasizing what can be done further to increase the sale of its products.

2 The product is a new brand of perfume. Outline five tie-in approaches toward acquiring free exposure on TV programs.

3 The product is a well-known brand of coffee that ranks fourth in sales in a large New England city. Plan a promotion tie-in with supermarkets that would get their maximum cooperation in advancing sales.

4 Write and suggest illustrations for a short pamphlet (reading time, four minutes) for retail sales personnel at department store counters selling a client's brand of electric razor.

5 Outline a complete program for a sales convention to be attended by two hundred salesmen in a resort hotel. The convention has the general purpose of reenergizing sales efforts with unchanged product models. The management is concerned with falling morale and general apathy.

6 (a) List elements that should be contained in the release of an announcement by a utility corporation of an application for an increase in rates.
(b) Using a typical big city utility company, write a statement for its president that could be the basis for the release in (a).

7 An old established bank is about to open a new branch in a recently developed neighborhood. Outline a campaign for that branch that would reach grass roots levels of the business and consumer communities.

* See Appendixes C, D and E for specimen material outlined in this chapter.

the practice of public relations

8 A large suburban real estate development is offering homes at about the $25,000 level within easy commutation distance from the nearest big city. Submit a prospectus to the developer containing a rudimentary publicity program that would attract the $15,000 wage earner.

9 How would you publicize a radical departure in architectural planning for urban redevelopment with the objective of obtaining acceptance by a city planning commission?

10 (a) Outline a six-month campaign for a western railroad having the purpose of increasing passenger traffic through scenic areas.
(b) Do a single-fold promotion pamphlet for travel agencies' racks for the same railroad.

11 An editor of an important travel magazine has been convinced that it will be advantageous to do a two-page spread on a client resort in color photographs. Suggest a shooting plan for the assigned photographer.

12 (a) Dummy a brochure for a new resort hotel in Florida. The hotel is a luxury enterprise and seeks to attract a wealthy clientele.
(b) Explain your proportions of picture and copy.

13 The client is a large chemical company that manufactures a synthetic fabric for use in the fashion industry. A decision has been made to introduce the fabric by a series of fashion shows. Do a plan for one of the shows to be held in an important hotel in New York City and explain the reasons for the arrangements recommended.

14 Pertinent Case Exercises (See Appendix A)
a. ACE OF CLUBS
b. THE MANOR BORN
c. ALL WASHED UP
d. POWER PLAY

SUGGESTED SUPPLEMENTAL READING

Aszling, Richard A. "Consumerism—and the PR Response." *Public Relations Journal.* New York: Public Relations Society of America (Oct. 1970)

Hayes, Charles E. "This Way to Suburbia." *Public Relations Journal.* New York: Public Relations Society of America (March 1969)

Lindquist, Robert. *The Bank and Its Publics: Philosophy of Bank Public Relations.* New York: Harper Brothers, 1956

Nader, Ralph. *Unsafe at Any Speed.* New York: Grossman Publishers, Inc., 1965

Packard, Vance. *The Hidden Persuaders.* New York: David McKay Company, Inc., 1957

Plummer, Gail. *The Business of Show Business.* New York: Harper Brothers, 1961

Public Relations for Your Bank. New York: American Institute of Banking, 1956

Stark, Jack. *Successful Publicity in Real Estate.* Englewood Cliffs, N.J.: Prentice-Hall, Inc., 1958

institutional public relations

5

FUNDS FOR HEALTH, WELFARE AND EDUCATION

More than twelve billion dollars are contributed by Americans each year to health, welfare and educational institutions. The augmentation of this fund by federal expenditures is increasing at an annual rate that may equal this amount in a very few years. Together, these two sources of enormous funds have attempted to give the American people the finest health, welfare and educational institutions existing anywhere; but increasingly, the supply of funds is not able to meet the demand for facilities. It is a tribute to American philanthropy that our privately endowed and partially government-subsidized health and welfare institutions are struggling to keep pace with the nation's needs.

Three factors have contributed most heavily to the generosity quotient in American fund raising. Foremost is the corporate and personal tax exemption enjoyed by the giver. Second is the high degree of unprecedented prosperity of American business since the advent of the Second World War. Third is the sharply increased feelings of responsibility that corporations and wealthy individuals have for social progress and the elimination of want in the American structure.

The American will to give expanded, rather than declined, with the federal and state assumption of responsibility for the indigent and unemployed. Emergent social needs on the family welfare level, or the direct-support level, have gradually been removed from the purview of private philanthropy, and the word *charity* in its ancient meaning is slowly disappearing from the American philanthropic scene.

In the educative field, which is also the recipient of ever-increasing government subsidies, cultural development has now assumed a top-rank status. Museums, concert halls and cultural complexes such as Lincoln Center in New York have now come into ascendancy, so that today philanthropy has as its main objective community building for all members of the community regardless of financial or social standing. Civic pride in architecture and in cultural achievement has almost assumed a competitive status with cities vying with each other for recognition.

The first problem for the practitioner in an approach to institutional public relations should be the consideration of who gives and why in the national community and, more specifically, in his own.

There are four principal private sources of funds: corporations, foundations, the individual big donors and the general mass fund-raising drives. The corporation ranks first.

During the last decade, large individual donations to American philanthropies have been replaced to an enormous extent by the contributions of corporate business. Unless individual tax schedules undergo radical changes in structure, the importance of personal contributions to the nation's major health and welfare institutions will continue to diminish. Large-scale support from business sources will assume an ever-increasing proportion of the burden.

In the face of these facts some new evaluations must be made of the effect that a philanthropic contribution has upon the corporate donor, and of the various factors that determine the plus or minus values resulting from each donation.

American history is replete with examples of individuals and families of great wealth who, through their philanthropies, have established great institutions that will forever bear their names. In a like manner, local philanthropies such as orphanages, homes for the blind and hospitals have, through the years, become identified as the projects of prominent citizens within these communities. These identifications of individuals with the public good and with social progress will, in the nearby future, be replaced by corporate names. To some extent this has already occurred, particularly in the research field. During the Second World War this trend toward corporate giving became even more pronounced by pressure of the Red Cross and USO campaigns. Although great stress was laid on the importance of the individual donor, enormous quotas made corporate aid mandatory.

Of course the individual who contributes to a favorite cause will remain the core of our philanthropic scene. The part of the volunteer who contributes service and time as well as money is the very soul of our voluntary health and welfare systems.

Several years ago, my firm was assigned a routine public relations task by a large textile corporation in New York City. In a conversation the president of the corporation told me about his family and the great burden they had shouldered in raising one of their children who, through an accident at birth, suffered from cerebral palsy. In the discussion that followed, he made me aware of the fact that there were tens of thousands of cerebral palsied children throughout the country, and that in each case medical help rarely went beyond the diagnosis. From there on therapy became a family affair and in cases where there was a lack of money, the children were usually hospitalized in institutions under state auspices.

In conversations that ensued from this first meeting the suggestion developed of a national cerebral palsy organization that would not only thoroughly research possible causes of the malady, but would also develop proper courses of therapy and care. There were a few statewide organizations that were trying to do this exactly, but because of their limited fund-raising activities their efforts were improperly supported and never sufficiently publicized.

What was needed to launch a national drive with sufficient press support to arouse enthusiasm for this cause in the general public was a dramatic demonstration to remove the cloak of secrecy that, because of parental attitudes, had hidden the extent of birth defect incidences from the public view.

At my suggestion an international conference, which represented twenty-three countries, was convened at the Hotel Statler in New York City. Two thousand parents of cerebral palsied children and four hundred physicians anxious to tell about their experiments and experiences with corrective therapy and to learn whatever they could elicit from their colleagues attended.

In the first session in which the doctors and parents met there occurred one of the most remarkable phenomenons I have ever witnessed in my career. It took less than ten minutes for the doctors to realize that the parents knew more than they did and had become, by trial-and-error methods, the experts in therapeutic treatment and devices. It was a four-hour session and those who attended it never forgot it.

From this session a national cerebral palsy organization emerged and has developed into one of the most successful health and welfare fund-raising campaigns in the world.

CORPORATE DONORS

But in replacing the large individual donor of the last generation, the corporation is inevitably guided by the same basic motivations. And the first of these is as sacrosanct with a corporation as it is with a school-child. There must be a will to give and it must be impelled by the loftiest motives stemming from the desire to help mankind.

However, from this point forward the corporate problem becomes more complex, mainly because the donation is substantial and, therefore, newsworthy. Anything that helps to shape public attitude toward a corporation that directly or indirectly sells to a mass consumer market is vital to the life of the corporation. Therefore, policy that directs the giving of funds, no matter how beneficent the motivation, must take cognizance of the pitfalls latent in bad public relations. Consideration must be given to these dominant facets of the philanthropic field:

1 Community relations (restricted locally to the support of institutions operating in the community in which the plants or offices are located).
2 Public relations on the national scene with the general public.
3 Public relations on the national scene with the consumer public.
4 Public relations on the national scene with dealers and distributors.
5 Public relations on the national scene with employees.
6 Public relations on the national scene with stockholders.

All six of these corporate relationships are involved each time a treasurer's check is issued as a contribution to a philanthropy. The more sizeable the contribution the greater is the need for caution. Each of these groups is acutely sensitive and sometimes sharply critical of the corporation's objective.

There are three main categories of philanthropies particularly deserving of corporate support:

1 Local medical and welfare institutions serving the needs of the immediate community and wholly dependent on the citizens of that particular community for support.
2 National health and welfare agencies operating on the national scene whose programs are of such magnitude and scope that they require nationwide appeals to achieve their objectives.
3 Educational and research institutions such as colleges, universities, professional trade schools, vocational guidance institutions and postgraduate professional schools.

The first of these categories has budgetary needs that are easily ascertainable by the community and are ideally handled by collateral appeals through a community chest. Such chests are administered by boards cognizant of the community's social welfare requirements and democratically representative of the various factions responsible for community welfare. In a community chest of this kind, caring only for local needs, the corporate contributor receives due recognition for assuming a substantial portion of the burden. By participating in the community chest the corporation is further integrated into the life and consciousness of the community. If sufficient identification is made with a few well-known local philanthropies, corporate support of the local chest located within the environs of its principal plants and installations is sound policy, and generous support should be accorded.

The second category for many corporations is the trouble area. It is the area in which the greatest degree of confusion exists and, incidentally, its appealing institutions represent the greatest national need. These institutions enjoy the greatest popular appeal of hundreds of thousands of zealous volunteers who are jealous guardians of their chosen organization's progress.

The greatest single misconception regarding these national health and welfare organizations is their number. Too often one hears the cry, "There are too many appeals." How many and what are they? There are, it is true, approximately four hundred national annual drives conducted legitimately in the United States. But the vast majority serve only special interests or exist on capital funds or other endowed income. They do not ask for general community support nor do they offer general community services. Corporations' donations, unless made for special reasons that relate to the work of the corporation, cannot be justified to most of them if the corporation respects its obligation to its stockholders.

American health and welfare depend to a great extent on the success of these drives. Unless generous corporate support is provided, the future of many of these organizations becomes highly problematical. But from a business viewpoint, an identification with individual causes is of inestimable value in the maintenance of maximum corporate good will.

It is therefore important that the link between the corporation and its chosen philanthropies be kept inviolate. Any system of fund raising or fund giving that, for the sake of convenience, breaks this link and substitutes itself as an agent can only succeed in eventually rendering both the corporate giver and the cause anonymous.

The millions of Americans who have aligned themselves with favorite causes and charities are, in great measure, responsible for our great strides in social progress. To allow the dissolution of these armies would also be a great disservice to the institutions that they have served so faithfully.

Corporate giving should never threaten the position of, nor sub-stitute for, the individual volunteer. However, this does not preclude keeping inviolate the identification of the corporate giver and the cause served.

The last category, which includes all types of aid to education, is a fluid field with many opportunities for a highly individualized giving program. As a community service, the corporation can make contribu-tions to institutions in its locale for general expenses, new buildings or other expansion, and for scholarships and fellowships. This can be supplemented with help that is mutually beneficial, such as providing educational aids and in-plant training. Research in areas of the com-pany's interest can be arranged on a contractual or endowment basis with schools, and provision can be made for the graduate and advisory staff of the project. With a view to employee relationships, many firms have established scholarship awards for workers' children. As an ad-junct, some give an additional grant to the institution of a student's choice. Corporations can adopt any combination of these philanthropic devices and tailor them to their own and to their communities' needs. Industrial gifts stimulate the private educational system. Identification with these schools creates much good will among the general public, customers, employees and the school alumni.

THE ROLE OF FOUNDATIONS

For the individuals or families who have amassed or inherited gigantic estates, the foundation organized as a tax-exempt corporation has become the most popular philanthropic channel.

Actually, the foundation idea did not originate because of tax pressure. It was the result of the extremely negative publicity given to the profligate living habits of some of the very rich during the first two decades of the twentieth century. There was also considerable public prejudice at this time against the accumulation of tremendous fortunes without a concomitant heightening of responsibility toward the public from whom the fortunes were made.

At about this time several of the country's wealthiest families estab-lished philanthropic enterprises managed by efficient executives with social work background or training. Sharply increased income tax rates during the Great Depression accelerated this method of giving, which continued to proliferate as individual incomes of substance became increasingly numerous.

For the practitioner, a knowledge, as well as a listing, of these foundations is a necessary ally for effective operation in this field.

Foundations specialize in a single philanthropic endeavor or a combination of them, so that the particular institution represented must be matched to the policies of the foundations specializing in that field.

In soliciting funds from a foundation there is a formularized approach that is usually engineered by the fund-raising organization engaged on the assignment. However, within the purview of public relations falls the duty of preparing a presentation for the client institution that is calculated for a maximum effect on the foundation's professional and lay boards of directors. This presentation should graphically portray the history, care and services rendered; necessity for maintenance, expansion or new construction; personalities involved along with their scope of responsibilities; a balance sheet covering the last year or two of operations and a specific-use budget for the amount being solicited at the time of presentation.

Ideally, the presentation should be in the form of a flip chart on an easel, from which the person making the presentation can provide illustrated material for his talk. The suggested length of time for such a talk is twenty-five minutes, after which a question-and-answer procedure is invited by the speaker. Presentations should rarely be made by a professional. They should be made by the lay president or other high lay official of the institution being presented. A much greater degree of mutual trust is engendered by an appeal from a philanthropist to a philanthropist. The complete text on the spoken presentation should be left with the foundation board to study at its convenience; also suitable printed material should be left.

Practitioners should also be aware that an appeal to a foundation is under no circumstances ever announced to the press. It is a confidential procedure. If the results are satisfactory and a contribution is received, it is incumbent on the foundation to make the announcement to the press, not the institution benefited. If the foundation prefers not to make the announcement, its volition to remain anonymous must be respected. It has also come to be considered good form that each foundation be told of solicitations made to other foundations.

THE INDIVIDUAL DONOR

Although both corporations and foundations have become the major sources of important philanthropic funds, the big donor remains dominant in America's fund-raising network. Every city, town and village in the United States has its individual name, or coterie of names, associated with the support of local health and welfare institutions, which more often than not bear these names carved in granite.

The motivations that inspire big gifts are so numerous and so complex, and so intricately and deviously interrelated, that any study in depth would require a volume of analysis.

However, the practitioner, in accepting an assignment in which a major portion of his efforts will be directed toward large donors, must become familiar with some of the surface motivations before he can be effective in this area. For some peculiar reason the very rich often feel very guilty, and large checks to worthy causes work miracles in assuaging guilt.

The public relations approach on this score, whether spoken or written, should evoke a consciousness of guilt without tactless or invidious reference. The usual line, and probably the best, is the subtle reminder of mortality, with the less subtle indication of how wonderful it would be to be remembered for the good deed from which posterity will benefit. Because ego projection beyond the grave molds the frame of mind conducive to generous giving, it is good policy to name a project for its donor.

The individual large contributor in the big cities of America is also very often motivated by the enhancement of social status. A large contribution is easily translated into a board membership or chairmanship among confreres of equal rank. The bridge between the public announcement of a large donation to an important community project and an invitation to membership in the right club is narrow. This commentary is not meant to be cynical. In this writer's opinion there is no more beneficial way for an individual to seek social rank than through the channel of well-planned philanthropy. Our country's philanthropy no longer is controlled by McAllister's Social Register of the last century. The sons of the immigrant laborers of that day have prospered and have given great amounts for the common need. Here again, tact is of the greatest necessity as a high priority in the practitioner's approach.

Another motivation of considerable influence is political. An identification with good causes means frequent appearances in the press in an unassailable context. A man or woman giving to institutions serving urgent human needs and active in his or her unpaid administrative management makes a good candidate for appointed or elected office. Political leaders are well aware of this fact and make frequent choices from this ever-growing roster.

Whatever the motivation, the approach to the big giver is always personal and the first interview has by this time become ritualistic procedure. The public relations man, in the company of a lay officer high in business or social prestige, arranges the meeting with the potential donor. The tenor of the meeting should be guided by as accurate an appraisal as possible of the motivations and personality traits of the interviewee. The more accurate this appraisal is, the less pressure will be needed. The agenda of this initial meeting should not include a direct appeal for funds but rather a full discussion of the business of the organization and how the interviewee can participate in it.

Despite many opinions to the contrary, it has been found, generally, that the hard-boiled business approach is not effective in a discussion of a particular philanthropic project. In the average American community, vanity builds hospitals.

MASS FUND-RAISING DRIVES

The genealogy of American philanthropy is denominational in character and, to a preponderant extent, religious institutions, or institutions religious in background, remain the dominant channels of funds. The great exceptions are the health and welfare drives, which in a historical sense are fairly recent arrivals. Less than a century ago, denominational groups controlled, almost in their entirety, all educational institutions outside the public school systems. The same holds true for hospitals, orphanages, old age and foundling homes and many other similar institutions. Incidentally, the various denominations started and maintained for many years a primitive variation of what we know today as foreign aid through their missions abroad.

Even though the various central churches still exercise an enormous influence in American philanthropy through their control of the channels that are traditional sources of funds, the great growth of the nation's population and the diversity of religious and ethnic pluralism have contributed heavily to nondenominational fund raising.

However, for the practitioner the religious divisions in any given community should control, to a great extent, his approach to the fund-raising problems of his client institution. Only a deep-level study in each case can guide the practitioner as to whether a broad-level nonsectarian approach would or would not be more yielding.

The dramatic drives on the American scene are the large nonsectarian health and welfare organizations' national fund-raising efforts. The senior drive, of course, is the Red Cross, and they then range out to embrace most of the medical disciplines to include heart, cancer, cerebral palsy and others, running the gamut of nearly all the unconquered mortal and crippling diseases.

These drives are almost all similarly organized, consisting largely of national offices administered by experienced professional staffs, and local or regional offices with small professional staffs aided by numerous volunteer workers on whom community enthusiasm really rests.

The public relations aspect of these national drives assumes such an important part of their working effectiveness that unlike other categories in public relations, the practitioner's influence is weighty on every level of the institution served. Financial support depends solely on public contributions and the main business of these organizations is to prove their worthiness of public support.

The public relations assignment for a national health or welfare organization is usually a three-part task. The first and most sensitive part is the day-to-day operation of an information program that reports on the actual work—care and research—of the projects supported by the funds collected. Media of all kinds look to these public relations sources for a never-ending stream of scientific disclosures and research development, dramatic human interest stories in hospital care and statistical revelations gauging the health and welfare of the nation.

Because the work of institutions dealing with health and medical research enjoys a high degree of public interest, extreme care should be exercised by the practitioner not to be influenced by the demand for news of dramatic medical content.

Unfortunately, the environment of our present-day world has made the modern scientist conscious of the renown potential in publicity. To balance this comparatively new urge, the practitioner must exercise conservative strength and become a monitor of prematurely announced scientific research results to prevent the negative boomerang reactions. Not yielding to temptation in this regard is difficult indeed for the practitioner who is constantly conscious of popularity inroads made by competing campaigns. Publicize objectives and proximity regarding substantial results, but be very careful about hinting or claiming research successes. The public supports effort and is fully cognizant of the cost of effort in overcoming medical problems. The sincerity of the effort and the progress toward the achievement should be reported without seeking the sensational headline that, too often, is a prelude to disappointment.

During the last half century, national campaigns proliferated. Budgets burgeoned into the tens of millions and the competition between worthy causes occasioned confusion and friction among the groups in the community supporting them. This gave rise to the United Fund movement, which has grown so continuously that, for the most part, the medium and large cities in the United States have interlocking boards of directors representing all major national health and welfare campaigns. Through their auspices, collective drives are supervised and the monies collected are allocated by their various member organizations.

Although this would appear to be a happy solution, unfortunately there is much opposition to it. The opposition stems, naturally enough, from the prerogative the board exercises in making the allocations according to its studied considerations. Many organizations have refused the umbrella of the United Fund movement and maintain fundraising organizations within cities in which the United Fund operates. This has caused some acrimony and in some instances has been harmful to individual campaigns. However, this situation has been aided by a spirit of compromise on both sides, and it appears that independent and collective fund raising will operate successfully side by side.

The practitioner, in representing an organization within the collective fund-raising drive, must constantly seek the maintenance of a strong identity for his cause so that it is not enveloped by the collective strength of the United Fund-raising organization. This is accomplished by a year-round public relations campaign acceding to the United Fund only for the duration of the actual fund-raising drive. On the other hand, if the client is not within the United Fund apparatus, seek a timing agreement with the United Fund administrators that would separate by a substantial period of weeks the two fund-raising drives.

The actual publicity for a health and welfare organization falls into two separate concurrent programs. The first is based on the work of the organization—its accomplishments within the field of its endeavors —and reflects all the work of the professionals engaged and involved. The second part revolves around the lay half of the organization, the volunteers, the national and local committees and the organizational events that are part of the program.

These two areas of work are quite separate and it is perfectly possible for a news item telling about the progress or results of a line of research to appear on the same day in the same paper as a social event that is part of a fund-raising campaign for the same organization. There is no conflict in the editor's mind about these items.

However, to the practitioner, the treatment of publicity in each area is entirely different. Scientific and medical research or medical care in the instances where they become usable for news items have to be approached on as an austere professional level as the work being reported. Sensationalism of any kind should be assiduously avoided and accuracy of detail sought for in every case.

On the other hand, wide latitude in consonance with dignity is permissible in the handling of social events. It is well to remember that all personalities involved in the lay efforts to raise funds look toward the mention of their names in the releases as eagerly as the professor looks for his name in the scientific report. Personalities lose enthusiasm in proportion to the depth of their anonymity.

Very much as in corporate public relations, the annual report has become the prestige place for health and welfare institutions. It is the annual task for the practitioner that requires the most care and proficiency in production. At this point the analogy ends, for many reasons, the most important of which is that the annual report for a health and welfare institution is calculated to show a soul-searing deficit that, if left to remain unfunded by public subscription, would cause all the good work described in the annual report to cease.

Therefore, the annual report should consist first of 1500 well-chosen words, pictures and captions depicting with utmost clarity the work of the organization; and secondly of a financial statement showing how this work was supported and the deficits sustained while supporting it. This should be followed by a projection into the next year emphasizing two salient factors: (1) that a still greater deficit is to be anticipated; and (2) that default would mean a serious rupture in public services. This should be followed by a poignant paragraph that in essence amounts to an appeal for more efforts on the part of the volunteers. It is preferable to couch the first part as a letter from the president over his signature. The rest of the annual report should consist of a full roster of the board of directors, professional and advisory boards, and all executive personnel.

Although the annual report, in intent and purpose, is usually the basic piece of literature for a health and welfare organization, serving as a brochure descriptive of the organization's range of activities, other literature to supplement it is required. The foremost of these is an envelope stuffer for enclosure with organizational mail to volunteers and contributors. This should be designed as a synthesis of the larger annual report, giving in reduced phraseology the desirability or necessity for public support of the work and services provided to the public by the organization. Other pamphlets along the same order are usually published during the fund-raising campaign for distribution at meetings, in mailings, and at various vantage points during the course of periodic solicitation.

To the practitioner, these pieces present no unusual problems. Generally, their thematic material is suggested by the fund-raising group engaged in the campaign. However, one continuing irksome problem to the practitioner is the succession of mailings. Sometimes these are directed to blind lists and at other times are targeted at former contributors and community volunteers. The same letter is never used twice. Each one has to fit in style and mood the cause for which it is soliciting.

A most successful technique has been the use of a prominent lay person's private stationery with his or her signature. But whether it is signed by a high-echelon dignitary or by the chairman of a local fund-raising committee, or even by a professional, it must evoke a quick and powerful sympathy and empathy with the cause. This objective must be reached in the first forty words of the letter to guarantee that the next fifty will be read. The lead is what is important. A self-addressed envelope enclosed is an aid, but try not to use gimmicks or tricks, or to use giveaways, or even religious paraphernalia. Giveaways have been used by so many completely phony organizations that the public has come to suspect any organization, no matter how legitimate, that reverts to their use.

If it is at all possible, use a sampling as a test before you incur the cost of a general mailing. Make the letter simple, but do not patronize your public. The composition of a letter that is effective is always a gamble. The date of a mailing is also a gamble. Experiment before you spend. Listen closely to the fund raiser. He knows the giving mood of his community. When the practitioner is asked his advice, it is wise also for him to know the moral and mental fiber of the particular community before giving it.

Fund raising has adopted wholeheartedly the technique of combining elaborate social affairs with the solicitation of funds. These affairs, largely speaking, divide themselves in two categories. The most common charge a high price for seating ranging from $50 to $250, and some are as high as $1000 per plate, with the organization profiting from the overage after hotel and food expenses are paid. Great successes in this system have been enjoyed, particularly when the affair takes the form of a ball handled ornately and assumes the posture of a social event of great prestige.

The second category uses the device of calling the roll of guests from cards bearing the diners' names. The theory behind this method is that a few planted inflated donations will encourage overgiving by appealing to the normal competitive spirit among donors. Although conceived in bad taste, this latter technique has been found to be so effective that fund raisers are loath to drop it.

Another popular channel developed for the raising of funds has been the formation of volunteer committees within the various industrial categories. This technique allows fund raisers to solicit a group in which all are known to one another and all vie with one another for a ranking position within the grouping. The effort is calculated to make each business head donate in proportion to his firm's standing within a given industry. A weak donation by any member of this group, or the absence from the affair by a member of this group, is thought to generate an atmosphere of gossip. The method is dirty, but effective.

A good rule for any practitioner to follow in the supervision of a public relations campaign for a health and welfare institution is never to deviate too far from the distaff side of the organization's fund-raising volunteers. Women are indefatigable workers for good causes and if mobilized into a harmonious program that properly balances their efforts with that of others involved, their contribution very often achieves success where the efforts of others fall short. The practitioner will find that the female zealot is his best ally and can usually enlist any community's human assets faster than the best professional action.

EXERCISES

1 Prepare a welfare fund analysis of a community with which you are familiar, preferably your home community, describing the efficacy of the various drives and the public attitude toward them.

2 Describe the benefits and dangers inherent in United Funds as compared to individual campaigns.

3 (a) A client is a large corporation accustomed to making annual philanthropic contributions of about a million dollars. The company manufactures farm machinery. Prepare an advisory plan for the distribution of such contributions and state the reasons for the recommendations.

(b) Describe in depth a recommended approach by a client voluntary hospital to the corporation for a substantial contribution.

4 (a) Outline a public relations campaign to be launched simultaneously with a fund-raising drive to build a new library on a large university campus. The university has national status with a large postgraduate roster.

(b) Prepare a presentation to a foundation with a time limit of fifteen minutes for delivery to the board. This presentation should be made orally to the class.

5 (a) Write a formula for organizing a membership drive for a local community organization that, for half a century, has tendered to the welfare needs of the small city's children. The caseload has grown so great that the original families who donated support find it necessary to increase substantially the number of contributors.

(b) Describe the social nuances of such a campaign.

6 (a) Prepare a dummy of an annual report for a research institute dealing with the problem of cancer, which is already a substantial beneficiary of American Cancer Society funds. It is partially supported by individual donors.

(b) Write in full the president's message urging expansion of the institute's field of work.

7 Prepare an annual mass mailing for the United Fund drive of your community.

8 The problem is to choose a board of directors consisting of twenty members to direct the affairs of a new institution dedicated to service to the blind in a large city. From what population elements of the community should this board be chosen? How should it be chosen to be truly representative of a supportive community?

9 Write the lead paragraph of a release reporting the speech of a Supreme Court Justice who was the honored speaker at a welfare agency drive dinner.

10 Pertinent Case Exercises (See Appendix A)
  a. WORTHY CAUSE
  b. SCHOOL DAZE
  c. MEDICAL MILESTONE
  d. WEALTH SHARING

SUGGESTED SUPPLEMENTAL READING

Andrews, F.E. *Corporation Giving.* New York: Russell Sage Foundation, 1952

Eells, Richard. *The Corporation and the Arts.* New York: The Macmillan Company, 1967

The Foundation Directory. (3rd ed.). New York: Russell Sage Foundation, 1967

Grief, Edward L. *The Silent Pulpit: A Guide to Church Public Relations.* New York: Holt, Rinehart & Winston, Inc., 1964

How 300 Companies Handle Contributions. Chicago, Ill.: Dartnell Corporation, 1959

Kindred, Leslie Woodrow. *School Public Relations.* Englewood Cliffs, N.J: Prentice-Hall, Inc., 1957

Kurtz, Harold P. *Public Relations for Hospitals.* Springfield, Ill.: Charles C Thomas, 1969

McCloskey, Gordon Ellsworth. *Education and Public Understanding.* (2nd ed.). New York: Harper & Row Publishers, Inc., 1967

Schmidt, Francis (ed.). *Public Relations in Health and Welfare.* New York: Columbia University Press, 1966

governmental public relations

6

INFORMATION VERSUS PROPAGANDA

It is well known historically that the world's most catastrophic wars occurred when diplomacy failed. It is less well known that diplomacy failed when public relations was poor or nonexistent.

The first priority of diplomacy is the inculcation of understanding, mutual understanding. Understanding emanates from the fullest possible exchange of information. When the dissemination of full information becomes subsidiary to intrigue, it becomes propaganda and propaganda is the antithesis of public relations. Propaganda is the promulgation of a point of view that obviates the element of truth on its path to a purposeful objective.

Governmental public relations is the presentation of fundamental truths on which a logical attitude can be based by the process of balancing negative and positive values without the coercive influences of emotional mendacity. For a government there can be no good public relations without good policy or without a beneficent objective. Where this equation does not exist, the practitioner becomes an agent rather than a counselor, and he can only answer to his own conscience.

All embassies of all governments have as their principal occupation the establishment and maintenance of a political, cultural and commercial environment conducive to a harmonious, if not a preferred, relationship between the country they represent and the country in which they are located.

In line with this objective, diplomatic establishments are divided into three parts: political, commercial and cultural. The same general formula exists in the municipal consulates throughout the world.

In addition, embassies of the larger countries have military attachés whose purpose, in theory, is to develop a cordial working relationship between the military establishment of their country and that of the host country. Practice and theory in this case occasionally bow to less innocent purpose, but because these matters do not relate directly to the practitioner, we will not expand on them here.

All embassies and important consulates have either a press bureau, information office or a public relations agency for the distribution of informational material relating to the activities of the embassy, as well as to important news emanating from the broad stream of life in the home country.

These news items stem from the areas handled by the various embassy departments or are rewrites of pertinent material disseminated from news agencies in the represented countries. However, before we analyze the nature of this flow of information, there is another category of public relations for foreign governments with which the public is far more familiar, and that is tourism.

PUBLIC RELATIONS FOR FOREIGN TOURISM

In Chapter 4 we described briefly the general nature of foreign travel from the United States abroad, and the remarkable growth this industry has enjoyed. But there is another aspect that is far more important and much more sensitive in its effect on the relations between countries of which the public relations practitioner should be aware. First in importance is the economic effect of tourism, and secondly, there is the public relations effect of tourism.

The volume of American tourism abroad has reached such great proportions that it has become an invisible facet of foreign aid. Every tourist is an exporter of dollars to the countries he visits. While he is enjoying his visit he is buying accommodations, services and consumer goods in dollars. The effect of this flow of money abroad is impressive merely in consideration of the staggering amounts spent. However, there is another consideration that the public relations practitioner delving into economic affairs should know.

According to the Treasury Act of 1934, American citizens holding dollar balances were restricted from converting dollars into gold or gold notes by federal statute. However, this restriction could not apply to the citizens of other countries who, as individuals, or through their banking institutions, could convert dollars to gold at will at a set price of $35 an ounce fixed by the Treasury Act, which forbids purchase of gold by Americans. From 1934 to 1954 the United States enjoyed such an overwhelming advantage in its trade balances because of a disastrous depression in Europe and then a catastrophic war, that the American gold hoard at Fort Knox was unthreatened. Then the American urge for foreign travel became epidemic and with European recovery the dollar balance became more and more unfavorable. Now the Fort Knox gold reserve balance has been halved and the Swiss franc and the German mark have become the strong and unthreatened trading currencies. In great part, the American tourist trade has helped to create this situation.

There are many other factors also present that are irrelevant to this particular subject. But tourism, in its present proportions—a great American industry—remains a great American problem as well. In the light of these facts, the practitioner should understand that the advertising and public relations campaigns instituted in the United States by foreign tourist offices and foreign carriers are to a great extent subsidized by their government with funds allocated for the specific purpose of drawing dollars into their countries. The second purpose—the public relations purpose—is that the American traveler favorably impressed with the country he visits becomes a permanent public relations asset when he returns to the United States. He is a little more sympathetic to the aspirations—cultural and political—of the country visited and is perhaps a little more vocal than his untraveled neighbor. More important, he is more likely to be a purchaser of consumer as well as durable goods manufactured in his favorite foreign country.

To the practitioner a tourism client represents a multifaceted assignment. Full justice to a major tourism account requires at the outset a thorough research and analytical process from which the practitioner should get a deep-level understanding of the geographical, ethnic, industrial, cultural and climatic facts about the country represented. In this kind of an account a political understanding, unless it is essentially hostile, is not important. Along with this research, a knowledge of all carriers servicing routes to the client country should be studied. Hotel accommodations of all kinds and on all economic levels should also come within the ken of the practitioner's knowledge so that at least basic information can be cleared and disseminated. The most advantageous way to conduct this research is on the scene, and an extended tour before commencing operations is always highly advisable.

Because an extraordinarily high percentage of all travel business originating in the United States is arranged through travel agencies, it is mandatory that the practitioner be knowledgeable, if not conversant, with travel agency operations. Travel agencies are well organized, through a trade organization known as ASTA (American Society of Travel Agents, Inc.), which is in itself a powerful influence on the travel recommendations of individual agencies. Most travel agencies exhibit racks of literature that deserve the careful perusal of the practitioner. Always remember that the travel agency is the final advisor before the traveler's mind is made up. The man in the agency to whom he speaks is in a position to emphasize or denigrate the advertising and publicity that originally attracted his client. In most cases, the travel agency is the final clearing house for recommendation or discouragement. For these potent reasons, the practitioner must prepare a better than adequate servicing of the more than 6500 travel agencies throughout the United States.

After a careful collation and consideration of all the research material gathered by the practitioner, there are three remaining steps before the start of activities:

1 A careful examination should be made of all publicity efforts, going back at least twenty-five years, that had been undertaken up to the time the assignment was received.
2 It is always valuable to spend an afternoon in the morgue of a good newspaper to acquire a cursory understanding of the public attitude shaped by the press toward the country involved.
3 A series of coordinating conferences should be arranged with the advertising agency responsible for all appearances of the client country in paid space, so that the themes in paid and editorial space will conform.

The first campaign objective is the travel section, now a feature department of every important newspaper in America. These travel sections have become the dream pages of middle-class America with leisurely Sundays supplying ample time allowance for discussion about where to spend the next, or first, trip abroad. Although the advertising in these pages is read almost as avidly as the editorial copy, feature articles, because they are presented in familiar journalese, are absorbed as the opinion of an unbiased editor. For this reason the sections of the Sunday and daily press must be given the highest priority by the practitioner.

Copy for these articles should be replete with actual recommendations of specific locations to visit, outstanding points of attraction, and be broad enough in coverage to suggest native foods that might appeal to the American gourmet. The same course of editorial treatment prevails for magazines, especially those particularly oriented to travel. Many of the larger newspapers and magazines have found travel such a profitable source of revenue that they employ correspondents who continually visit points of interest for direct on-the-scene reporting.

We have discussed the approach to these editors in Chapter 2. The same rules apply. Probably the most important adjunctive aid for the proper servicing of the American press is a complete photographic file in color and black and white of the client country. Very few travel stories should leave a practitioner's office without supplementary photographs. Cultural events that might attract tourists are especially useful to travel editors and deserve well-documented background stories that will encourage an annual coverage of the occasion.

Some of the great metropolitan dailies publish advertising supplements on individual countries that have been found to be an extremely successful medium for travel promotion. These supplements are the products of joint efforts by the newspapers' advertising departments and the public relations and advertising agencies servicing the account. They are made economically feasible by the sale of enough advertising space to make publication financially profitable. The advertising space is provided by hotels and resorts, carriers, banks, travel agencies and shipping interests.

The editorial copy contained in the supplement is usually supplied by the public relations practitioner and, in most cases, is frankly slugged as advertising. It is this writer's opinion that travel copy is not diminished in credibility by the advertising slug and that the general tone is not injured in either its promotional impact or in the veracity of its subject material. Travel copy is expected by the reading public to be romantic so that on these pages, at least, lush descriptions are forgivable.

Literature for display, carrier distribution, and mailing is controlled in volume and in lavishness of production by the budget. There is practically no limit any longer to the absorption level of the American travelers' appetites for reading material about where they might go. But there is a definite limit as to how many American dollars a foreign country will pay to satisfy this appetite.

The practitioner's first efforts in the field of literature should be to publish two basic pieces. The first is commonly called a throw-away, a one-fold pamphlet sized to fit a No. 10 envelope. This piece must fit the travel agent's rack as well as be convenient as an envelope stuffer for all types of promotional mailings. The second piece of literature should be an ornate brochure featuring the highlights of the country from the viewpoint of a traveler. It should be done in color and be profusely illustrated. It should be edited with a view toward making it date slowly. If radio and television are being used by the advertising agency, the slogans on all printed material should be the same as those used in advertising.

FOREIGN AGENTS REGISTRATION ACT

At this juncture of a tourism campaign for a foreign country, the methods to be used by the practitioner coincide with those described in the section on travel promotion in Chapter 4. A further expansion of this phase would be mostly repetitive. However, before continuing with another phase, and far more important—the sphere of public relations for foreign governments—it might be well to bring to the practitioner's attention the legal restrictions governing all representation of a foreign state.

Shortly before the Second World War, Congress passed the Foreign Agents Registration Act, which enabled the Department of Justice to enforce the full disclosure of all activities of American citizens representing foreign countries. These disclosures are required in the form of full reports covering regular periods as designated by the Act, which was written to protect the national interests of the United States from activities that might be subversive or calculated to pervert popular attitudes. Along with the disclosure of activities, the Act requires that all fees and financial arrangements, including campaign budgets, be revealed in their entirety so that not only authorized agencies of the United States Government have access to these facts, but so that the general public can be fully informed about the true source of influences designed to affect their motivations.

For the guidance of the practitioner, a copy of the Act can be found in Appendix F. (See Appendix G for a specimen prospectus for a foreign tourism account.)

TECHNIQUES OF FOREIGN INFORMATION PROGRAMS

In the handling of a public relations assignment for a foreign government, the practitioner must always remember that the prime responsibility of the job is to maintain, to the greatest extent possible, a nonfluctuating, favorable news environment for the client country. It is the stability of a continuous flow of factual information that builds the public relations position of health resilient enough to resist or offset negative developments. Unlike any other area of public relations work, a client nation's too-frequent appearance on the front page of the press usually signals the creation of a negative attitude. A front-page headline often spells crisis and continual crises can only result in long-lasting unfavorable opinion. In this regard, it is of little consequence whether the crisis is posed as cured or on the mend. A practitioner must know that the positive sign of an approach to stability is the return to page ten or a complete lack of coverage.

With this caution in mind, the practitioner should seek to establish a channel to the press that can assure editors of a reliable flow of supplemental and background information having, as its principal purpose, the statistical validation of wire stories serviced by correspondents stationed in the country represented. The second purpose is to supply human interest filler material that can stand independently as stories of the kind that would not ordinarily be considered important enough to be serviced by a syndicated wire service.

One of the most difficult rules to learn or, more properly, to gauge in the foreign relations field, is the curiosity quotient that exists in the American public for news about a client country. The hard fact of the matter is that there are very few foreign countries in the free world for which the American public sustains a continuous news-information appetite. With the exception of a few large metropolitan dailies and the principal news magazines, along with the major networks, widely covered foreign news usually emanates from points of catastrophe. A case in point is Vietnam, which a comparatively short time ago was a country so obscure to most Americans that it was hardly known at all. As this is being written, it is a focal point of national attention because it is in a state of war in which the United States is involved. But from the public relations viewpoint, its thrust into public notice will assure it a negative public relations reaction for at least a generation to come.

Therefore, do not exhaust a normal curiosity level for the sake of front-page placement. Tranquility in national terms means happiness, and tranquility plus happiness are not front-page items.

An example of the reverse function of public relations can be illustrated by my first important assignment in public relations. The year was 1931, which in its economic aspects was one of the most baleful in American history. It was a year of bankruptcies, declining markets, closed factories and dim horizons.

As was expected, nearly every government in South America defaulted in interest payments on the various bond issues they had sold in the United States. One of these governments honored me with an ambassadorial visit to request that I mobilize an American press so apathetic and so unaware that they would not report this nation's default. I told the ambassador that I did not think I could quite prevent the appearance of an item reporting default, but that if his government would wait until the right moment, I might be able to keep the news off the front page. He agreed that this would represent success to his foreign office. I would call him within two weeks to give him the date.

The subsequent series of events is another proof that an effective public relations practitioner must be aware of the general flow of world events in order to give full service to the client assignment. I knew from financial reports that Brazil was about to default, and what I did was to find out the date the next coupon interest payment was due. I told my client that this day was ideal for his announcement. Brazil made the front page and my client nation had forty words of type as an addition to the Brazil story, deep in the financial section of the paper.

A public relations assignment for a government is usually defined by a contract between the embassy of that government and a public relations firm. Such a contract rarely, if ever, includes tourism publicity if the country involved is a first-class power. Generally tourism contracts are awarded by tourism agencies, which are usually wholly or occasionally partially controlled by the country involved.

Every embassy is staffed with information personnel headed by an attaché who, under direct ambassadorial supervision, guides and monitors the public relations operation. Because the news disseminated falls into three categories—political, cultural and economic—the attachés in charge of each are more or less involved. It should be remembered that these attachés are also in close touch with their respective ministries in their home capital, so that instruction to the practitioner is invariably a reflection of considered policy.

In the dissemination of news items containing official quotes, a high degree of accuracy must be maintained. Meticulous care in the translation of statements and documents is a prerequisite of accurate reporting. If the practitioner feels that rewrite, addition or deletion is properly suggestible, the English version should always be retranslated into the home language for approval before use is made of it. A public relations practitioner is not a diplomat, nor does he have to be informed about the genesis of policy. The service should be confined to giving his client embassy a maximum degree of communicability in proportion to the editorial importance of each individual item. A further duty of the practitioner is to give the embassy his professional judgment on the public relations values, negative or positive, contained in the items to be released.

However, a good practitioner, in carrying out an assignment for a foreign government, must be fully aware of the political environment not only in the country he represents but in that country's multiple relationships with the major countries in the world. This is not as complicated as it sounds. It simply means that no action of a government in the furthering of its foreign policy is a political abstraction. Everything that the government does in this context is done within the framework of a political atmosphere mainly composed of what is going on at any given time. The practitioner should be an avid reader of sophisticated journals reporting on the political scene. He must know about existing conflicts of viewpoints not only regarding his particular charge but regarding those pressures that touch indirectly on his client's problems. This is one field of public relations in which the practitioner must become an avid reader if he is to become an effective writer.

The United Nations enclave in New York City, with its attending corps of ranking diplomats, has complicated substantially the function of international public relations. It has in effect established two capitals in the United States, each one housing its own corps of correspondents servicing journals and networks throughout the world. For the practitioner, these two establishments each provide their own sets of chores and good protocol requires equal attention to both.

SUPERVISING VISITING DIGNITARIES
FROM FOREIGN GOVERNMENTS

Among the functions found to be most complicated in the international area are those devoted to the visits of heads of states and other high dignitaries to the United States. These assignments are complicated and the practitioner is only concerned partially.

For the most part, in concert with the State Department, the embassy programs the visit. In these programs every hour must be clearly accounted for and even rest periods must be clearly designated. More important, the meeting between the visiting head of state and his party with their counterparts in the United States Government are usually held within the bounds of an agreed-upon agenda completed well in advance of the occasion.

For the practitioner these meetings pose no problem because the press office of the embassy, the White House and the State Department are responsible fully for joint or separate communiqués. Usually a date and time for a press conference are announced to follow the climactic conferences of the visit. In Washington, D.C., this is traditionally held in the National Press Club, whereas in New York a hotel room of sufficient size is engaged, or ocassionally the facilities of the Overseas Press Club are used. In these conferences the intrusion of a public relations representative in any capacity other than observer is barred. All servicing of the press on these occasions should be handled by the press officer of the embassy acting directly under the ambassador.

The practitioner's responsibility is mainly directed toward servicing the press with background material that will enhance or expand the story elements of the visit. An example of such material would be full biographies with supplementary photographic material of all the principals making the visit including, of course, background material on their wives or other family members in the party. Then there should be a professional scanning of invitation lists to receptions or other planned social events so that no mistakes of omission or commission are made.

Because the visit is front-page material, it is usually a perfect opportunity for placement in the press and on the air of financial and cultural material not directly relating to the immediate business of the high-level meetings. The practitioner should also keep a weather eye out for the trivial experiences of the visiting dignitaries that make for human interest material both during and following the visit.

All these activities are routine. The important factor that public relations counsel must always be aware of is this: the visiting dignitaries consider their press in America a poor second in importance to their press at home. Their reason for coming is to prove to the people that their government rates high in the councils of the world and that the President of the United States and the Secretary of State have taken counsel from it.

Usually these trips are made in the company of a full squad of newspapermen who are not foreign correspondents in the ordinary sense; they are local political reporters sent with their head of state to report on the conferences and other salient features of the visit on the scene. Full television teams often accompany the group. The practitioner usually shares the responsibility for the comfort and working facilities of this group of newspapermen as well as for easing any difficulties they may encounter in a strange land.

Before leaving the problem posed by official visits of dignitaries, this writer would be remiss if he did not remind the student of some of the psychological aspects of these visits. There is a peculiar neurosis extant in the community, shared by many to an aberrated degree, of the benefits to be derived from closeness to the great. It is not an uncommon sight to see people wait for an hour on the reception line to shake hands with a president, king or chancellor and, after one handshake, move off into the throng with a beatific expression that is at once omniscient and socially uplifted. The omission of those who feel this way· rrom the invitation list can create an implacable enemy for the visiting regime. For this reason reception lists are swollen, and kept swollen, so that no one who is regarded as "belonging" can be offended. Some of the world's juiciest rumors have begun on these reception lines, and no nation's government enjoys immunity.

However, very often the practitioner can serve a noble purpose by seeing to it that the head of state does not get cornered in a long conversation that usually takes the form of a protracted political speech and that is, surprisingly enough, often rehearsed. A rescue from this kind of torture is a service strictly within the call of duty. Incidentally, the embassy attachés cannot accomplish this without embarrassment.

Quite another aspect of public relations in the governmental field, and very likely one of high priority for the practitioner, is the plethora of friendly and unfriendly organizations whose sworn raison d'être is to make the client country look good or bad. The specific purpose is usually contained in the organization's charter, and for many of these organizations it is not only an objective, but the sole objective. Very often the practitioner finds his client harmed by the friendly organization as much as by the enemy group, particularly in times of heated controversy. Of course, the partisan organizations are composed of American citizens who are usually, but not necessarily, descendants of native homelanders, so that control is impossible and inadvisable. These organizations have press departments of their own and throughout the years have developed a working channel to the daily papers that, especially when they are in communities with large minority groups, tend to service the desires of their subscribers. Practically no great nation is exempt from these pressures.

It is incumbent on the practitioner to research the organizations related to the minority groups interested in his client. Research must be done on their constituencies, their general lines of procedure, their credos and their leadership. Good public relations requires a working acquaintance with all organized proponents and antagonists in the community. When this relationship is heightened to a point of confidence that invites conferrals on projects rather than actions of impulse, a great success has been achieved. But when an organization's emotions take the shape of a picket line in front of an embassy or consular office, the best principle is to remove oneself and one's representatives from the scene and allow time and weather to dissipate the demonstration. No purpose is ever served by pitting emotions against emotions. One thing to remember in these instances is that the ambassador's or consul general's door must always be kept open to a properly designated committee so that the petition of the moment can be properly served.

REQUISITE PUBLICATIONS

One of the most important assignments falling within the purview of government public relations is the preparation of literature to be distributed by embassy mailings.

The foremost piece of regularly distributed material is usually the publication of the official newsletter of the embassy itself. Titled innocuously, it is usually a monthly or bimonthly issue with its principal contents devoted to a liberal scanning of its home country's national press. In addition to this, there are important statements of policy from ministerial sources as well as news about the visits of dignitaries from the home country to Washington. This Bulletin, as it is usually called, is sent to foreign editors of the national press, foreign correspondents stationed in Washington, political science, history and economic divisions of all universities and schools above the secondary level.

The preparation of this paper should be delegated to an experienced editor who is either bilingual or is assisted by a translator. The job requires the daily reading and clipping of a cross-section of the national press of the home country as well as the assembling of items having the most significance to American readers.

To be effective, the editor should strive to make this paper as objective and as unbiased as possible. To allow a seepage of promotional material into the embassy publication would make it valueless to its sophisticated readership. It is always a good idea to include in each issue at least one report on the client nation's economy.

Other literature bearing the embassy imprimatur has a wide range of purposes and forms. It is usually educative in nature and its publication is usually inspired by a public relations rather than promotional or publicity motive. For instance, the issuance of a good map designed for schoolroom purposes is a sound device to make vivid a territorial contention without resorting to an argumentative text. If the map is accompanied by a piece of simple literature depicting agricultural and industrial regions and a demographic population analysis, its use in the classroom is considerably augmented and client policy is furthered.

Literature designed to show investment opportunities for the American financial community in the client country is also valuable and here again the dry fact is of far more use than promotional exaggeration, especially if the practitioner's client is an underdeveloped country. Economic literature should be targeted to its purpose—and that target is usually the cynical businessman whose normal doubts must be overwhelmed by irrefutable evidence.

The practitioner should also avoid the old stratagem of expecting a montage of all clippings to attract interest. A single reprint of a good magazine article is effective, but a piece of literature containing a collection of photographed articles suggests, if indeed it does not prove, that a publicity campaign has been launched in an attempt to distort by amplification what might be a kernel of truth.

However, much more latitude is granted literature in the cultural field, where the terminology of the theater has become accepted usage. Therefore, make use of cultural events, especially in the fields of art, theater, opera, music and ballet, by the occasional publication of an attractive brochure that has as its principal purpose an educative or almost encyclopedic guide to the cultural life of the client country.

RADIO AND TELEVISION PUBLICITY

The media of radio and television offer a wide range of possibilities for servicing with material from the client country. Whereas the news departments of the large networks are always anxious to supplement stories with background material and supplementary comment, the educational networks will very often use regularly scheduled program material. Political content, particularly in the controversial event field, is welcomed rather than avoided because the network news departments usually take the responsibility for presenting both sides either by quoting an opposing viewpoint or by editorial comment.

In handling a governmental account, placement is never as difficult as discretion. This is particularly true in the radio and television presentation of personalities, such as visiting heads of state, or other high officials, along with permanently stationed embassy and consular staffs. The tradition of interview programs has become fixed in their purpose of extracting sensational revelations from highly placed officials who have had a lifetime's experience in maintaining diplomatic vagueness. The result has been the development of verbal fencing matches for the edification, if not the amusement, of the audience.

The practitioner should remember that not all diplomats and statesmen are adept at this kind of game. The baiting to which they are sometimes subjected can stretch patience to the breaking point and a flare of temper can cause an unfortunate incident. Study the show; know who the interrogators will be and know that your client's representative can deal with them. Do not permit the glamour of a network show to distort your judgment.

EXERCISES

1 In about a five hundred-word essay, discuss the essential differences between propaganda and a public information program.
2 Outline a series of advantages for the registrant of the Foreign Agents Registration Act and describe how this act protects the citizens of the United States.
3 Prepare a prospectus projecting a tourism program for a European country.
4 Do a dummy clearly depicting the use of art work for a pamphlet to be included in the literature on travel agency racks.
5 (a) Prepare a memorandum for a client who operates a chain of luxury hotels and is about to open a new one in Brazil, covering all publicity arrangements involving the opening of the hotel.
(b) Do an outline of a story on the same opening for a first-class American travel magazine.

6 Prepare a detailed plan for a visiting head of state whose mission is to confer with the President and Secretary of State in Washington. The duration of his stay will be five days, including the one day in Washington covering the conference. The objective is a maximum favorable press.

7 The ambassador of a client African nation that has recently acquired independent status is invited to address a luncheon meeting of important businessmen. Outline your suggestions for the important elements to be contained in this speech.

8 A photographic file is about to be compiled for a client nation to service the American press. What should be suggested as a basic list of photographs with which to start an operational file for press servicing?

9 Design a minimal program for an ambassador of a client country who seeks a continuing contact with minority groups formed from immigrants and the children of immigrants from his native country.

10 An action by the government of a client country has been taken that has received an unfavorable and highly critical press in the United States. Prepare a memorandum for the ambassador of the client country that attempts to neutralize the editorial havoc.

11 Pertinent Case Exercises (See Appendix A)
    a. YANKEE COME BACK
    b. STATE VISITOR

SUGGESTED SUPPLEMENTAL READING

Cater, Douglas. *The Fourth Branch of Government.* Boston: Houghton Mifflin Company, 1959

Goulding, Phil G. *Confirm or Deny: Informing the People on National Security.* New York: Harper & Row Publishers, Inc., 1970

Lee, John (ed.). *The Diplomatic Persuaders: New Role of the Mass Media in International Relations.* New York: John Wiley & Sons, Inc., 1968

McGinniss, Joe. *The Selling of the President, 1968.* New York: Trident Press, 1969

Meyer, D. Swing. *The Winning Candidate: How to Defeat Your Political Opponent.* New York: J. H. Heineman, 1966

Wyckhoff, Gene. *The Image Candidates: American Politics in the Age of Television.* New York: The Macmillan Company, 1968

impact of television on public relations practice 7

THE POWER OF THE MEDIUM

Some ten years ago on a pre-jet, slow overseas flight this writer had occasion to engage in conversation a seatmate who at that time was a highly placed executive of a large motion picture company. His stories about Hollywood were a conglomeration of legend and facts typical of America's most colorful industry. But something he told in passing was unforgettable to a public relations practitioner. It seems that his studio released a film, *Talk of the Town.* It starred Ronald Colman portraying an associate justice of the Supreme Court of the United States. Mr. Colman received more than 4000 pieces of mail from all over the United States asking for legal opinions and advice on matters covering the entire range of jurisprudence. As if this was not frightening enough, my traveling companion added that a substantial number of letters came from lawyers. That picture was made about twenty years ago and its name has long since been forgotten, but consider that the step from that point to Ronald Reagan's role in California politics today is a very short one.

What we are discussing here is human credulity and how public relations, making full use of technological tools, has produced a hyper-suggestible mass that may eventually make George Orwell's *1984* look like Pollyanna's concept of social design.

Although the moving picture, radio and television industries usually are classified within the general category of entertainment or amusement businesses, they unquestionably rate as the most powerful public relations devices of our time. In its zenith year—1948—the film industry reported that the national film audience was 3.4 billion people. Actually, each week some 65 million Americans, about half the population at that time, were exposed to Hollywood products. However, by comparison with today's day-and-night total-family exposure to television, the direct and subliminal effects of the movies up to twenty years ago are almost insignificant. A massive mold has been created in which the viewing public has been poured and cast.

If buying habits alone had been formed by this mold, the blessings and sins would merely be commercial, but the process has worked a far wider effect. Human mores in America have been changed; behavior patterns of a lifetime's duration have been changed and the individual's relationship to reality has been changed.

The housewife pushing a cart down the aisle of a supermarket filled with wares shown on TV commercials is a basic factor in the national economy. However, the same housewife daily exposed to the synthetic philosophies and moral teachings of a combination of favorite soap operas may become, at best, a family irritant and, at worst, a social problem.

In a nation afflicted by steep rises in alcohol consumption and drug usage the problem of addiction to harmful behavior patterns is of grave concern. The television screen in the American household has developed addictive patterns that have affected to some degree, positive or negative, the mental health of the country.

Very little mention is made of the positive effects TV has had on the American consciousness. Many writers on the subject have restricted themselves to the problem of violence on the TV screen. From this uneven criticism rises the error that television influences the youthful mind mainly or exclusively. The contrary is true.

There is a high quotient of educative values in noneducative program material. Favorite TV serials, whether they be the daytime soap operas or the features shown on evening prime time, have changed adult speech patterns, dress and social philosophy. Most of the changes have served to improve the mass condition. Although the highly literate and sophisticated few may voice skepticism about this general effect, there is no other educative medium that could have accomplished the same broad effect in as short a period of time. While all the negative nuances of the dramatic shows, particularly within the realm of sex and violence, continue to inflict a cumulative attrition on our society, in the main the bad are punished, and the good are rewarded by their own righteousness.

The communications industry, particularly public relations, must accept the daily TV program as the norm of the American market, whether it be in the field of entertainment, news, sports, philanthropy, politics, religion or, most important, the commercial as the vehicle of commerce. The daily environment of the American stream of life is now shaped by television to a far greater extent than it was in the past shaped by the press. Although mention is made of the power of the TV screen in all the facets of public relations covered by this book, the subject requires study in a deeper dimension for the proper understanding of the medium.

THE FUNCTION OF TELEVISION NETWORKS

To the practitioner the function of the network and individual station in the news field is of first importance. The major networks have assembled fully integrated staffs that, on a worldwide basis cover, photograph, report and comment on each day's news to an extent very few published newspapers can afford. This coverage is effective, accurate and edited expertly to hold the viewers' attention. The daily news programs are supplemented by well-produced interviews, as well as by the documentary coverage of political and social situations backgrounding the news. The American public has never been so well informed.

For the first time, a great number of Americans in both city and rural communities are exposed daily to at least the highlights of international events, rarely covered in the greater part of the American press. For most, it was the introduction to a new world and was a great factor in creating the appetite for nonfictional reading that resulted in a book publishing boom. It is often said that a little knowledge is a dangerous thing, but no knowledge is even more dangerous. For a long time the great mass of Americans lived in dream world isolation. The television news programs have served a great purpose in transforming a lack of awareness to an appetite to learn more. The local fire, or police raid, is still front page in the local newspaper. But on the network news show it is an insert at the end of a broadcast. The viewer is left with a sense of balance instead of a distorted sequence of values. More than this, almost every corner of the world, its people, its cities and its problems, has been brought into the viewer's living room to give him a cumulative sense of familiarity. Ancient geographical prejudices have been lessened and an important sense of closeness or kinship has been substituted. Resistance to foreign accents and products has been dissipated to a great extent and a new understanding of the common destiny of the world community is beginning to dawn.

TELEVISION'S ROLE IN POLITICS

Television is the only medium that can promise the communications industry an approach to the theoretical saturation of the population. Because this saturation point is so nearly fulfilled on some of the evening-hour telecasts, new conduct for political campaigning has been formulated.

For the practitioner television has developed an entirely new phase in the public relations business, and during the last ten years this has steadily mounted in importance until today it would be unthinkable for a major candidate, local or national, not to use television as the foremost medium in a projected campaign. A television campaign in an election is so volatile in its effect that it overshadows all other devices used in ordinary media, so that if a negative effect is created, a fatal imbalance can be produced that can lose an election for the candidate. How best to present a candidate on TV can become a practitioner's nightmare in a technical area of production that is as yet experimental.

Let us examine some of the pitfalls. Political success is very rarely based on intellectual prowess or incisive logic. The public demands a candidate who is most like its image of itself, but also one who can control situations, even in the glare of a spotlight or the discomfort of facing a TV camera. In newspapers and radio the written and spoken word created the entire posture of a candidate. The press carried photographs of situations manufactured for the purpose of favorable presentation, and radio depended on vocal commentary to present statements of political position and to describe the occasion and environment of the speech or interview. Television goes much further. It picks up the grimace, the gesture, the tic, the perspiration, the anxiety or, worse still, the overconfidence. Even on tape it allows for very little second guessing, and usually it is very good, or it is awfully bad.

Campaigning on TV usually takes three standardized forms: spot announcements, forums (more popularly known as debates) and news coverage. Spot announcements are very expensive, and they usually dominate the budget of a candidate. Their actual production should be left in the hands of professionals experienced in this very highly specialized technique.

But the planning of the presentation is the responsibility of the practitioner. Very often this planning must be as much devoted to obscuring the personality faults of the candidate as exposing his attributes. TV audiences have been weaned on and trained by a profusion of highly professional presentations acted by skilled veteran performers. Their assessment of a poor performance is instantaneous. Therefore the most effective spots are the shortest, using the maximum histrionic output that good direction can possibly extrude from an amateur.

The best results are usually obtained from scripts that attack the opponent's contentions rather than defend campaign issues. The reason for this is that anger and indignation are much more reliable emotions to communicate than sincerity and beneficent intention. If only this rule is adhered to, the practitioner's success potential with spot announcements will be heightened substantially.

The following suggestions are important factors to remember in preparing short spots—that is, spots whose duration is from fifteen seconds to half a minute. Keep the camera in close-up contact with the candidate speaking directly to the audience. Do not have him sitting at a desk not knowing what to do with his hands. Do not have him walking around or demonstrating the homeyness of his badly decorated living room. Resign the assignment if he insists on placing his wife and kiddies in focus.

Try to use scripts without other voices, such as interrogators or simulated constituents. Audiences subconsciously resent rehearsed scenes and lines. Direct confrontation is the most acceptable presentation.

Be wary of the use of humor. In a heated election the issues are not comical to the voters. Candidates who amuse do not usually win.

If possible, unless your candidate is experienced in debating technique, avoid a head-on television forum in which two or more candidates take part. This is usually a high-risk gamble. Spontaneous brilliance is not a commonly found asset and the heat of argument is far more likely to expose negative personality characteristics than a winning charm. Frank and open discussion of the issues is the purpose of a campaign, but if these issues are relegated to a debate format, semantic counterpoint very often beguiles the audience away from the issue, with the stronger personality prevailing.

On the other hand, too strong a personality can cause an arousement of underdog favoritism that can again result in a distorted conclusion. Try to meet all the issues of the opposition, but meet them with your candidate in solo appearances rather than in a discordant duet.

The walk through crowded racially imbalanced neighborhoods has become traditional for TV campaign news coverage. It is very difficult for a candidate to come off well through a welter of handshakes, baby kissing and split-second sidewalk dialogue while he chews enthusiastically on a morsel native to the particular ghetto being covered. The practitioner here should implant in his client's mind the necessity of making the walk without condescension and with a maximum of dignity in an effort to convince the voters that the sojourn is, in fact, a frank solicitation of votes.

The practitioner can determine the political climate of the nation more easily by a study of daily television than by editorial comment in the press. The national environment created by TV actually forms the public attitude, which by impulse accepts or rejects editorial recommendation. Action scenes on TV depicting violence and the destruction caused by violence completely overwhelm in the public consciousness the appeals to reason, compassion and consideration appearing in print the next morning. Political exponents on either side of any question compete for support not so much with each other as they do with molded attitudes aroused or set at rest by the sheet of glass permanently established in the national living room. Never before has the tide of events had an instantaneous channel of communication and, when it has developed momentum, it is almost a hopeless task to attempt the manipulation of reversal.

The practitioner must develop a time sense that can tell him when enthusiasm or momentum starts its ebbing process so that he can advise a political client properly on the timing and efficacy of counteraction. Of course, if the momentum is in his client's favor, he should make full use of it by allying him with all the elements enjoying ascendance. But then he, too, must know and be able to judge the subtle points that indicate exhaustion.

The effect of television on national campaigns is very diverse and so complicated that it demands a demographic study of each section of the nation before proper evaluations can be made. Network television presents a fairly consistent reportage to the entire nation. However, this reporting is in pictures, and sometimes local narration and comment can change the meaning of the pictures on the screen. It can also shorten the picture, lengthen the picture, delete the picture or distort the interpretation, depending on its catering to local feelings or prejudices. Networks are prone to minimize their control over the interpretation of local stations that are influenced frequently by their anxiety to achieve the fullest presentation of feature entertainment material carrying the maximum advertising potential.

Therefore political impact that is highly satisfactory to a viewpoint in Texas may work great injury in Illinois. Even in national campaigns with multimillion dollar budgets, it is good policy to sectionalize the buying of time and to prepare for each section specially designed presentation material.

Even more than the daily press, television has become the open forum of daily politics—national and local. The annual election is the only time during the year that the public is actually aware of a contest, but the political forces of the country vie for each moment of each day for what possible aid their cause can be given. An interesting survey, not yet made, might be the determination of what proportion of TV viewers is aware that fully half of the program material results from public relations efforts for one cause or another. Every committee of the Senate and Congress has an information officer engaged in television placement. Multiply this number by state and city departments of government, all legislative branches of these governments, and you will still get only a partial picture of the influence of public relations on TV. Add to this projection every important, or would-be important, executive of these three tiers of political operation and you come closer to measuring the pressure exerted. Thankfully Mr. and Mrs. Average Viewer are unconscious of the genesis of this portion of TV programming because the number of disguises used to capsulize politically influenced programs is infinite.

HUMAN CREDULITY

At the beginning of this chapter reference was made to the human credulity factor. For the gauging or measuring of the impact of TV, the credulity quotient of the American population must be the prime consideration of a practitioner before he accepts or rejects script material or production ideas. This is particularly true for programs touching on or directly based on political issues. There is something about the public relations industry that encourages a healthy cynicism in an approach to any philosophical preaching. This tinge of cynicism is a good defense against the hypersuggestibility that plagues the professional area of communications generally, and TV specifically.

But for the general viewing public quite another mental environment holds true. Just as for many centuries the printed word was fact merely because it appeared in a face type, today what is viewed and heard on TV for the greater part of America becomes gospel. There is some subconscious belief that a divine monitor stands at an enormous switch and if an untruth is spoken, he will pull the switch and black out everything.

This perplexing and so far ungaugeable credulity level in the American population is at one and the same time a nightmare to the agencies of government whose assignment is the "control" of television fare and the licensing of commercial television.

The contest between the Federal Communications Commission and the television industry will in all likelihood outlast a few of the coming centuries. The public relations practitioner need only be acutely aware of this extraordinary credulity that makes America the most profitable of all world markets for the propagation of sales or philosophical ideas.

Unfortunately this all-encompassing will to believe exists in the very literate or so-called sophisticated levels of American society as much as in the less aware and more apathetic sections of the population. Perhaps the point can be made clearer by an incident experienced, or rather suffered, by this writer.

Some ten years ago I was a guest at a dinner party numbering about forty people whose occupations included high-level executive positions in publishing, advertising, public relations and merchandising. They were about as sophisticated a group as a New York hostess could arrange in planning an "interesting" evening. Conversation at dinner centered on a very popular quiz program that was enjoying the highest TV audience following recorded to that date. Prizes ranged in fantastic sums up to hundreds of thousands of dollars. No human being ever having enjoyed life on this earth could have had his mind cluttered with the desiderata that the answers to the quiz questions demanded. In fact, very few libraries contained the research material necessary to ascertain these answers or even to approach them intelligently.

One of the quiz participants was an 11-year-old child who week after week blithely answered the most complicated questions on America's corporate history—questions that could not have been answered by any major bank president living then or now. The categories of questions involved in the program covered the whole intricate range of human interests, knowing no bounds or limits to show off the sensational capabilities of the participants. A guard from a famous New York bank delivered the questions to the interrogator who in turn asked the questions of the contestants locked in a soundproof booth, all of which made the operation faultlessly credible to the multitude of viewers.

It had been on the air a long time when this dinner party conversation took place. My fellow guests believed so devoutly in the authenticity of this program that when I mentioned that it might be one of the greatest hoaxes ever perpetrated on the American public, I met such indignation that I was almost forced to leave. I was declared subversive, irreligious and an obvious degenerate.

Six months later everyone connected with the program was indicted for criminal fraud and the television industry was shaken down to at least the fifth floor of the network building that had devised it.

Nothing ever told to the American public in words or in pictures, in print, on radio or television could have been more incredible than this program. It challenges the imagination to think that the huge mass comprising the viewing audience of the entire United States could be hypnotically entranced by an inconceivable and obvious fraud week after week with the religious zeal and conviction that viewing this program required. And yet it happened, and it will happen again.

Television's first big business victory over a competing medium was marked by the demise of the SATURDAY EVENING POST. Although there has been no end to the analyses attempting to give the reasons why a publication that became a national institution could not compete successfully in its space selling, there is no doubt that for the audience of this particular magazine the television screen became the far greater lure. The cycle of this effect in the contest between TV and the nation's most important consumer publications is not yet complete. The casualties of the future are already aware that they have received mortal wounds.

In surveying the channels of greatest productivity for a client, whether it is in the field of paid advertising or in the placement of the most effective publicity, the practitioner should always be aware that to the great mass market, television has become king.

In the near-term future, in the course of the normal development of techniques already available, it should be possible to telecast news as it happens directly from a location anywhere in the world. Satellite transmission and intergovernmental cooperation bringing news and pictures to worldwide audiences in color, or black and white, with coverage in depth, need no longer wait for the presses to roll. The huge circulation picture magazines have cause for grave concern.

However, television may well prove to have been of more benefit to the publishing industry than injury. It has been the direct cause of a prodigious increase in public awareness of the widest spectrum of problems confronting humanity, and more people than ever before are looking for more than superficial understanding. The result has been the creation of the greatest market for books in world history, with all the dramatic increases in demand dating from the advent of television.

Also there has been an ancillary effect on intellectual or "think" journals, many of which have become profitable for the first time since television. This process will unquestionably continue, mainly through the inability of TV to grant sufficient time allotments to supplementary material. Those who seek the added dimension will always need to seek recourse in publications.

In properly gauging this trend, the practitioner must always be aware that the attraction of TV lies in its ability to entertain. When it whets the appetite for education, a book must be purchased. This writer is aware of the great strides made in educational TV and the growing use of ultra high-frequency channels to supplement the school system. Nevertheless, it can be safely assumed that if television deserts the Western and the suspense thriller for educational fare, it will simultaneously lose the interest of the media director who buys space and time.

EXERCISES

1 Pertinent Case Exercises (See Appendix A)
   a. NOVEL ATTRACTION
   b. PRINTS INVESTITURE
   c. NOVA
   d. SELECT SENATOR

SUGGESTED SUPPLEMENTAL READING

Barnouw, Erik. *A History of Broadcasting in the United States.* New York: Oxford University Press, 1966

————. *A Tower in Babel.* New York: Oxford University Press, 1966

————. *The Golden Web.* New York: Oxford University Press, 1968

————. *The Image Empire.* New York: Oxford University Press, 1970

Barrett, Marvin (ed.). *Survey of Broadcast Journalism 1969–70: Year of Challenge, Year of Crisis.* New York: Grosset & Dunlap, Inc., 1970

Friendly, Fred W. *Due to Circumstances Beyond Our Control.* New York: Random House, 1967

Hodapp, William. *The Television Manual.* New York: Farrar, Straus & Young, Inc., 1953

Kendrick, Alexander. *Prime Time: The Life of Edward R. Murrow.* Boston: Little, Brown & Company, 1969

McLuhan, Herbert Marshall. *The Medium Is the Massage.* New York: Random House, 1967

Steinberg, Charles S. *The Communicative Arts: An Introduction to Mass Media.* New York: Hastings House, 1970

Walters, Barbara. *How To Talk with Practically Anybody About Practically Anything.* Garden City, N.Y.: Doubleday & Company, 1970

the art of getting, holding and losing clients

8

WHO NEEDS PUBLIC RELATIONS

Up to this point this textbook has been concerned mainly with the background necessary for the servicing of clients engaged in the main fields of institutional and commercial enterprises requiring public relations counsel. However, recognition must be made of the fact that nearly half of a senior practitioner's time—that is, the proprietor of a firm—is absorbed by the acquisition of new business and the maintenance of a stabilized contact with old business.

The first axiom to be learned in the technique of acquiring new accounts is that counsel is sought as soon as there is a focal point of pain within the organization or the institution under solicitation by the practitioner. This pain need not only be symptomatic of a poor relationship with the consumer public, stockholders or employees, but very often may be found to emanate from frictional relationships among administrative executives.

PINPOINTING THE PROBLEM

One of the first experiences this writer had in soliciting a new account involved a large manufacturer of toothpaste. Being a young hopeful, I had prepared a twenty-page prospectus that I thought covered every element of the company's business existence, and I applied in its pages every panacea that could possibly stem the downward sweep of a very doleful sales curve.

After having submitted the prospectus I was called in to attend an executive board meeting where for the first time I met the principal officers of the company. I was all prepared to enlarge on every detail in my prospectus, which I quickly discovered had never been taken out of its envelope. (By the way, they rarely are.) The atmosphere of the meeting was tense, if not outrightly acrimonious. I did not know why, beside the public knowledge that the company had fallen from second to eleventh place among its competitors. At the end of a series of lengthy harangues that were concerned with things other than my business there, I was told very curtly that I had been retained at a nominal fee for a one-month trial.

I left the meeting more than slightly confused and was somewhat stumped by what my very young organization could do in four weeks that this mighty corporation could not figure out in twenty years. On my way home that night I was inspired sufficiently by having received my first important assignment to walk into a drugstore and buy a tube of my new client's product. The next morning I tried it and it tasted like something that had been brewed by the witches in *Macbeth*. It was just awful!

I telephoned the client requesting another appointment with the executive committee. At the meeting I made the startling announcement that the reason for the toothpaste's dwindling popularity was its taste. Everyone smiled—everyone knew. The members of the executive board, either singly or in concert, could not bring themselves to tell it to an eighty-year-old president whose pet gripe in life was sweet-tasting, pleasantly flavored toothpaste. He believed that anything popular before the Spanish-American War—even though its taste was medicinal —would remain the people's choice in the early 1930s, when one of the few pleasures left to a Depression-ridden country was the taste of the morning toothpaste.

It very quickly developed that the reason I had been hired was to take on the onerous assignment of informing the president of my profound findings. Of course I was expendable and for a small fee they could risk having me thrown through the plate glass door. All would be safe until next year's sales declined. I was ushered out after I said my piece—fortunately not violently. Three years later the company went out of business.

NECESSARY OBJECTIVITY

Very often public relations counsel is sought by organizations having internal difficulties requiring an outsider's objectivity. Usually, the necessity for outside counsel is predicated on a decline of public appeal evidenced by loss of sales volume or competitive status.

In these situations the practitioner should never volunteer possible changes of policy or specific recommendations for activity before he is given a chance to investigate fully the underlying factors contributing to the condition at hand. The first perfunctory interview resulting from a direct solicitation or an invitation for a discussion sometimes ends with a request for a memorandum or a prospectus. Even the most expert public relations man cannot analyze a situation and suggest methods to cure faults without an opportunity for sufficient research to reveal possible policy defects. It is therefore far more reasonable to refuse a potential client's request for a prospectus on the basis that it would be an effrontery to assume a knowledge of a unique combination of circumstances greater than that of an experienced management.

Expertise in these cases revolves around two specific methods of attacking the problem: First, the practitioner must be relatively sure that the problem concerns the client relationship to the public and that the techniques of communication are heavily involved. This is to assure the qualifying of public relations as the determining factor in the client's problem. Secondly, the practitioner must be sure that within the area of public relations he is assured a part in the making of policy.

This may seem so obvious in the beginning of a client relationship not to bear mentioning, but the practitioner will soon learn that most potential clients have an erroneously expanded idea of the function of public relations to the point that disaster situations often develop. Unfortunately, more in the past than in the present, the business community romanticized the function of the public relations practitioner to the extent of obscuring the true nature of the public relations assignment. The success or failure of a public relations assignment is measured by the ability to reach specific or general groups of people through media with which they are familiar and in which they have confidence. The practitioner must be the master of the techniques necessary to accomplish just this. Qualifying the nature of the assignment establishes the best working arrangement between client and practitioner.

This necessity for proper boundaries being placed around the work area at the outset brings to mind many personal experiences, which may contribute to illustrating the importance of definition. The client in one such instance was a large manufacturer whose plant was in distant Michigan and whose posh executive offices were in New York. This is procedure in big business. When my firm was retained the president and I clearly outlined the fairly routine assignment, which was to give his company and its products a maximum degree of exposure in both the trade and consumer press. I assigned an account executive who had some knowledge of the client's particular industry, and at the start all went well. Before long, however, I began to be disturbed by the condition of my account executive after his return from frequent lunches with the president of the company. He would invariably return so drunk that he would have to spend the afternoon behind a closed door in a somnambulant effort to recover. His recovery was mandatory; he had to accompany the client on a round of fashionable bars and night clubs in the evening. I was unaware that my account executive was an alcoholic. He took to the task with extraordinary enthusiasm. Of course the client was also an alcoholic. My employee became the fair-haired boy who could do no wrong. When anything important had to be done I either attended to it myself or sent an abstemious nondrinker to fulfill the task. The climax of this unhappy arrangement came when I had to make a progress report to the executive board of the company. After a short wait the president returned to his office from a liquid lunch with my account executive. The president opened the meeting saying, "Well, Mr. Blumenthal, what have you done to earn your keep?" and the next words came from my account executive, who said, "Yeah, try to answer that one!" I resigned the account, fired the account executive and apologized to the board for not being able to alter their real problem, an alcoholic president.

Although practically all large corporations in the United States either retain public relations counsel or have a department delegated to public relations, new problems arise constantly requiring new approaches and making solicitation by new agencies welcome. By definition, the word *problem* used in the preceding sentence means difficulty. A conference with a prospect that starts with the declaration, "We have no problem" usually means that the practitioner will get no business. It also means that the man to whom he is speaking is concealing the truth. There are no corporations, profit or nonprofit, business or welfare, without problems—hurtful ones. When these problems concern communications, internal or external, a public relations prospect is born.

PROPER PRESENTATION

The practitioner's choice of approach to the prospect is smoother if he is armed with at least a vague knowledge of how his services can be applied. Usually a prospect who feels urgently in need of counsel will ask his law firm, advertising agency or officer most closely related to public relations duties to seek a number of public relations firms for interviews. The wrong way to represent your firm at an initial meeting of this kind is to exhibit more than a cursory knowledge of the potential client's business or problems.

Correct procedure requires that you make a presentation of your agency—its history, its staff, its general scope of experience and its flexibility—to show how it could concentrate on new business with sufficient intensity to get quick results. The choice of an agency by a prospective client is usually made on the assessment of agency maturity and/or confidence in the conceptual abilities of its principals.

The most successful presentations at initial conferences are usually straightforward spoken declarations of agency strength without recourse to slides, charts and other illustrated gimmickry—which usually depresses rather than impresses. If the prospect discloses his trouble, use it as an opportunity to ask for a second conference after a sufficient period of time for study and consideration.

The most productive cold approach to a prospective client is a well-written brief letter. This letter must do one thing: it must stress the importance of maintaining a continued access to public opinion while that opinion is as yet unfrozen. The letter should end with a request for a short interview and an assurance that an exchange of thoughts would be both provocative and productive.

Even a superficial reading of a good morning newspaper will uncover at least a dozen cold-approach prospects. An imminent proxy fight, a new product threatening many old ones, an international dispute, a precipitate drop in the value of a security or a politician hit with a tomato are all in dire need of a good practitioner, and these are only surface examples. Practically every item in the daily press has a direct impact on public opinion with both positive and negative effects. The victims of the negative side need and deserve counsel. They are usually the ripest prospects for a campaign.

Methods of operating a public relations account are as varied in the systems the practitioner might use as the number of his clients and potential clients. There are no set rules of procedure, just as there are no duplications of client problems. The more conceptual an approach to the problem, the less routine is the program of activity. The practitioner must institute his own system of communication with the client mainly for the purpose of affording the client an opportunity to gauge progress. Periodic reports are most commonly used and they usually cover a period of a month. They can be written or oral, depending on the client's preference, and they should contain a detailed review of all the activities engaged in for the client within the period under review. However, the practitioner should be guided by the adage that nothing ages quite as fast as yesterday's publicity. Therefore, effective reporting includes a glossary of past achievements, but emphasizes the projected program. The accent should always be on tomorrow.

If possible, a report should always be made on a calendared occasion in a formal manner in the office of either the client or the practitioner. Informal luncheons do not lend the environment necessary for the serious discussion that should follow the delivery of a report. They do not allow the practitioner to supplement his review with statements from personnel who were engaged on the account; nor do they allow for materials to be presented for reference. Short, pithy memorandums are recommended between meetings with a client rather than frequent personal meetings in which conversation becomes repetitive and might falsely indicate difficulties or even stagnation. Keep the client well informed but do not bore him with lengthy tracts that make hearing from the practitioner a chore.

The most common mistake practitioners make in communicating with a client is in trying to maintain a high excitement level. A good client seeks a steady rate of progress, not a pyrotechnical display that usually ends in a misfire. Hard work engenders more confidence than a scintillating idea that is usually too complicated or too dangerous to exploit. Public relations is a service industry and a part of the business process. A client expects his agency to provide an even, steady flow of work. He will not continue paying for occasional flashes of genius offered as a substitute for a satisfactory rate of activity.

A CASE IN POINT

Sometimes the practitioner is faced with the task of exerting a disciplinary force within the client organization in order to properly attack the assignment. A maximum amount of tact and subtle firmness is required, but if the client recognizes the need, and the pressure is deftly applied, successful results can be obtained. Let me give you a good example of a case of this kind:

Some years ago a formidable author wrote a book devoted entirely to the exposure of certain practices common to the funeral industry as it operates in the United States. The book received wide acclaim, much favorable publicity, good reviews and was a best seller almost immediately after its publication. The entire price structure of the funeral industry came under direct attack in the news columns of the nation's press, and legislative investigations threatened the equanimity of a comparatively unregulated, very lucrative American industry. If ever there was a situation requiring emergency public relations therapy, this was it.

My firm was called in for consultation by one of the largest trade associations representing a membership of funeral directors doing business in all the major cities of the United States. At my first meeting with the executive council of this group I encountered unbending indignation and threats of a libel suit against an author whom they were sure was part of a subversive conspiracy that planned to bring ruination to a large group of innocent, honorable businessmen.

At this first meeting I volunteered little more than a thorough researching of the entire industry. Because of the emergency nature of the situation, I tried to accomplish this research discussion in as little time as possible. What followed was both harrowing and depressing. I made personal visits to some of the largest and some of the smallest funeral establishments in the country, investigating their selling methods, their price structures and their advertising, as well as the community channels through which they solicited business.

My findings revealed that a substantial majority of the country's morticians was indeed on a par morally with the ethical level for general business conduct in industry. However, a far too numerous minority had adopted substandard procedures and were definitely casting a shadow that would quickly lead to legislation for the protection of the public. As soon as I was sure of the authenticity of my research I wrote a memorandum assembling the facts and recommending that the abuses could only be controlled by the adoption of a code of ethics that would in effect police the industry. I told them that although my suggestions might seem defensive in nature, control of the offenders in their industry was essential. Only this could place them in a position invulnerable to the public clamor for governmental control which, of course, was their great fear.

Organizational protocol required that I discuss this with all six regional boards before I could bring the matter before the entire organization at their national convention, which had been called into emergency session a month hence. At each of these regional meetings I had to face attacks by members who told me in no uncertain manner that I had not been hired to become the spokesman of their enemies. They wanted to know what I had done to quiet the public clamor and to discredit the author of the book. My rebuttal was to recite my personal experiences during the period of investigation and that the most good counsel could do for them was to suggest that they clean their own house before it was done for them. Patiently I lectured them on how to use public relations; that there could be no good public relations without sound internal policy, and that effective public relations had to reflect truth and not contrivance.

Slowly and painfully I won them over to my viewpoint, but they revenged themselves by naming me the principal speaker at their convention. I wrote a thirty-minute address in which I clearly set forth all my recommendations for internal reform and advised the expulsion from membership in the organization of all who would not conform

111

with the ethical conduct required by the code, which they would write and enforce.

I shall never forget the terror I felt when I walked into the assembly hall where 1000 dour-visaged morticians were waiting to be told the extent of their collective sins by the "expert" from New York who had never buried anyone. It did not lift my spirits when they opened the meeting by singing "There Are Smiles That Make You Happy." I delivered my speech, which evoked no ovation, but it did succeed. The resolution containing my recommendations was passed.

Following this convention, which was given national press coverage, the clamor began to recede with several important editorial comments praising the decision to police the industry from within. Several months later a Senate investigation concluded with a commendation to the organization I represented for their meritorious work in bringing forth a morticians' industry the public could trust. The moral of the story is that the practitioner must sometimes take on the onerous task of washing a client's hands before he exhibits them to the public.

The problem of vanity, previously mentioned in this book in Chapter 5, is ever present in the operation of an account. Corporations and institutions, regardless of their purpose or size, are composed of human beings, and publicity often presents an overwhelming temptation for them that it is impossible to resist. Yielding to the vanity motivation in the operation of an account is a matter of degree, and containing it within a noninjurious degree presents difficulties. The authenticity of releases is dependent on the ability to quote a named spokesman of sufficient status to bear responsibility for the release. The practitioner must be cognizant of the human condition that makes it as important to recognize the competition among the high echelon of the client company for who will be chosen as the spokesman, as it is for the company to compete for news space in the daily press.

The experienced practitioner knows that a picture and description of a new product on Page 34 is worth infinitely more to the business of a company than a first-page portrait of the company's president published in connection with his appointment to an officership in a philanthropic cause. But the assessment of this balance of values will never be gauged purely by business measurements. To get both items in the press should be the practitioner's purpose, but if a choice must be made, take the front-page portrait. Whose picture is used, and whose is not used, in an annual report can sometimes determine the renewal of a practitioner's contract. The practitioner's only defense is to remain *au courant* with the internal affairs and, more important, the internal jockeying for power within his client's councils.

High-ranking corporate executives, no matter how overtly they exhibit their aggressiveness, can suffer from very deep feelings of inferiority. To be unaware of this is to court disaster in the handling of an account.

I remember one occasion that changed the attitude of a client corporation's president toward me from positive to negative in an instant.

We were headed uptown in my client's limousine after a long conference in Wall Street that took us well past the dinner hour. He had offered to drive me home and I had accepted the invitation. At one of New York's busier crosstown streets he stopped the car, turned to me and said "I'm buying a newspaper. Do you want me to get you one?" With this, the newsstand owner came over and said "What will you have, mister?" My client bought a then-popular sensationalist tabloid and I asked for THE TIMES.

The contrast between my choice of newspaper and his was evidently too marked. I was never able to recover from the effects of this error, and eventually I lost the account because of it.

STAFFING THE ACCOUNT

Every client large enough to require a campaign of long or continuing duration will insist on a permanent staff being assigned to his account exclusively. Depending on the size and the scope of the operation this staff sometimes becomes sizable, made up of copywriters, researchers, media and art personnel and, of course, supplementary clerical staff. This group, occupied solely with the affairs of one account, is usually placed under the supervision of an account executive or supervisor directly responsible to the head of the public relations firm.

The choice and assignment of an account executive to a specific account is one of the most sensitive areas of a practitioner's operation. The account executive, besides the numerous duties attendant to servicing the account, serves as the communications channel between the practitioner and the client and very often performs the dual task of interpreting the needs and motivations entailed in the operation from one to the other. A good account executive frees the practitioner's time so that he can apply himself to directing and ordering of priorities rather than get bogged down in the morass of mundane details involved in the successful pursuit of the objectives of the assignment.

A well-chosen account executive can be the backbone of a successfully operated account, and the choice must be carefully made, taking into serious consideration the client organization and what qualities would make for maximum compatibility. However, there are certain qualities that apply to any account executive and that should be basic to the process of employment. An account executive should have a background of more than five years in public relations work either for an agency or in a department devoted to publicity. His appearance and personal habits should be good without being studied, and an easy social grace is useful. He should have an ability to write, with a comfortable command of the language in a fluid, rather than a florid, style, and with a minimum of affectation. He should also be skilled in editing copy written by others. Most of all, a good account executive should have an awareness and a curiosity about the world in which he lives that can only be satiated by far more than an average amount of reading. More specifically, this reading should consist of at least two daily newspapers, two books a week, and three weekly news magazines, as well as a fair amount of reading in whatever special interests he has adopted for his own intellectual pursuits. In the opinion of this writer this is a bare-minimum schedule to provide the working literacy necessary to service adequately any modern business or institutional client.

It is not necessary for the prospective account executive to have had previous experience in a business that is similar or related to the client's. A good public relations technician can service an account of almost any kind after a short period of orientation, concentrated study and research in the problems at hand. Just as a newspaper reporter covers a wide variety of stories having no relationship in fact or background, a good account executive wastes no time in assembling the vital facts basic to establishing an effective channel of communications with the public.

EXPORTING PUBLIC RELATIONS

Probably the greatest single accomplishment resulting from the widespread use of public relations in the United States was the export of the concept abroad. The idea caught on so fast in Europe that in most countries the American methodology was adopted in unabashed frankness without even translating the words *public relations* into other languages. The concept of the philosophy of the public relations industry has now permeated free Europe, and the Near East, Africa and Australia, especially in the highly industrialized sections, have rapidly followed suit.

This phenomenon has widened considerably the range and profit possibilities of the American practitioner. In every country having industrial and financial aspirations in the United States there is an opportunity for a successful solicitation of new business. The launching of a foreign marketing operation in the United States, with all its concomitant complications in every instance, finally devolves on the development of public acceptance. It is in this field that public relations offers the most economical and fastest working key to sales. The American market is replete with examples of highly profitable markets that developed, in some cases almost overnight, leaving little doubt of the high degree of permanence of the establishment of European product distribution in the United States.

The American practitioner should scan European trade publications to be constantly on the alert for new products for which a substantial demand in America could be developed. Solicitation should be made by letter, preferably in the language of the country to which it is sent, stating first an educated estimate of the numerical and financial potential for the product's use and then retail price scales of domestic competitors, along with a brief but accurate research paragraph on the tariff regulations governing the import of the product under consideration. The letter should also contain an offer to visit the prospect at the prospect's expense if he desires further consultation about his export potential. If the prospect is of sufficient size and prestige to make practical the consideration of an advertising as well as a public relations budget, offer consultation on both, with the enjoinder to help him choose an effective ad agency if a decision to export is made.

When solicitation reaches the conference stage in either America or Europe, depending on who makes the visit, discussions usually cover a far wider area than do preliminary talks with domestic prospects. There are a number of problems involved requiring serious planning in which public relations counsel will act not only as an adviser, but also as an organizer. The importation of a product into the United States in volume requires a distributional and sales apparatus, warehousing and effective display facilities, so that maximum dealer and consumer exposure can be effected simultaneously with the launching of public relations and advertising campaigns. In the greater number of cases the public relations organization is responsible in its entirety for the formative stage of these developments—that is, the public relations firm is responsible for recommending either contracting with an existing dealer network or organizing a factory-owned dealership for the exclusive servicing of the exporter. In either case, negotiations and personnel choices become the responsibility of the public relations counsel.

Because of these other considerations, substantial amounts of money are involved and the responsibility is weighty. The client has the right

115

to demand, and should expect, a thorough researching of the American market for his product as well as a complete marketing program, on the basis of which intelligent decisions can be made. If the public relations practitioner does not have the facilities to conduct such a research assignment properly, he should without hesitation recommend employing research institutions experienced in this highly complicated area. The more research that is done in the beginning, the fewer agonizing mistakes will confront both the practitioner and his client in the future.

As his experience with European business increases, the practitioner will become qualified to operate for American firms in Europe. This is by far the fastest growing tangent of the American public relations industry, and it should continue to grow for the next decade.

Financially strong American firms have found the Common Market area of Europe, with its lusty appetite for American products and American services, the most lucrative market outside the dollar area. These countries (the Netherlands, Belgium, Germany, France, Italy and Luxembourg) have become hard-currency countries with a fluid parity and convertibility with the dollar. Under the European Common Market system of eliminating tariff barriers among the member states, they have become a solid and integrated buying pool enhanced each year by rising living standards and swollen bank credits.

There are very few American companies of a size sufficient to export to this Common Market that have not already made substantial investments in manufacturing and distributional facilities. Some of them, in a comparatively short time, have become mature profit-making establishments. Although most of these companies use European advertising agencies (a good many are American owned), there is always a demand for American public relations practitioners, some of whom have opened offices abroad to supplement extensive publicity campaigns in the journals of Europe with American methodology. The theory behind this practice is that only American public relations firms can convert staid European buying habits by transferring the elements that created the demand for those American products in the United States to the population of Europe. Many Americans are amused on their trips to Europe when they hear radio commercials with which they are familiar translated into the language of the country they are visiting, using the same music, the same intonations, the same humor and, most important, enjoying the same consumer reaction.

No American practitioner should consider the solicitation of an operation of this kind until he is well versed in the commercial and financial environment that a client will meet in Europe. Certainly he should not consider the expensive experiment of opening a foreign branch until he was quite sure of his clientele and his ability to serve them effectively. It is far more expeditious to start this operation by an arrangement with a European public relations firm as an affiliate until sufficient knowledge is gained to own or control the operation. It is not a territory that lends itself easily or sympathetically to the inexperienced, but it certainly will become, if it has not already, a most lucrative source of business. The American investment in Europe since the Second World War has become one of the dominant factors in the world's economy and, with the European Common Market at the beginning of what may be the most extraordinary economic growth in modern history, a second market equivalent in size to the United States looms in the not too-distant future.

EXERCISES

1 Pertinent Case Exercises (See Appendix A)
   a. SCOTCH ON THE ROCKS
   b. BRAKE THE BANK
   c. INDUSTRY INVITATION

SUGGESTED SUPPLEMENTAL READING

Adams, Alexander B. *Handbook of Practical Public Relations.* New York: Thomas Y. Crowell Company, 1965

Baker, John Newton. *Your Public Relations Are Showing.* New York: Twayne Publishers, 1958

Harlan, Gene, and Alan Scott. *Contemporary Public Relations: Principles and Cases.* Englewood Cliffs, N.J.: Prentice-Hall, Inc., 1955

Lesly, Philip (ed.). *The Public Relations Handbook.* 3rd ed. Englewood Cliffs, N.J.: Prentice-Hall, Inc., 1967

Roalman, Arthur R. *Profitable Public Relations.* Homewood, Ill.: Dow Jones—Irwin, 1968

the ethics of public relations

9

THE CONCEPT OF THE "IMAGE"

As the reader probably will have noticed, the word *image*, which has become a cliché in the public relations and advertising fields, does not appear in this textbook. Through the years that it has been bandied about it has come to mean what an individual, corporation or product looks like but really is not. Sadly enough, to give someone or something an image has become such common purpose in the pursuit of public relations campaigns that very often the actual personality of many clients far exceeds in total asset value the false façade.

It might seem to the young practitioner wading through the morass of commercial campaigns or examining the techniques of noncommercial campaigns that the American public will accept aberrations, distortions or exaggerations and totally ignore any approach that attempts to use the truth. In advertising, the claims made for a product are subject to the painstaking scrutiny of governmental agencies. Indirectly, the same holds true for public relations copy in either press or pamphlet publications. But the newspaper editor who reads and edits public relations copy is the final judge and, therefore, in the exercise of his responsibility to his readers separates, by discretion, truth from falsehood.

However, the concept of the image is more subtle and more sinister. To create an image is to create an exterior mirage to conceal for self-serving advantage an unattractive but ever-present core. What is most perplexing about the process of image building is the bald assumption that the image is necessary regardless of the truth, efficacy or good character of the beneficiary.

Although contemporary history is replete with examples of the boomerang factor that lurks constantly in image building, the process goes on without any analytical attempt to determine how and when the facts about a client or his product became so vague or so uncertain that some palliative cocoon had to be woven for presentation to the buyer.

Perhaps some discussion of the ethical environment of American business would be of value before attempting to analyze the conditions that call for, or preclude, the manufacture of the image. The Industrial Revolution is little more than a century old and with the ability to mass manufacture came the necessity for mass selling. At first the distance between the manufacturer and the user was very small and then confined mainly to special lines of consumer goods.

In the middle of the nineteenth century, when a locomotive was sold to a railroad, the transaction usually involved the president of the locomotive company and the president of the railroad. Whether their images were good or poor had little effect on the sale. In consumer goods, the owner of a store during the period following the Civil War would often follow up a customer complaint by writing a personal letter to the proprietor of the factory that produced the faulty merchandise.

Today a wide gulf separates manufacturer and consumer. In between them lies a most complicated distribution system designed for ease of marketing huge quantities at a maximum yield. The actual relationship between these two poles has almost ceased to exist and the communication apparatus, which is advertising and public relations, is a one-way street. Talking back to the manufacturer requires not much less than a congressional investigation.

The practitioner, whether he is a counselor in an independent agency or an employee of an industrial or nonprofit organization, controls communications traffic along this one-way thoroughfare. What are some of his ethical considerations; what are the traffic lights that should guide his actions and recommendations?

A PRACTITIONER'S RESPONSIBILITY
FOR CLIENT CLAIMS

First of all, in the publicizing of a commercial product or service, is the practitioner responsible for the claims made by his client? With the exception of outright fraud, the practitioner is in charge of the *techniques* of transmission and carries no burden of investigation or analysis in his responsibility to either the client or the consumer. He is an adjunctive arm in the process of distribution; the legality of claims is a decision relegated to scientists and attorneys in their respective areas. Even in cases where the practitioner feels it is incumbent on him to invent slogans that occasionally imply claims, permission to use them must come from the client who, it must be assumed, has recourse to advice.

However, once the area of claim is established, it is the practitioner's duty to extrude the most from it. In most instances the legitimacy borderline is vague, but falling sales does not always mean that the claim area must be expanded. It might, and often does, mean that the approach is wrong.

The rules guiding advertising are somewhat more relaxed than those that restrict editorial access to the press. However, care must be exercised not to make them too divergent. It is difficult to be convincing if one or the other goes out of bounds.

An interesting example of this was a recent news item that told of a tenant in a luxury apartment who had received a bill for $130 from his utility company for his household consumption of electricity for one month of service. He had just moved into a new building that was the first completely electric building erected in his community. The utility company had printed several pieces of literature to aid the landlord in persuading prospective tenants that all electric appliances would mean enormous savings. The error was compounded by the fact that the landlord had built the building after having read advertisements and magazine pieces extolling the economy of electricity. Technically, no exaggeration was intended by either the builder or the utility company. When used in vast quantities electricity is cheap, but in a high-rise apartment house electrical heating can prove a disturbing expense to tenants.

The public relations lesson in this is that a product must be explained and sold in terms of need to the individual consumer. The appearance of this one item in the press can, and did, prove disastrous to a long-range public relations campaign.

Truth, reality and human credulity are going through a strange orientation daily in America by virtue of exposure to television advertising. The result has been an erosion of the viewer's line of tolerance, which will probably never be reconstructed. The situation soap opera technique of the commercial has come to be accepted by the viewer in very much the same way as the acceptance of the fictional skit. This process has given the advertiser a latitude bounded only by the taste limits of wit and whimsy. Comedy has become a substantial part of the technique so that claims, no matter how fantastic, are couched in slapstick humor intended to make the public laugh its way to a supermarket or drugstore counter.

This is not the public relations practitioner's orbit of endeavor. But it is his environment.

EVALUATING A PROSPECTIVE CLIENT

What kind of an account should be rejected by the practitioner? In general practice a full financial and character investigation should be made of all prospective clients. Of course this is unnecessary in cases where corporations or individuals are very well known and accepted in their areas of activity.

When investigation shows financial instability, the assignment is usually offered on a contingency basis that, in effect, makes the practitioner a partner in the operation and his own client. Sometimes this kind of deal is obscured by the offering of stock options or participation in a profit-sharing plan. Usually the outcome of this type of arrangement is poor, with an almost certain litigious termination. There have been many exceptions that have developed into happy relationships, but these exceptions do not prove the rule. The rule is, avoid them.

Financial substance does not always mean safety for the practitioner. The moral character and ethical behavior of a prospective client bears even deeper research. Be especially wary of campaigns having exotic objectives under the cover of a routine assignment. A common type in this category is defamation. This kind of campaign is usually targeted at racial groups, commercial competitors or political candidates. The practitioner very often falls heir to the public onus, or even legal procedures, in these campaigns, whereas the client is protected by a routine contract requiring an innocent series of assignments. In other words, the practitioner becomes the classic "fall guy" at the instant the project boomerangs.

Never accept a client whose account you might not be able to resign. Unfortunately, the last forty years have witnessed a huge infiltration of the American business community and labor unions by organized racketeers. In most cases, these organizations are so well masked that only deep-level investigation can reveal true ownership. Some particular businesses have become almost monopolies in the territories in which they operate and the network of these operations challenge even the investigative resources of the FBI. These accounts entice the unwary practitioner with fees and budgets that are swollen purposefully. Once they are accepted, extrication becomes difficult.

Never accept an account in which the client, or one of his designated principals, demands a percentage of the fee in the form of a personal cash rebate. In doing so, the practitioner becomes an active accomplice to an evasion of the federal income-tax law. Apprehension can mean a heavy fine or prison sentence. In the course of a public relations career the practitioner will be offered, on many occasions, clients in exchange for a commission agreement with the agent. Although there is nothing illegal in this kind of arrangement, it is ethically questionable. It is highly preferable to require the receiver of the commission to perform an actual partial assignment that will contribute toward the success of the operation.

PUBLIC RELATIONS AND LOBBYING

Lobbying is not a public relations function, but it is one of the most frequent causes of campaign fiascos. In its most fundamental sense, it entails the exertion of influence, pressure and other coercive means to extract a favorable attitude toward a private individual or corporation in order that a legislative vote or an administrative decision can be effected.

Lobbying and lobbyists are controlled and even licensed by most American legislative bodies and their work is subject to official scrutiny under the various permissive acts governing their behavior. Their work is usually confidential and carried out on a person-to-person basis. It is private, rather than public, relations and so sensitive in its procedures that the risk quotient for the client usually far outweighs the advantages sought.

However, a good public relations practitioner, when given a legislative problem should explain to his client that the greatest lobbyists are the voters at the polls. A good public relations campaign that sifts and analyzes the issues in a manner that molds public sentiment will have infinitely more effect on a legislator's decision than any number of whispered conferences in the halls of the various capitols. If it is an honest issue, give it a forthright public campaign. If the motive is clouded, the practitioner would do well to pass it on to a professional lobbyist.

No practitioner's career is complete without the repetitious introduction of polls in conjunction with every assignment. Opinion polling has become a vital adjunctive service of both advertising and public relations. It has also become an industry—possibly one of the most remunerative among the quasi-scientific services. In the political field, polls have replaced demographic analyses and all former systems of predicting election returns.

For the most part, with some disastrous exceptions, they have proved an accurate guide to the final results. The mathematical "infallibility" of the electronic computer has expanded opinion polling substantially and has made the use of periodic analyses almost mandatory in such fields as radio and television, in sociological surveys for governmental agencies and in the large-scale merchandising of products in speculative territories.

There is so wide a scope for the legitimate use of opinion polling and so much value to be derived from these polls that the practitioner need have no hesitancy in recommending them whenever the element of doubt about public feeling exceeds the spectrum of knowledge or experience. However, the practitioner should be wary of suggestions for polling in which results are planned to support a viewpoint already formed for any of a multitude of self-serving purposes. The practitioner should know that polls and pollsters, interviewees and interviewers are usually honest. However, the programming of a poll, the questions asked and the categories, the economic levels and neighborhoods chosen can materially affect the results. These can be maneuvered so that an erroneous self-serving interest can be sustained by an "honest" poll. Even if the circumstances are forceful enough to engage in such a polling operation, good ethical conduct would require the practitioner to point out to his client the fallacious elements involved. For the practitioner to recommend such an operation is unethical and bad public relations.

Fund raising and public relations are different disciplines but are very often mutually dependent. A good fund-raising campaign always requires the aid of a simultaneously operated public relations campaign. At times, especially in instances where a direct public appeal is made, the practitioners of each operation work closely together, but the functions are not related and do not belong under one roof. It is very possible to have a fund-raising campaign fail while a good public relations campaign is in progress because of improper fund-raising techniques. The reverse can also occur, but experience has proved that failure is more likely when the control is exclusively with one or the other.

FORMULA FOR FEES

Every practitioner is confronted with the problem of what it is fair to charge for a contracted assignment. Accepted procedure has, over many years, evolved a formula that approximates the following: the cost of actual personnel involved on a full- or part-time basis plus the proportionate share of general overhead consumed in terms of time and material should amount to two thirds of the total fee. The remaining third is profit—or, more politely called, consultative charges. This equation is not presented as a rule or even as a guide because each practitioner has a right to set his own value on his or his firm's services.

However, a formula that far exceeds this equation is unconscionable. The time is long past when the practice of public relations requires clients to pay for a mastermind process that promises to cure all ills in cloistered thought. Public relations is not a process in an ivory tower. It is hard work intelligently directed and, for the most part, routine enough to equalize the effectiveness of experienced practitioners. The public relations practitioner who charges astronomical fees is usually the one who has been more successful in publicizing himself than his clients.

CLIENT-PRACTITIONER RELATIONSHIP

The ethical considerations in a client-practitioner relationship are not the sole concern of the practitioner. They also are the concern of the client. Too often public relations counsel is sought for risk-laden responsibilities in which the client fears involvement in case of either a misstep or bad judgment. In other words, management often seeks an outsider's shoulders to burden with speculative ventures. In the event of failure, the public relations practitioner is dismissed and management denies any authorization of his actions. This has not yet become a frequent event in the practice of public relations, but it has happened too often for the practitioner to be blind to the possibility.

For this and many other obviously sound reasons, public relations counsel should always seek to render his service on a policy, as well as a functioning, level. To take part in planning and to know intimately the *raison d'être* of a campaign permits a clear understanding by all concerned of the methodology to be pursued by the information arm of an enterprise. Not only does this create an effective and thoroughly coordinated management orientation toward a campaign, but it lifts the level of public relations above the mundane publicity status. Always seek to have the broadest managerial support for the design and pursuit of public relations activities so that a minimum of internecine friction can be anticipated.

Another tangent of public relations practice to avoid is the glib application of Freudian therapy to corporate problems. Although there are indeed many crises in business life that might be attributable to deep-seated mass-motivational causes, the public relations practitioner need not play the role of a therapist. There are clients who at first flush may be impressed greatly by Freudian patter, but experience teaches that the client's trance is short-lived with a pronounced inclination to transfer his business to a counsel who talks hard facts and works hard to convey them to the public.

the practice of public relations

Industrial psychology has its greatest application in the field of labor relations and it hardly ever breaks down in its therapeutic routine until the subjected employees become aware of it. Brainwashing, no matter how beneficent its purpose, can be fiercely resented and then violently rejected. Even when some special reason exists for its use, the public relations practitioner should not attempt the fulfillment of this kind of assignment.

THE PRACTITIONER IMAGE

Present-day public relations practice, because of uneven historical development, has given the business community a rather distorted picture of its practitioners. After the First World War, and possibly until the middle 1930s, the public relations man often posed as an omnipotent seer whose cogitations only required a problem to be presented in order for its solution to be forthcoming. Some of these solutions were as exotic as the fees that were charged for them.

This condition was never true for a majority of the practitioners of this time, but it described accurately so many of the more colorful people in the field that a public concept was established. Unfortunately, it was not a favorable light that was cast on all the personalities involved in public relations.

Time has long since erased the soothsayer type, but he has been replaced, also in a minority, by the high liver, big spender, playboy type. The injury to all is just as great.

The ethical consideration in this regard lies in the approach to the client and the prospective client. The American business community has ceased for some time to regard public relations as a luxury. It is a working arm of every large business and many medium-sized businesses in the United States. Every government department—municipal, state and federal—has information offices. The armed services train personnel to do public relations on all echelons. All health and welfare organizations have designated public relations departments and officials. A great degree of maturity has been established, but there are still many private practitioners who lean heavily on a romanticized version of the role they feel required to play in order to make a great impression. This group chooses restaurants for their outrageously overpriced menus and will give an overwhelming tip to headwaiters to be sure a name will be remembered. In fact, their whole life—business and private—consists of little more than cutting a wide and noticeable swath through an offended public.

Exactly the contrary pattern is recommended for the practitioner.

The maximum impression of confidence is gained by an aura of conservatism. In demeanor, dress and social behavior, the practitioner should avoid what is ornate and overaccented.

One of the most sensitive areas of ethical behavior lies in account solicitation. When is it proper to solicit an account serviced by a competing public relations agency? The answer is mainly in the degree of aggressiveness used. It is perfectly proper to suggest to a prospective client that certain special areas in his campaign are not serviced, or that a more complete saturation might be produced by the use of specialized applications available through the facilities of the applicant practitioner. No criticism of the incumbent practitioner should be made or implied. Solicitation in this case would be the offering of an ancillary or supplemental service. However, this does not apply when solicitation is invited by the account. Even then, when a prospective client is seeking a replacement of public relations counsel, it is his ethical duty to notify his old counsel that he is making inquiries.

The most unethical solicitation procedure is that of attempting to procure business by the enticement, with money or rank, of employees of other public relations firms. There is no excuse for this behavior and the sin is compounded when the original approach is actually made by the employee of the competitor. Complete rejection of the proposal, as well as the man, is the only proper procedure. Incidentally, this method of getting business is also illegal because of the conspiratorial nature of the negotiations.

The ethical public relations practitioner should always be aware throughout his career that he bears a public responsibility. By giving corporate entities, government and governmental agencies and private individuals access to public exposure, he becomes the instrument by which reputations for credibility are made. This credibility very often, and sometimes very quickly, grows to a point at which the public relations counsel loses the power to exercise control, and the utterances and actions of the client property develop a publicity momentum that needs no tutelage or aid. The power to warrant, or even command, press notice is much more respected by the professional practitioner than by the people he services. To build a respect for the influence that can be wielded with this power is part of the duty of the ethical practitioner.

The education of the client in the civic responsibilities he assumes on the launching of a public relations effort should continue throughout the lifetime of the effort. No campaign falls outside of the slip stream of the daily historical process of mankind. All public relations, to be successful, must fit within the context of the multitude of daily occurrences that merit public notice. To build a story worthy of editorial exposure within this context is the public relations man's function. To build it beyond its rightful proportion results in the exaggerated anomaly that enjoys the most temporary praise and is rewarded eventually by complete oblivion.

EXERCISES

1 Pertinent Case Exercises (See Appendix A)
   a. CLEANED OUT
   b. ACCOUNT IN QUESTION

SUGGESTED SUPPLEMENTAL READING

Golden, L. L. L. "Difficult Years: Past Concepts and Present Trends." *Saturday Review* (May 10, 1968)

———. *Only by Public Consent: American Corporations Search for Favorable Opinions.* New York: Hawthorn Books, Inc., 1968

Houser, Theodore V. *Big Business and Human Values.* New York: McGraw-Hill Book Company, 1957

Rockwell, Henry T. "A Press Release Goes to Court." *Public Relations Journal.* Public Relations Society of America (Oct. 1968)

Safire, William L. *The Relations Explosion: A Diagram of the Coming Boom and Shakeout in Corporate Relations.* New York: The Macmillan Company, 1963

Simon, Morton J. *Public Relations Law.* New York: Appleton-Century-Crofts, 1969

APPENDIXES

case exercises

1. BOOKED FOR TAKE-OVER

Runyon & Mason, a privately owned publishing company established in 1912, has been one of the most successful and prestigious
purveyors of trade and textbooks in the United States for three
generations. It has on its roster many celebrated American and
European writers, and notable experts in most fields contribute to
its various educational series. Philip Runyon, grandson of the
founder, is president of the company, and Dale Emerson is its
lengendary editor-in-chief. They are particularly proud of their
carefully culled staff of editors and sales representatives.

The past year, although not overly profitable for any publishing
house, was especially unfavorable for Runyon & Mason. Few of the
expected best sellers excited the reading public; sales of first serial,
reprint and film rights were as rare as were college adoptions of
textbooks. As a result, Philip Runyon found it expedient to enter
negotiations for the sale of the company, as a wholly owned subsidiary, to XYZ, an industrial complex that umbrellas an electronics
empire, a domestic airline, an international hotel chain, a broadcasting network, a supermarket chain and a cigarette manufacturer.
Runyon has been assured by the powers at XYZ that his own company will remain autonomous, and under his direction, despite the
change in ownership. However, in other instances of XYZ acquisitions, a directed push toward more profits through a lowest common
denominator mass appeal has tended to cheapen the products involved. This facet of XYZ's reputation is as well known as is its
so-called Midas touch.

Customarily, Runyon & Mason holds two conferences each year
for its salesmen, fifty in number, who cover all sections of the United
States. One group represents the paperback division; another, hard-
cover books to traditional book stores; and the third, to textbook
outlets. The first meeting is held early in January in the company's
New York offices to announce the firm's spring and summer editions.
The second is scheduled for mid-June, when the fall and winter
lists are presented. This early summer meeting is also a social event
and combines business meetings with recreation. Salesmen and
participating company officials are encouraged to bring their wives,
at the firm's expense, and the locations for the convention are in
some resort near New York City: Atlantic City, Montauk, the
Poconos or the like. This year, the company has commandeered the
Seneca Inn, on Lake Holly in upstate New York.

Runyon has decided that the summer sales conference is the
best possible time to release the news of the sale of the Company
to his valued staff, as well as to the general public. He is hopeful
that his editorial and sales personnel will be convinced that the
quality of the Company's publications will not change and that their

faith will be communicated to authors and clients. He does not want to lose any of his staff of experts, nor his reputation in the literary world.

1. Make notes for a speech by Runyon explaining his move and justifying it.
2. Outline a program for any complementary public relations events at the sales conference to substantiate Runyon's plans.
3. Draft a release for the XYZ acquisition announcement.

2. PRACTICAL PHYSICIAN

Dr. Frank Hulbert, a general practitioner in Shaw Corners, N. H., is also a laboratory researcher in his spare time. Because three members of his family have been afflicted with severe sinus disorders for many years, he has investigated the field of remedies for this particular ailment with special interest. In his cellar laboratory, he has finally developed an anticongestant tablet that has brought rapid and consistent relief to his wife and daughters with no disadvantageous side effects. When his neighbors learned of the "miracle" medication, there was such a demand that he personally packaged the formula for distribution at cost by the local druggist. He named the pills MPH (his wife's initials); the boxes and labels were designed by his eldest daughter who is studying art in the local high school. Meanwhile, he patented the formula.

Dr. Sam Rogoff, the village druggist, sent a write-up on this success with MPH to the monthly publication of a trade association to which he belongs. Always alert for new discoveries, three major pharmaceutical companies tested Dr. Hulbert's product, discovered its excellence and attempted to break down its component parts and to duplicate it in their own workshops without using the exact patented formula. They were not successful. Thus, Dr. Hulbert had three offers for the outright sale of the rights to produce MPH. Astutely, he accepted only a long-time royalty agreement from Dorcis, International, one of the big drug firms, which cleared the necessary licensing procedure with the Food and Drug Administration and prepared to produce and market MPH nationwide. Because he was still in control of his discovery, Dorcis officials decided to use Dr. Hulbert as the keystone of their advertising and publicity campaigns—"Country Doctor Strikes Golden Medication."

1. Draft a release in which Dorcis announces the production of MPH.
2. Scout the competitive anticongestant claims and determine areas wherein MPH might be better.
3. Outline a publicity tour for Dr. Hulbert in ten major market areas of the U.S.

3. DOLLARS AND SCENTS

In 1938, the Colorado Brass Corporation (CBC) built a plant on an isolated tract overlooking the Cotton River, ten miles outside the small Kentucky town of the same name. Its product was, and still is, industrial dyes. This is a relatively small operation compared to the many other establishments making up the giant chemical and metallurgy combine. At the time of its opening, it employed 150 people from the town's population of 3500.

Cotton River was then the market and banking center for a farm area and had no other industrial activity. CBC selected the location for its plant because land and construction costs for the site were reasonable, as were state and local tax assessments. Also, a work force, at a relatively low wage level, was immediately available.

A few years later, a bourbon distillery was opened in Cotton River, followed soon by a beet sugar processing plant and a factory for manufacturing electric blankets. The municipal chamber of commerce is working actively to attract new business to the town, which has grown in population to 15,000.

Residential areas have radiated to take over surrounding farm and woodlands. Near the CBC plant, a real estate project, River Heights, to include about forty homes costing no less than $50,000, has flourished. This development covers the bluffs overlooking the south shore of the Cotton River, and has a particularly pleasant vista.

Jerry Kinzer has managed CBC's Cotton River plant for the past twenty years. He, and all his employees, are well aware that the three smoke stacks of the factory occasionally exude an unpleasant odor, which is not overly objectionable or offensive, to their point of view. Also, formerly, there were no neighbors to complain. Now, a citizen's committee from River Heights has petitioned Mr. Kinzer to get rid of the "noxious" smells.

On his own initiative, Kinzer and his plant engineers have made a survey and determined that the odors could be obliterated by adding special filters to the stacks, the installation of which would cost an estimated $750,000. He sent a comprehensive report to the CBC home office in Denver.

Meanwhile, the parent company, which is having many more serious problems with air and water pollution in other parts of the country, does not want to invest this amount of money in the Cotton River plant for at least two years.

1. Outline a program for placating the River Heights residents temporarily.

136

2. Outline a campaign to bolster the prestige of the CBC plant in the Cotton River area to help combat local antagonism.
3. Outline a program to recruit CBC employees in these community public relations projects.

4. PLANT FOR PINA

Xerxes Electronics, a wholly owned subsidiary of the XYZ behemoth (see Case #10), has thirty plants across the United States and eighty-two in other parts of the world. Business is booming and sales potential necessitates further expansion. High priority is being given to the construction of a new factory to make transistors. A team of experts has explored many possible areas in which the plant might be located. Their final report, based on space, site cost and available labor, recommends the purchase of an abandoned Second World War Air Corps Training Camp near the farm center of Pina, Texas.

Pina has a population of 4000. Other towns within a thirty-mile radius are of about the same size. Agriculture is the local industry, and individual farms and cooperatives in the vicinity grow lettuce, spinach, carrots and melons as their chief money crops. Pina supplies an auction market and a processing plant for cleaning and crating the produce, which is then transported by truck to onward-shipping depots outside the area.

The two-block business district of Pina contains three grocery stores, one department store branch of a statewide chain, two drug stores, a few speciality shops, two cafes and a pool room. There is one movie theater, but no public library. The school and medical facilities of the town are just adequate for serving the community. A sixty-bed hospital with a resident surgeon and two general practitioners minister to the needs of the townsfolk. There is no hotel, but three or four householders will rent rooms to transients. The Pina Endeavor, a weekly newspaper, reports community happenings.

Xerxes will require 300 pretrained workers to operate the Pina plant, which it plans to open for production one year hence. They must be imported from other parts of the country. In addition, the company will seek to employ about 500, without previous experience, from the area around Pina.

Adequate housing and other necessary accommodations for the workers and their families who will move into Pina must be carefully resolved without unsettling the present residents. The local labor force must be carefully recruited in order not to create undue competition with the farmers, whose wage scale is lower than that intended for the Xerxes plant.

1. Draft an initial release for the Pina Endeavor, the town weekly newspaper, announcing the purchase of the Pina Air Base for a future Xerxes plant.
2. Draw up an agenda for a meeting between Xerxes repre-

sentatives and the leading citizens of the Pina community to discuss and air any potential problems on either side.

3. Outline a program for recruiting trained electronics workers for employment in Pina.

5. FREE WHEELING

Rico, the Italian automobile manufacturer, has decided to enter the American market with its products. In the wake of many other more popular, less expensive foreign models, the Italian firm plans to offer six current designs, ranging in price from $6000 to $16,000, port of entry New York, to American car buyers. The line will be introduced at the New York International Automobile Show in April.

It is now November of the previous year. New Rico models have been displayed to great public enthusiasm at the annual automobile shows in London, Paris, Turin and Geneva.

The Rico Company, which is located in Pisa, Italy, was organized in 1901 by Roberto Rico, a carriage maker and amateur machinist. He built his first operative automobile in 1897, and after a series of successful experiments was encouraged by fellow automotive buffs in Pisa to go into quantity production. With an initial working force of six neighbors, he started turning out two machines per month. They were made-to-order models. The Rico name gained increasing renown as Roberto and his colleagues successfully entered races and rallies that were gaining in popularity throughout the world. Although his output was considerably more limited, Rico was acknowledged along with Benz, Daimler, Fiat, Peugeot and Renault as one of the European automotive pioneers. Until the end of the Second World War, the Rico was still virtually a custom-made car.

At the end of the Second World War, Renaldo Rico, eldest son of Roberto who was in semiretirement, found new financing through government supports and enlarged his plant facilities to produce in modified assembly line fashion about 500 cars each month. These were still luxury models and had maintained the Rico hallmark for style and precision engineering. Renaldo set up showrooms in Milan, Paris, London, Nice and Zurich. Only a minimum of sales effort was necessary to market the 6000 models produced annually.

Renaldo intends to increase his production by 25%, without excessive plant expansion and has earmarked 600 cars annually to the American market. He has decided to open sales and service offices in New York and Los Angeles. An English-speaking sales manager, who has been factory trained, and a similarly indoctrinated engineer, will be sent to each of the two locations to work with the American staff.

Renaldo Rico, who does not speak English, arrives in New York, coincident to the announcement of his plans for selling his automobiles in the United States.

1. Outline a publicity program to cover Mr. Rico's visit to New York and Los Angeles in November.

2. Draft a press release announcing the coming introduction of Ricos in the United States.
3. Draw up a press list to whom this release will be sent.
4. Outline a publicity campaign for Rico from November to April, when the line will be debuted.
5. Outline the contents of a press kit to be distributed in connection with the New York Automobile Show.

6. ARTISTIC ENDEAVOR

Abbot Abbotson came from Bay City, Ill., where his father operated a bicycle repair shop. Starting as a tinkerer, young Abbotson emerged early as a mechanical genius, and his many inventions during the course of a long and productive life greatly increased the efficiency and comfort of American automobiles, as well as modern airplanes. He amassed an enormous fortune, and when he died at the age of 82, his major bequest was to his home town for a cultural center to rival the most impressive in the country. He specified that the complex should contain an art museum, for which he left his own extensive collection; an opera house; a concert hall and a library. The foundation established by the Abbotson will to create the center was adequately endowed to sustain the project on an efficiently operating basis, without resource to principal, for at least thirty years. There would be absolutely no cost to the citizens or government of Bay City.

Reginald Tyler, the American architect, and one of the most venerated creative artists in the world, has a new commission. He has been selected by the trustees of the Abbot Abbotson estate to design the Abbotson Cultural Center in the Midwestern metropolis.

Mr. Tyler enjoyed his first acclaim at the age of 23 when he designed and supervised the construction of a revolutionarily styled hurricane-proof hotel in Palm Haven, Fla. He went from there to many triumphs and worldwide acclaim, and a cult grew up around his very personal philosophies of design. Although he has been less active as a practicing architect in recent years (he is 79), he is frequently consulted by younger colleagues and occasionally chairs architectural seminars.

The model and plans that Mr. Tyler presented and that have been approved by the Abbotson trustees will come as a shock to most modern critics and editors, who consider the designer a peer of Wright, van der Rohe, Gropius and Niemeyer. This cultural complex will be of an entirely classical construction—Greek revival, in fact.

The New York headquarters of Abbotson Enterprises has been selected as the location for a press conference at which Mr. Tyler will appear, and at which his model will be unveiled.

1. Plan the program for the press conference.
2. Draft an invitation to the conference.
3. Draw up a guest list.
4. Outline the contents for a press kit.
5. Draft an initial release for the press kit.
6. Word arrives one hour before the conference is scheduled that Mr. Tyler has died of a heart attack. What should be done?

7. SURPRISE PARTY

The Para-American Rubber Company (PARCO) has developed a revolutionary new automobile tire that has tested out to be veritably accident proof. In extensive and exhaustive experiments, the tire has resisted blowouts, punctures and skidding. This is a genuine breakthrough in the tire industry. Although the retail price of the tire will have to be higher than the most expensive one currently on the market, PARCO is confident that its durability and security qualities will make it worth the premium cost.

PARCO, which has been manufacturing a wide variety of rubber goods since 1910, has a worldwide sales gross of $1,679,420,000 annually. In domestic tire sales, however, it ranks as number four in the industry. This new product could raise PARCO to first position.

The development of a new tire, called the Creon, has been a top-secret project and absolutely no news of its existence has leaked outside the company. The first announcement is certain to rate as important news by the business and consumer press alike.

To present the Creon for the first time in a properly impressive setting, the Company plans an elaborate press party to be held in New York. In the course of this party, PARCO technicians are prepared to exhibit the tire's invulnerability to many hazards: brads will be driven into the casing with sledge hammers, without damage; razor cuts will be made and heat and friction stresses will be caused through contact with a rotary emery wheel. A ten-minute motion picture has been produced to demonstrate the holding powers of the tires on water, oil, ice and snow.

1. Outline a plan for the party: where and when it should be held; suggested decor; refreshments; events and entertainment.
2. Draft an invitation, which must not reveal the reason for the party.
3. Draw up a guest list.
4. The evening before the party, an automotive trade magazine editor telephones a PARCO executive for a company reaction to the announcement of a new, invulnerable tire just introduced by PNEUMA, the Italian manufacturer. What happens next?

8. BRUSH UP

After eight years of research, experimentation and market surveys as to the wants and needs of the buying public, the Lois Corporation, one of the country's largest manufacturers of soaps, cleansers and dentifrices, has decided to introduce a new toothpaste. Lois executives have decided that a novel combination breath-freshener and stain-remover brand of paste will find rapid acceptance, although toothpaste buyers are known to try one tube of a new brand and then revert to their former favorite. Lois expects that the newest entry into the market will not only lure users but will also hold them.

The name is Spark. It's tasty, spicy, invigorating and not too sweet. And it does remove difficult stains more effectively than any competing brand. The packaging is attractive: a tube and its enclosing box in gold on white. This color scheme complements the paste itself, which is white with flecks of gold.

At present, there are fourteen brands of toothpaste on the market drawing an annual sales of $234,600,000. The best selling brand, not a Lois product, has 32% of the market. Lois has two very popular brands, one of which is in second place nationally with 21%. The other has 14%. To be classified as a success and to justify permanent production, Spark must attract at least 2% of the toothpaste buyers in the country within one year after its national introduction. Furthermore, the top-selling toothpaste has the endorsement of the American Dental Association.

Rumor has it that all stain removers contain abrasive material that is harmful to tooth enamel, although this is not true in the case of Spark.

Lois Corporation will test market the product in Cleveland, Des Moines, Houston and Seattle.

1. Draft an initial release for the four test-market cities announcing the introduction of the new product.
2. Outline a program for approaching dentists for endorsement.
3. Outline potential article ideas about Spark and its qualities that might intrigue:
   a. LIFE
   b. READER'S DIGEST
   c. COSMOPOLITAN
   d. DENTAL SURVEY
   e. MODERN PACKAGING

9. HHV IN JEOPARDY

The HHV Company, named for its founders, Roger and George Hurst and their brother-in-law Sam Verdon, commenced operation in the village of Leesville, Va. in 1879. Its principal product was burlap, along with slightly more refined sacking materials. By 1900, the Company had become successful enough to afford a take-over of a less fortunate competitor whose plant was located in the neighboring Virginia town of Pineland. This latter factory was also equipped to manufacture canvas and other rough cotton materials.

HHV continued to flourish and rode the crest of a wave of prosperity with multiple contracts from the United States Government during the First World War. From the mounting profits, additional expansion seemed requisite, and six more plants were purchased or constructed between 1917 and 1921, in North Carolina, South Carolina and Georgia. With these supplementary facilities, HHV ventured into domestics, threads, hosiery and toweling. During the Depression years, the Company exercised many practical economies, but managed to maintain its labor force, even with lowered pay scales. Thus, HHV managed to survive the most dire economic pitfalls of the early 1930s, and was poised to accept the renewed capacity output required by the demands of the Government and the public at the outset of the Second World War.

In 1948, with the death of the last surviving founder, George Hurst, the Company became a public corporation, although it continued under family direction. Robert Hurst II and John Vernon now hold the positions of chairman of the board and president, respectively. The Company has 1,220,110 shareholders, 35% of the stock belonging to members of the HHV official family and other employees. Dividends have been relatively small, but regular. There is now a total of twelve plants located in four southern states, employing about 3500 people, some of whom are third-generation HHV workers. Sales for the previous year totaled $142 million. HHV has $2 million in cash and Government bonds on its balance sheet.

The Company management learns that an investment group headed by New York financier David Abell has been buying HHV stocks heavily. Abell has a reputation for taking control of small successful companies, milking them dry and dumping them. This is obviously the beginning of a raid by Abell and his associates for control of HHV, and a battle for proxies will ensue.

1. Plan a campaign for HHV management defense.
2. Plan a campaign for the Abell group's attack.
3. Draft an announcement for an HHV stockholders' meeting.

10. XERXES COMPLEX

Hiram Xerxes built his conglomerate, starting literally with his own hands. As an amateur radio operator using homemade equipment, he leapt into the arena of entertainment broadcasting by organizing a regular one-hour presentation of music (instrumental ensembles and vocal groups) from a popular Chicago restaurant. A licensed commercial station was one result of this early experiment, and WCHI became the keystone of the future Zodiac (Hiram was also interested in astrology) network. The stars evidently favored him. Within a few years, he had added stations in Cincinnati, Detroit, Boston and, finally, New York and Washington. This owned-stations group formed the nucleus for a network of affiliates throughout the central and eastern states.

Meanwhile, he purchased a small factory adapted to making home radio receivers under various patents. This shop, located in South Bend, Ind., burgeoned into Xerxes Electronics, which now manufactures a complete line of household appliances, computers and other business machines, as well as a broad spectrum of adjuncts to modern technology.

In 1926, Hiram offered stock in these combined endeavors to the public, under the covering name of the XYZ Corporation (X for Xerxes, Y for euphony, Z for Zodiac).

XYZ acquired Central States Airlines in 1932, when the twenty-city passenger and cargo plane service almost foundered under a deluge of Depression debts. Government contracts helped considerably to bolster the line after Hiram's company took control. It now profitably serves a territory from Minneapolis to Dallas, with Newark and Denver as its east and west termini.

In 1948, the Zodiac network added television presentations to its family. In 1949, Cameo Hotels, located in twenty cities in the United States and in ten major capitals around the world, came to XYZ through a stock merger.

Hiram personally financed the innovators of Miraco cigarettes in their early experiments and directed the introduction of the new low-tar, filter product when it flashed before the public in 1952, with an enormous assist from first place on Government health test lists and a $25 million advertising budget. There is now a menthol twin, Miraco II.

The acquisition of the Astro supermarket chain came in 1957. This Midwestern organization consists of 720 stores in states bordering the Mississippi River. Most recently, XYZ has added the prestigious publishing firm, Runyon & Mason.

Although it is the thirty-second largest company in the United States, XYZ still lacks corporate identity. Its public personality seems to coincide with that of Hiram Xerxes, who is now 76 years old. The various entities under the XYZ umbrella seem to have no connection with the parent firm. In all probability, a majority of the 97,000 employees scattered around the world have no idea of the magnitude or make-up of the XYZ enterprises.

1. Outline a long range public relations program directed toward XYZ employees to familiarize them with the parent company, its history, its components, and each individual's part in the giant corporation.
2. Outline a long-range public relations program to acquaint the general public with the story of the parent company as the sum of its components.

11. CLOCK RUN-DOWN

The Enoch Mather Clock Company of Spruce Bay, Mass., has been an American institution for more than one hundred years. The name of the company has stood for excellence in timepieces, in the guarantee of precision workmanship and in the conservative elegance of design. Even though many more expensive and elaborate brands have been imported from Europe, the Mather products have maintained, until recently, a loyal public and ever-increasing sales.

Long a strictly family business, the company sold its stock to the public after the Second World War, when the need came to increase its capital in order to retool to meet increased competition from European imports. Ten years later, after the death of the then chairman of the board, who was also the last direct heir of the original Enoch Mather, controlling interest in the company was purchased by Daniel Sauk, who owned a national chain of discount jewelry stores.

Almost immediately, Sauk introduced a program to inflate the value of Mather stock. In the clock and watch production, through unnecessary economies and cutbacks, he reduced the quality of the materials used. In speeding up plant operations, he forced out of the company many dedicated craftsmen who took pride in their work. The resulting output was often shoddy, but the respected name of Mather temporarily camouflaged such defects, and the high prices for the merchandise remained intact. Sauk also increased the company budgets for advertising and publicity. Sales rose to a new high for the company and quarterly reports showed increasing profits. Accordingly, the market price for the stock climbed, until Sauk suspected that it had hit its limit. Then he sold out his holdings and left the company.

When a new management took control of the Enoch Mather Company, the stock had plunged to one fifth of its maximum height. Complaints about the poor quality of the merchandise and returned clocks and watches came pouring in from dealers and distributors across the country. Sales plummeted.

Naturally, the first activity of the new management was directed toward restoring quality control, and soon once again the plant was turning out clocks and watches meeting the former high standards.

1. Outline a program whereby the new management can win back the confidence of its distributors and dealers.
2. Outline a program whereby the new management can rebuild its good name in the financial community.

12. CLIPPED WINGS

Central States Airlines has been grounded. Its newly unionized clerical staff voted to strike when mediation toward a two-year contract did not materialize. Flight crews and maintenance workers refused to cross hastily set up picket lines. Planes, in transit at the time the strike was called, continued to their destinations, but passengers were delayed after landing by the inexperienced baggage handling by company executives. Twenty cities are affected, ten of which have no other air or rail service.

The strike comes as a result of a long-smoldering rebellion among the company's office workers against their low pay and lack of benefits. The union was formed under the leadership of Charlotte Rodgers, senior reservations clerk at Newark Airport. A veteran of almost twenty-five years with Central States, she faces ultimate retirement without a pension. She and her fellow workers, the ticket agents, secretaries, bookkeepers, and messengers, hope to present a solid front in requesting a more reasonable personnel program. Sixty per cent of the company's office staff have committed themselves to this action. Meanwhile, Jack Nasoff, president and operating director of the airline, has refused to recognize the group as legitimate bargaining agents.

Central States, a wholly owned subsidiary of the XYZ conglomerate, is an efficient, profitable operation. The equipment is first rate and service, in flight and on the ground, is superior. Complaints from passengers or freight clients are rare. Flight personnel and ground crews, who belong to major national unions, are well paid.

Nasoff's attitude toward office personnel is based on his experience that the supply of such workers far exceeds demand. Little training is required. Rapid turnover is to be expected, so benefits can be kept at a minimum. Accustomed to running his company with a firm hand, he finds it intolerable that a newly formed group, not even a majority of the workers they purport to represent, can paralyze Central States Airlines.

1. Outline a program to establish public identity for the Central States Airlines Clerical Workers Union.
2. Outline a program, for the ten isolated cities, by which municipal officials and business leaders are persuaded to protest the strike and bring pressure for early settlement upon the company management.
3. Outline a program to insure that the other airline unions continue to support the strike.
4. Draft a release from company management justifying the refusal to bargain with a nonrepresentative union.

13. ACE OF CLUBS

This year's sunning spot for the international "in" crowd will be Solaris—at least, such is the fond hope of a group of American entrepreneurs who are constructing a new resort facility on the island of Grand Bahama, in the West Indies.

Luxe Unlimited, the American corporation that is sponsoring the project, is headed by Wesley J. Newcombe, Jr., scion of a Houstonian oil empire. Mr. Newcombe is no mere figurehead for the organization. He was the originator of the idea and is actively pursuing its execution. He and his family are providing the financial backing, which will total $2,500,000. Mr. Newcombe's partners are Roy Ashmead, a former director of the Liberty Hotel chain, which consists of half-residential, luxury establishments in twelve major cities throughout the United States; and Carl Milan, former Davis Cup champion and current member of the New York investment firm of Brady, Milan, Inc. Mr. Ashmead, selected for his know-how in the operation of fashionable hotels, will be resident manager. Mr. Milan was picked by Mr. Newcombe because of his illustrious and wealthy contacts.

Solaris is intended to be an exclusive private club from November through March. During the remainder of the year, it will be open to the public. Membership in the club will be limited in number to 1000, who must be approved by a Board of Governors. Members may maintain accommodations throughout the club season, or reserve them for specific periods during these five months. Membership fees are $2500. Annual dues are $1000 and additional fees are assessed according to accommodations used. It is an expensive resort.

The club facilities will include a main house with accommodations for two hundred guests; two restaurants, one formal; a snack bar; two drinking bars; a cabaret and a casino. Twenty three-room cottages surround the largest of two swimming pools. Ocean swimming, with its adjuncts of surfing, skin-diving and water skiing, tennis courts and access to a golf course are provided.

The Bahamian Government has approved a gambling license for the Solaris casino, despite widespread publicity about American gangster elements involved in the operation of the public casino at Freeport, the island's largest city.

Grand Bahama has a temperate climate year-round, with temperatures ranging from 65 degrees in December to 90 degrees in July. December usually has a few days of rain. Humidity is low. There is a readily available labor force and wages are moderate, but the workers tend to be indolent.

Grand Bahama is easily accessible via short flights from Nassau Miami or Palm Beach and its many marinas can accommodate the largest of private yachts. It is possible that two major airlines will establish regular flights between New York and Freeport.

The month is January. The prospectus is in the making. Solaris is expected to be ready for the next winter season, commencing at Thanksgiving. The Board of Governors must be formed and a membership drive undertaken without delay.

1. Outline a plan for setting up a Board of Governors.
2. Dummy a brochure (prospectus) to attract club members.
3. Dummy a brochure to attract out-of-club-season patrons.
4. Outline a publicity program to give Solaris international recognition.
5. Outline a program to counteract gangster-taint publicity concerning Bahamian casino operations.

14. THE MANOR BORN

Four miles south of Willbury, Conn., just off the main highway to Hartford, there is a wooded tract of some 2000 acres, encompassing a range of hills that slopes down to a picturesque stream known as Nepeko Creek. This parcel of land, still family owned, was a part of the extensive estate granted to one Alwain Jones by the English Crown in 1745. It has remained in its sylvan state because the rocky and corrugated terrain is unsuitable for farming.

Willbury is having a mild population explosion. Heretofore noted only as the village surrounding Brookdale College, it has recently become the home of two industrial plants: a press and bindery for Runyon & Mason, the publishers, and a research laboratory set up by the Xerxes Electronics Corporation. Several hundred employees and their families are expected to move to Willbury in the near future. Also, there is a perennial influx of new residents who are attracted by the "ivory tower" charm of Willbury and the cultural and intellectual stimulation of its college community.

Jones Jones, a Willbury attorney, and the present owner of the Nepeko Creek property, has decided to develop this area as a housing project. The woods have been cleared to allow the initial construction of about four hundred houses. A two-lane road from the highway to the building site has been graded and paved. Streets are being laid out in the development, and a three-bedroom model house has been designed and is under construction. Plans call for a children's playground, four tennis courts and an outdoor swimming pool for summer use by the residents.

The property is now called Nepeko Manor. Intended for middle-income occupants, the half-acre plots have been priced by Jones at a par with the going real estate rates of the day. Terms of purchase are very reasonable. Costs of the houses are estimated from $30,000 to $40,000. The Millbury branch of the Patriots Bank and Trust Company stands ready to assist potential buyers with the necessary financing.

From the green in front of the Town Hall in Willbury to the gate in the stone fences that enclose Nepeko Manor the distance is exactly five miles. Eventually, Jones plans to build a shopping center adjacent to the housing area.

Willbury businessmen in general are enthusiastic about the development program. The only dissenters are a few hunters of small game who had used Nepeko Creek as a preserve and the local Boy Scout troop, which had commandeered a part of the hills for hiking and camping.

1. Prepare the outline of a prospectus offering Nepeko Manor to potential buyers.

2. Outline a publicity campaign to attract buyers in Willbury.
3. Outline a publicity campaign to attract buyers from other areas.

15. ALL WASHED UP

Superba, "the soap with the velvet lather," has been a household word for the past sixty years. Manufactured by the Lois Corporation, this particular brand helped to establish the company as one of the industry leaders. It is an all-family, all-purpose product, recommended for complexion, bath, dishes or laundry. It is made in three convenient sizes, to accommodate kitchen or bathroom use. The wrapper is pristine white, with gold lettering.

Advertising campaigns for the soap over the years have featured mothers, brides, teenagers, babies, noted athletes and movie stars. One of the first network radio series had Superba as its sponsor.

New cake soaps with perfume and cold cream additives, deodorants and detergents have entered the market year after year to pare off Superba sales. Lois executives feel that the venerable Superba badly needs an injection from some fountain of youth, although they have no intention of tampering in any way with its formula or its readily identifiable packaging.

1. Outline a program to develop new publicity for Superba.
2. Create an idea for an article on Superba for any specific national magazine.
3. Find an idea for a women's page article in a newspaper on Superba.
4. Devise a publicity photograph for newspaper use.

16. POWER PLAY

The Amalgamated Power and Light Company services a major city and four neighboring counties in a Midwestern state. It provides electricity, gas and steam to a residential and commercial consumer list of about 2,240,000 accounts. Like most similar utility operations, it holds a monopoly in this territory.

For many years, Amalgamated had a good public record. Recently, however, frequent dim-outs have occurred during peak usage hours in midsummer and one major eight-hour black-out throughout the entire area was caused by storm damage to vital equipment.

The problem is outmoded equipment. The company has not kept pace with the increasing demand for service, which came with a rise in population, wider use of appliances in every home and the influx of new industry.

Because the management of Amalgamated has presumed to place community service before an undue financial return, its rates have been moderate, while still guaranteeing stockholders a fair return in dividends. Thus, customers and investors have been satisfied. Now, a master program for completely modernizing the plant will require an enormous financial outlay. To maintain its profit margin and dividend pattern, a rate increase to consumers of about 30% will be necessary. Amalgamated has petitioned the State Utilities Commission to authorize this increase, effective within sixty days.

Amalgamated always has been most generous in contributing to community United Fund drives, local hospitals and a liberal scholarship program for the college in the city. Its 2000 employees are well paid, with broad benefits. The Company has had few labor problems and has managed to negotiate periodic union demands with a minimum of disputation. Amalgamated has 843,700 individual stockholders, of whom about 60,000 reside in the service area.

1. Prepare a publicity program to justify the rate increase.
2. Draft a notice to stockholders of the rate increase.
3. Draft a release to the press announcing the rate increase. To whom will you send this?
4. Prepare an agenda for a public meeting called by Amalgamated to answer consumer questions and complaints.

17. WORTHY CAUSE

Eyes in the Dark, Inc., is a nonprofit, tax-exempt organization located in South Wayne, Pa., a suburb of Philadelphia. Established in 1948, it is an institution for training dogs as guides for blind people and for educating blind students to work with the dogs. The school was founded by Lyle Livingston, professionally an insurance agent, who had become interested in guide dogs through the experiences of an older sister. She had lost her sight in a childhood accident. Mr. Livingston, in partnership with Rex Torrance, a trainer with fifteen years of experience in similar institutions, leased a farm in South Wayne and recruited a first group of ten students through the Philadelphia branch of the National Institute for the Blind. The operation grew quickly, first through word of mouth and then by solicitation for prospective students along the Eastern seaboard.

At present, the farm can accommodate twenty students, each in twelve classes per year. Classes run for one month. There are six instructors employed in addition to Mr. Torrance, and a kennel staff of four. Two former students of the school now work full-time as scouts and trouble-shooters. They travel about the country interviewing potential students, and they visit students after graduation to ascertain that all goes well in their post-training situations. A breeding farm for dogs has been established with an experienced manager.

Although many blind people are not emotionally, physically or environmentally suited to using guide dogs, Mr. Livingston feels that there is enough need for his school to justify its expansion. He would like to double the capacity of the Eyes in the Dark operation, and has conferred with an architect to draw up plans for such a program. There will be increased dormitory space, a new recreation hall, new and completely modern kennels and an addition to the breeding farm. The total cost of this expansion is estimated at $500,000.

Eyes in the Dark, Inc., is at present supported by hundreds of small donations brought in through an annual mail solicitation. Many of the donors contribute regularly. The mailing list, which was compiled in 1950, has been enlarged each year. Also, the school has benefited greatly from several bequests that bring in a yearly income of about $75,000. Students may or may not pay a token charge of $100 for their training and their dog. The annual operation of the school costs $150,000.

1. Outline plans for a survey to determine the prospects for a fund-raising drive for Eyes in the Dark.
2. Draft a letter to regular contributors asking for an increase in their donations.

3. Draft a letter to members of the Board of Directors for the institution asking for contacts with foundation trustees or corporate executives who might be helpful.
4. Draft a letter to the head of a foundation asking for an interview with Mr. Livingston.
5. Draft a letter to the Today Show suggesting a television visit to the farm and an interview with Torrance.
6. Draft a letter to READER'S DIGEST, suggesting an article.

18. SCHOOL DAZE

Brookdale College (2000 students) is a four-year, coeducational, liberal arts institution located in the town of Willbury, Conn. (population 5000, excluding the students). Its scholastic standing is on a par with the best colleges in the country, and its admission standards are more selective than for most others. The president of the school is Dr. Perrin Charles, class of '41. He is an able administrator who served his apprenticeship for this post as Dean of Studies at a leading Ivy League University.

Brookdale, as most institutions of this era, needs financial support from any possible source. Although its tuitions and fees should be almost adequate to support the operation of the school, approximately one third of the student body is on scholarship from funds provided by bequests and endowments from wealthy alumni. One of the richest of these is Arthur Lois, class of '07, chairman emeritus of the Lois Corporation, a major soap manufacturer. Mr. Lois is a trustee of Brookdale and has expressed recent interest in donating the necessary money for a much-needed new library on the campus.

Mr. Lois and three other equally affluent trustees are expected in Willbury for a weekend visit with President Charles. At this time, the latter hopes to persuade Mr. Lois to commit himself firmly to the library project. The honored guests will be quartered at the Willbury Inn, a historic hostelry located at the edge of the campus.

For the past three weeks, the few Brookdale members of the Students for a Democratic Society dissident group have staged minor rallies and protests on the campus, demanding undergraduate participation in the running of the school. On Wednesday, they were supplemented by one hundred or more agitators who were not members of the student body, but who had drifted onto the campus in small groups, spending the day disrupting classes and other regular student activities. That evening, the enlarged group attacked the Administration Building, attempting to occupy the president's office. They were turned back by campus security guards, without injury to either side. The greater majority of Brookdale students took no part in this demonstration, except as onlookers. Meanwhile, the rebels melted away into Willbury to organize their next move.

Faced for the first time with turmoil on his own campus, President Charles has to make many fast decisions:

1. Whether to increase the number of the campus security force.
2. Whether to alert the Willbury, county and state law authorities of possible need.
3. Whether to postpone the vitally important visit of Mr. Lois and the other trustees.
4. How to liaison with local news media to insure a fair, factual

158

and unsensational reportage on any further incidents at Brookdale.
5. You are the College Director of Public Relations. Please prepare for President Charles a memorandum with your recommendations on public relations policy for the present and immediate future.

19. MEDICAL MILESTONE

Next May 12, the Barnes County Memorial Hospital will attain a major milestone. On that date, seventy-five years ago, the institution was opened to its first patient, three-year-old Polly Fitzhugh, who had mistakenly swallowed lye. She survived, and is living in Barnesdale today: Mrs. Pauline Fitzhugh Haydock, mother of three, grandmother of eight, great grandmother of one.

The Barnes hospital was founded by Dr. Louis Haginian, a surgeon who had migrated from Philadelphia to Barnesdale with this specific aim. Dr. Haginian had come to the North Carolina town on two previous occasions to visit friends in the tobacco business. He had admired the friendliness and hospitality of the residents, the leisurely pace of their everyday life and the temperate climate of the area. He brought his new bride here to make a home.

The hospital at its beginning had beds for thirty patients. Six trained nurses rotated three each on twelve-hour shifts. They were aided by a dozen practical nurses. There were no resident doctors at this time. The local general practitioners tended their own patients in the hospital. Dr. Haginian performed all operations. The building, a two-story, red-brick edifice was the property of Dr. Haginian and three partners who were local businessmen. He later bought out the other interests. During the years that followed, the town, county and state subsidized additional wings and new equipment; by the end of the Second World War, the Barnes County Memorial Hospital had become an integral part of the North Carolina network of up-to-date medical institutions. Its executive director, Donald Furlong, is appointed by the State Bureau of Hospitals; the hospital is operated as a nonprofit organization. There are now facilities for three hundred patients. There are eight surgeons, a staff psychologist, twelve residents, twenty interns and a training school for nurses.

Dr. Haginian died, while still in active service, at the age of 73. His younger son, who had also studied medicine, is now attached to the hospital as an ear, nose and throat specialist.

As the day of the special anniversary drew near, the hospital board of directors decided to use the date as the beginning of an annual fund-raising drive, to supplement the state allowances for equipment and for treating charity cases. The first goal was set at $150,000. Director Furlong enlisted the cooperation of Fred Sanders, bank vice-president; Ed Marlowe, manager of the HHV plant; several other businessmen and three prominent local matrons.

A week-long celebration is planned with a homecoming theme. Invitations have been issued to prominent and wealthy ex-residents. Festivities are to include open houses at local factories; church socials; home talent entertainment; a town fair with the usual hog calling, husband calling, pie eating contests and, finally, a guided tour of the hospital.

1. Outline a fund-raising program for the hospital.
2. Outline a program of events for Anniversary Week.
3. Outline a program for an open house at the new HHV factory.
4. How can television coverage be secured?

20. WEALTH SHARING

As a part of its program to unify the various branches of its organization, the Board of Directors of the XYZ Corporation has decided to streamline and standardize its annual donations. Heretofore, corporate giving has been almost haphazard, with its six divisions making individual policies or delegating this authority to their own local components.

Now, each part of the conglomerate is requested to submit to the vice-president in charge of public relations for XYZ a projected budget for its corporate giving for the next year. The programs will be analyzed and consolidated and an overall standard will be determined.

One of the divisions of XYZ is the Astro, the supermarket chain. Astro consists of 720 stores located in nine states: Wisconsin, Illinois, Iowa, Missouri, Kentucky, Tennessee, Arkansas, Mississippi and Louisiana. Its head offices are in St. Louis. The company has a total of 24,138 employees. Last year's sales amounted to $982,485,190, with net earnings of $9,350,944.

Astro was founded in St. Louis in 1924 by Loy Astor and Paul Troban. The company originally consisted of four grocery stores in various areas of the city. Meat departments were added in the stores in 1930, and additional branches were set up throughout Missouri and across the Mississippi River in Illinois. The chain grew rapidly, despite the Depression of the 1930s. At the outbreak of the Second World War, when the labor supply diminished, the stores were converted into self-service markets. This is their format today. The Astro supermarkets stock merchandise that appeals to middle- and upper-class patrons and are usually situated in suburban shopping centers.

Astor and Troban were both public-spirited men, and they established an early tradition of involvement and participation in the communities they served. Particular efforts were made to hire handicapped people and to run special training programs for the disadvantaged so that they might have better opportunities for advancement. The present executives of Astro have maintained this tradition.

Despite such activities, the chain has been charged with racial discrimination. In the two hundred stores in the four southern states there is not one black manager. In the other markets in states farther north, 20% of the managerial staff is black. There is also one black vice-president in the St. Louis office.

1. Outline an annual donations program for Astro on each of three levels:
    a. national

b. state

c. local

2. Outline a program whereby Astro can combat the charge of discrimination in its southern stores.

21. YANKEE COME BACK

The island principality of Montemare had been in the doldrums both literally and figuratively. Fifteen years of civil disorder and a series of short-lived, unpopular (both with the Montemarianos and the outside world) governments had left the country teetering on the brink of bankruptcy. Its agriculture, which had produced sugar, coffee and tropical fruits for profitable export, was completely disorganized. Fertilizer, petroleum and other plants, built originally with foreign capital and later expropriated by one of the pro tem governments, were no longer in production. National utilities were in a state of semipermanent breakdown.

Then came a new head of state—General (now President) Tachi Machisto. Despite the fact that he took office first as Commander in Chief of the Army, Machisto is no stereotype of a Latin American strongman. He is honest, free of greed, and completely dedicated to the titanic task of nursing his country back to economic health. Internal politics on the island seem to have been stabilized. Machisto has been confirmed in his office by an open election, and the renegade factions seem fortuitously to have killed one another off.

The World Bank has faith enough in the Machisto regime to make loans that will finance his plans to reorganize and develop the country's resources. Private foreign investment capital has followed. However, for the quickest possible inflow of dollars, a stimulation of tourism, particularly from the United States, seems to have the brightest potential.

Montemare could be an Eden for visitors. Off the beaten tourist track for so many years, it now offers new horizons for most world travelers. The island, shaped roughly like a flatfish, is edged on all sides by broad beaches of almost every description, with sands in white, pink or black, practically to order. San Pedro, the capital and chief port, surrounds a deep water harbor, sheltered on three sides, that can accommodate even the giant transatlantic liners that have been impressed into cruise service. On the leeward side of the island, around San Pedro, the sea is usually mild. On the windward side, it is a surfer's paradise.

Behind the beaches, an oval range of hills and mountains rings the island. The tallest, La Torre, rises to the height of 13,000 feet. Within the bowl formed by the mountains, a tropical rain forest flourishes. And in this jungle, disregarded for the past fifteen years, are the fabulous Tupa ruins, the remains of an ancient pre-Mayan tribe that inexplicably disappeared before 1000 B.C. Archeologists were among the first to come back to Montemare after Machisto reestablished order. The temples of Tupa are remote from San Pedro, but can be reached by tourists via small plane or Land Rover.

At present, accommodations for luxury-demanding guests are limited, but the prospect is rosy. The Cameo Hotel System (an American subsidiary of the giant XYZ Corporation) is restoring the 600-room Castillo Tropicano, once one of the showplaces of Latin America. Completely modernized under a crash program, and with the addition of a gambling casino, the hotel should be open for tourists within three months.

Two international airlines are now making semiweekly calls at the San Pedro airport. These flights were originally set up to accommodate the many technicians and businessmen who are making regular visits to the island. Three cruise ships each will include San Pedro on the itinerary of one voyage next winter.

1. Outline a one-year program for bringing United States tourists to Montemare, fully utilizing tie-ins with airlines, shipping, hotel organizations and private industry.
2. Create four special events that spotlight Montemare as the place to visit.
3. Outline a program for publicizing Montemare as a logical locale for international investment.

22. STATE VISIT

André Bonaventure, the President of the African republic of Moldania, is planning a state visit to the United States. It will be his first trip to this country, although he has journeyed to France, England, Warsaw and Moscow since his country gained its independence in 1958.

Small in population and area as compared to the other emerging nations in West Africa, Moldania has developed a sudden potential affluence resulting from newly discovered deposits of oil, copper and zinc.

When the country separated itself from French rule, its leaders decided against membership in the French community. Nevertheless, they have accepted financial and technical assistance from France, and President Bonaventure is felt to have strong pro-French leanings. He was educated in a French mission school in his native village of Mbolgi and at the French university at the Moldanian capital, Obitele (formerly Unitéville). He was graduated from the Military Academy at St. Cyr, and served for four years as a lieutenant in the French Army. When the drive for independence swept through Europe's outlying possessions after the Second World War, Bonaventure was still a soldier. He resigned his commission in 1950 and returned home to take an active role in helping to win autonomy for his country.

Bonaventure is the second president of Moldania. He had been Secretary of State with its first independent government, and succeeded to the chief executive's post in a popular election three years ago.

The oil finds in Moldania were made by an Anglo-American consortium. The other new discoveries are credited to Russian mineralogists. President Bonaventure is particularly anxious that his country's new wealth be used to better the living standards of the people. He is setting up schools and hospitals, and he is advocating the earliest possible construction of a hydroelectric plant on the Itybi River, which would afford irrigation for an expanded agricultural program for Moldania and electric power for most of the country. He has been negotiating with Russian technicians on this latter project, much to the consternation of Western diplomats.

The visit to the United States is interpreted in State Department circles as a gesture of friendship. It is deemed probable that a counteroffer from American sources in support of the Itybi Dam project would personally please the Moldanian president.

Bonaventure will make this trip without his wife. His English is fluent. He will arrive in New York via Air France on Monday, and will visit Washington for a meeting with the President of the United States on Wednesday afternoon. An evening reception at the White

House will follow these official talks. On Thursday, he will fly to Houston; on Friday, to Chicago. He returns to New York on Saturday, and onward to Obitele, via Paris, on Sunday.

The Moldanian government maintains embassies in Washington and, for its United Nations delegation, in New York.

1. Outline a public relations program for President Bonaventure's first visit to the United States, with these primary goals:
   a. to dispel any stigma of friendship with the Communists
   b. to present him at best advantage to the American business and industrial community
   c. to avoid any possible racial confrontation, about which President Bonaventure, as a black, is particularly sensitive

23. NOVEL ATTRACTION

While working as a staff assistant in the Lois Memorial Library at Brookdale College in Willbury, Conn., Melanie Jones, 24, has in her spare time written a first novel. History was her major at Smith, so it is logical that her initial literary effort should deal with a bygone era. Also, Melanie's forebears were among the first English settlers of Willbury, Conn., and one ancestor, Alwain Jones, was one of the largest landholders in New England prior to the Revolution. This is the period she selected for her novel.

The young writer entrusted her completed manuscript to a family friend who managed the Runyon & Mason printing plant in Willbury. He was so impressed with the work that he sent it immediately to Dale Emerson, the editor-in-chief of the publishing company, in New York. Mr. Emerson was even more enthusiastic and snapped up the book for the earliest possible publication. He recommended to Melanie the services of a reputable literary agent who could deal with the legal aspects of her contracts and could also represent her in marketing subsidiary rights.

The world of books is a small one, and the excitement within the house at Runyon & Mason over this first novel was soon transmitted throughout the industry. Copies of the manuscript, Xeroxed for submission to book clubs, paperback publishers and motion picture producers, were in hot-cake demand.

THE VIRGIN OF NEPEKO CREEK is to be published in May, with a first printing of 50,000. It has been chosen as a primary selection by two book clubs, and the movie rights have been optioned by one of the most famous names in films.

According to forecasts in the book trade press:

"TVONC is written with a silver-bright literary style, untarnished by liberal portions of amatory interlude and violent action."

"The most un-put-downable novel in thirty years."

"History vividly transported to here and now."

One reviewer notes that the photograph of Melanie Jones on the book jacket might well serve as an illustration for the heroine of the novel, Emerald MacCray.

Runyon & Mason are naturally delighted at the advance word-of-mouth, which spells runaway success for the first novel. The author will make an excellent subject for publicity.

1. Outline a campaign to publicize TVONC and its author in the following media:
   a. trade press
   b. newspapers
   c. magazines
   d. national television
   e. local television and radio

24. PRINTS' INVESTITURE

The chemical division of the Colorado Brass Corporation has perfected a new synthetic fiber that is sparking wildfire excitement in the textile and fashion industry. Fabric made from this new thread is wrinkleproof, stretchproof, stain resistant and washable in cold water. It has the softness of wool and the resilience of silk. The looseness of its knit allows air penetration, rendering the material comfortable for all-season, year-round wear. It will be marketed under the name *Lanseta*.

Although this fiber is not expensive to manufacture, the management of Colorado Brass decides to introduce it to the public with an aura of luxury and exclusivity, and to limit its uses for the time being. HHV, a progressive firm long experienced in textiles, is now diversifying its activities toward a new line of dress and suit fabrics. This is the company selected to produce the first *Lanseta* knits. Hubert Scoggins, a vice-president of HHV, will supervise the *Lanseta* operation. He hires as his creative director a young woman already renowned as a graphic artist, Lysbeth Manson.

The textile specialist for Colorado Brass, Don Moore, works very closely with Scoggins and Manson through the months of the *Lanseta* debut. Colorado Brass absorbs the costs for trade advertising; HHV has responsibility for the consumer press. Both companies will share the expense of mutually beneficial promotions.

Through Mrs. Manson's wide contacts, many well-known artists are commissioned to submit fabric designs and patterns. These original sketches and their knit counterparts will be displayed later in a special, limited-run exhibit at the Museum of Modern Art in New York. The show will then tour similar art establishments across the United States.

Mr. Scoggins, meanwhile, has persuaded the best-known designers of women's and men's fashions in this country, England, France and Italy to create styles in *Lanseta* from HHV materials. A collection of their styles will be photographed on location at Aspen, for winter scenes, and in Acapulco, for summer atmosphere. The pictures will be used for future advertising and promotion. A fashion show, benefiting a worthy charity, will be presented in the auditorium of the Costume Institute of the Metropolitan Museum in New York, and will show off the best of these creations.

The combined impact of these activities should spur manufacturers and designers all over the world to work with HHV *Lanseta* fabrics. Advertising will keep the product before the public eye, but the budget is not limitless. The most extensive possible publicity is required.

1. Outline a program for obtaining maximum free publicity for HHV *Lanseta* on television.

2. Draft a letter to a top fashion designer that will incite his interest in HHV *Lanseta* fabrics.
3. Draft a letter to a major manufacturer of expensive women's clothing extolling the values of *Lanseta*.
4. Outline a program for minimizing the costs of the photographic junkets to Aspen and Acapulco, through all plausible tie-ins.

25. NOVA

Ted Enriques is a quintuple-threat entertainer. He is a singer (baritone); comedian (keen and subtle humor); dancer (agile); guitarist (proficient) and impersonator (barbed but benign).

At 24, he was a minor luminary in night clubs in his native (born Rosario) Argentina. He had first taken a degree in law, and then taught legal history for two years at a university (Santo Tomas Diaquino) in Buenos Aires. Meanwhile, he moonlighted as a cabaret entertainer and discovered that this was his preferred vocation.

In 1969, a world-famous director, who was a judge at the Argentine Film Festival, saw Enriques perform in a club and offered him a minor role in a movie to be made in Hollywood. This was a first flash toward international stardom.

In the motion picture, "Tijuana," he appeared only in three scenes. Afterward, he found a job (third billing) in a floorshow at the Gallo Rojo, a Spanish-language cafe in a Los Angeles suburb. An immediate hit with his Latin audiences, he was soon the leading attraction at this club.

Edward Beach, president of the Zodiac Television Network, was vacationing in southern California, and happened to catch Enriques' act at the Gallo Rojo. A second stroke of fortune! With a past-proven eye for incipient talent, Beach offered Enriques an exclusive contract, to guide the performer's career in films and nightclubs, arrange his television appearances and, when the time was ripe, to star him in his own TV series.

When "Tijuana" was released, despite the brief appearances, Enriques' presence was noted by several major reviewers. Fan mail gushed in; interviewers followed. He was offered larger parts in two additional movies and his first stand at a club in Las Vegas. Meanwhile, he broke the language barrier between Spanish and English, with the remaining accent and occasional grammatical lapses endearing him more strongly to his audiences.

In September of next year, the Zodiac Television Network will present "The Ted Enriques Hour," from 10 to 11 on Thursday evenings. In the planned format, he will be able to demonstrate the full range of his talent. He will be supported by the Muchachas, a troupe of eight pulchritudinous singer-dancers. To supplement the Latin atmosphere (and to shave production costs), the shows will be taped in San Juan, Puerto Rico. Guest stars will be imported from all over the world.

The Lois Corporation has announced full sponsorship of the new variety show for its product, Superba soap.

Both Lois and Zodiac are intent that this will be the most popular show of the next season.

1. Draft a release announcing the new television series.

2. Outline a publicity campaign for the six months prior to the first telecast.
3. Outline a campaign to counteract the possible union charges of "runaway" production, as a result of the use of San Juan.
4. Outline a one-year build-up of Enriques as an international personality.

26. SELECT SENATOR

United States Senator Livingston K. Rice, from the sovereign state of Connecticut, has announced that he will retire at the end of his current term of office, for reasons of ill health. He has selected as his heir apparent the incumbent Lieutenant Governor, Ellery Martin.

Martin is a lawyer, hailing from Hillside. He will stand for election in November of next year, following his party convention in May and the primary in June. His party support is in question, however, despite the sponsorship of Senator Rice. In his present office, Martin is rumored to have spent too much time in personal pursuits. His acquaintanceship with personages with an underworld taint has been widely bruited, and recently a national magazine openly accused him of receiving bonuses from a construction company that had been awarded lucrative state contracts. Although Martin immediately instituted a suit for libel against the magazine, his constituents remain restive. Even Governor Barnard Bailey, the grand old man of state politics, is loath to voice support for his beleaguered colleague.

Party officials began quietly to search for a replacement for Martin. Governor Bailey does not choose to move from the comfort of his present post. Congressmen throughout the state have various ethnic, religious or political limitations that could curb their drawing power outside their own districts.

Finally, a suggestion came from Arthur Lois, retired chairman of a national soap company and chief fund raiser for the party. His choice is Dr. Perrin Charles, president of Brookdale College in Willbury. A native of Connecticut, Dr. Charles has an excellent record as a scholar and administrator. He is an impressive speaker and is prominent, not only in the state but throughout the nation, for the calm control of student activism he displayed on the campus during the previous year. His book on this subject, TO THE BARRICADES, was almost a bestseller. Dr. Charles has been persuaded to throw his hat into the Senatorial ring.

The party convention was a riotous affair, with the Martin bloc putting up a stiff fight for their candidate's nomination. They failed, however, and Charles won by a narrow margin. It is inevitable that he will face Martin and at least one other candidate in the party primaries.

Through Mr. Lois and other influential and affluent friends, Dr. Charles has accumulated a campaign chest of about $1,500,000.

1. Outline a television campaign to elect Dr. Charles for United States Senator:
   a. the month before the party primary
   b. five months before the election

2. What other media might be used?
3. Outline the format of a television debate between Dr. Charles and
   a. Lt. Governor Martin and the other candidate in the primary
   b. the opposing party candidate in the election

27. SCOTCH ON THE ROCKS

Everyman Beverages Corporation is one of the largest distributors of soft drinks and liquors in the United States. This firm controls the bottling concessions for a popular cola and a wide range of flavored sodas. It owns and operates domestic distilleries for making bourbon, rye, gin and vodka. It imports a variety of French, Italian and German wines and liqueurs and Black Watch, the venerable scotch whiskey.

The production of scotch (and only the malt beverage distilled in Scotland can legitimately bear the name) is strictly controlled by a British trust, the Distillers' Corporation, Ltd. The DCL, as it is known in the trade, regulates the annual output of each distillery and selects importers and distributors for individual brands throughout the world. Companies in this country bring in about fifty different brands bottled in Scotland. Many other well-known labels are shipped by barrel and bottled here.

Black Watch is produced by MacVertie & Son, of Tavish, Scotland, a distillery founded in 1882. It was once the acknowledged favorite drink of three European monarchs and has garnered medals of merit at expositions and trade fairs all over the world. Its tartan-banded bottle is instantly recognizable. For many years, it has had an international renown, and its global sales today still rank it as number eight among competing brands.

In the United States, however, it has greatly declined in popularity in the last fifteen years. J & B, Cutty Sark, Dewars, Ballantine —all so-called light scotches in both color and taste—are now the best sellers. Black Watch is, admittedly, a "heavy" scotch, with a distinctive smokey taste and dark color.

The Board of Directors of MacVertie & Son, which is headed by Ian MacVey, is much concerned over the plummeting sales of Black Watch in America. The contract with Everyman as importer is effective for one more year. At the end of that time, DCL will decide whether a competitor might be able to market Black Watch more profitably than Everyman.

For its own balance sheet, Everyman would like to increase the sale of this scotch and does not want to lose the prestige of the name on its list of imports. The company needs desperately to upgrade the reputation of Black Watch to attempt to curb the ever-increasing preference toward light scotch and to erase the impression that Black Watch is an old-fashioned drink.

1. As a public relations and publicity counselor, draft a presentation to Everyman for a one-year program aimed toward accomplishing the needs cited here.
2. Outline a publicity program covering visits to New York and Los Angeles by Ian MacVey.

28. BRAKE THE BANK

Spruce Bay, Mass., has a year-round population of about 12,000, which swells to 15,000 during the warm months when summer residents come to occupy their cottages along the shore.

A former fishing village, and once a prosperous mill town (Halo Hosiery, 1921–1933), Spruce Bay now boasts as its only industry the Ethan Mather Clock Company. Many residents commute to employment in neighboring communities.

The semiweekly newspaper published Tuesdays and Fridays is read by most people in town. About 3000 also subscribe to daily papers from Boston.

There are two banks in Spruce Bay: The Whalers Union, an institution that was practically founded with the town; and the Otis County Savings Company, started shortly after the First World War. The latter has always been more progressive, more liberal in its loan policies, more apt to fluctuate interest rates as prosperity waxes and wanes. It handles 60% of the banking business in the community.

The present chief executive of Otis County Savings is Graham da Cunha, a state university graduate active with the local chamber of commerce, school board, Masons, Kiwanians and Elks.

The Whalers Union president is Thaddeus Sears IV, Amherst and Harvard Business School, a banker's banker, and no joiner except for the Episcopal Church and the Country Club.

In New England, one of the largest financial corporations is the Patriots Bank and Trust Company. It has its headquarters in Springfield, Mass., and branches in eighty-four localities throughout the six northeastern states. It has just added its eighty-fifth branch, with the absorption of the Otis County Trust Company in Spruce Bay.

1. Plan a publicity campaign to introduce Patriots as a benign giant to Spruce Bay.
2. Plan a publicity campaign to convince Otis clients, current and potential, that a branch of Patriot will offer better service.
3. Plan a publicity campaign to dramatize Whalers as "Still the Spruce Bay Bank."

29. INDUSTRY INVITATION

Barnesdale (population 15,000) is located in the Piedmont section of North Carolina. It is about sixty miles from the state capital at Raleigh and the famous Research Triangle, wherein three universities offer their pooled resources to assist local industry. A major north-south highway runs adjacent to the town, which also features service (two local passenger stops daily) by the Seaboard-Coastline Railroad. It is the county seat of Barnes County, and a banking and shopping center for the dairy, tobacco and cotton farms of the surrounding countryside. It has a thriving tobacco market (September-November) and two hosiery mills, originally independent but now a part of the Clayton Corporation. Doelger Bros., the meat packer, recently built a small plant near Barnesdale to produce sausage.

The Boost Barnesdale Association, made up of local businessmen and headed by Fred Sanders, a vice-president of the Croatan Bank & Trust Company, is most interested in drawing other industry to the town. Not only will additional paychecks and tax returns stimulate the local economy, but also better schools and hospital facilities would inevitably result.

On a recent visit to New York, Sanders learned that the HHV Company, textile manufacturer, is considering the construction of a new plant for making towels. Because the eight other HHV factories are located in the South, it seems likely that further company expansion will take place in this same part of the country.

Barnesdale can offer HHV a site—six acres between railroad and highway—two miles outside of town. The land cost and local and state tax formulas are advantageous. The town is prepared to offer special inducements to any company moving into Barnesdale. For HHV, water mains will be extended beyond the city limits to the factory site. This will mean a sizeable expense for the town, and property tax rates will have to be raised slightly, but Sanders and his colleagues deem it a worthwhile investment for the future.

Barnesdale also can offer a readily available supply of semi-skilled labor, mostly from the black population of the town (6000). There have been minimal race problems, and school integration has been executed satisfactorily.

Among the dissenters toward further industry in the town are the Women's Club, worried about traffic congestion; local landowners who fear that factory sites will debase the value of their personal tracts for residential development; and property owners who object to any tax increase entailed by the watermain extension.

1. Outline a presentation to HHV recommending Barnesdale as the best possible site for a new factory.

2. Draft a release for the local newspaper explaining the benefits of more industry for Barnesdale and counteracting the objections.

30. CLEANED OUT

For three generations, the Blanquette family had been in the cleaning and dyeing business. Their first establishment was opened on the Rue de la Régence in Paris in 1910, and a son of the founding father still operates it. In 1931, Réné, a grandson, migrated to the United States. After working for a series of American employers in the same field, he eventually set up his own shop on East 60th Street, in New York City.

Réné Blanquette's services guaranteed meticulous individual attention. He or some member of his small staff of experts personally processed each article of clothing brought to him for cleaning or refurbishing. His unique techniques in treating furs and the most delicate of fabrics won him a wide reputation throughout the city, and his clientele included many famous and wealthy people.

By popular demand, and also to broaden his own horizons, Blanquette, with two assistants, opened a second shop, to operate during the months of May through September, in Southampton, Long Island, where many of his city patrons spend their summers.

His establishment in Southampton was much smaller than that in New York, and Blanquette underestimated the volume of business he would receive in the resort village as the summer population increased. Also, he hated to disappoint good customers by refusing to serve them. On June 30, prior to the long Fourth of July weekend, he had such an overload of clothing to be processed that it was evident that he would not be able to meet his deadlines without assistance. Instead of sending the excess work back to his associates at the shop in New York, he decided, as an expedient, to farm out some of the items to an assembly-line cleaning establishment in the not-too-distant town of Riverhead.

That night, the Riverhead plant burned to the ground and thirty articles of clothing belonging to several of Blanquette's most influential clients were lost in the conflagration.

The factory at Riverhead was fully covered by insurance, so there was no financial loss involved for his customers. However, the reputation of Blanquette and his firm were at stake.

1. How should Blanquette notify his customers of their losses?
2. Should he talk to the press, and, if so, what should he say?
3. Outline a public relations campaign by which Blanquette can re-establish his prestige in Southampton and New York.

31. ACCOUNT IN QUESTION

Ernie Ramfisk, a successful salesman of Long Island real estate, is also a sports car buff. He owns a Jaguar XKE convertible, and, as a spectator never misses the annual racing events at Southampton, Lime Rock and Glens Falls. He patronizes The Pit Stop, a service garage in Astoria, Queens, N.Y., which caters to a large number of sports car enthusiasts. Its owner, Aldo Fausto, was once a mechanic with a famous Italian racing team.

Fausto has a new invention. It is a small filter that may be easily fitted onto any carburetor. It is intended to screen out excess carbon, which would otherwise clog the engine and curb efficient operation. The device will supposedly increase pick-up and cut down on fuel consumption. It is called Generato.

It can be turned out in The Pit Stop machine shop for about forty cents per item and, with proper promotion, retail for ten dollars. Ramfisk has agreed to provide the financial backing for its manufacture and distribution in return for a profit percentage.

Fausto's name and contacts in the world of sports cars will be a definite asset in spotlighting Generato, and Ramfisk also knows many influential people in the same field.

There is the fact, however, that Generato is similar to a dozen other devices on the market, and many automotive experts deny the effectiveness of such an apparatus.

1. How can a publicity consultant evaluate this account before taking on representation?
2. Draft a letter to Ernie Ramfisk declining to accept the account, with valid reasons.
3. Outline a six-month campaign for publicizing Generato.
4. Prepare a list of trade press contacts.

an annual report

THE PRESIDENT REPORTS TO THE STOCKHOLDERS

The fiscal year ending October 31, 1962, was one of significant change, substantial growth and steady progress for Roadway Industries Corporation.

ROADWAY INDUSTRIES, INC.

Acquisition of the former Vee Industries, Inc., was completed as of March 1, 1962, and Roadway Industries Corporation assumed leadership of its fourth major industry. Renamed Roadway Industries, Inc., this new division is the world's largest builder of mobile homes, specialized classroom units and other types of industrial buildings. During the eight months it has been part of your corporation, operations have been at a profitable level and have been a significant factor in the increased sales and earnings of Roadway Industries Corporation.

This acquisition has also demonstrated the value and importance of Roadway Industries' long-standing policy of assembling an outstanding management group of seasoned, young, and vigorous executive talent, with a marked ability as a team, to absorb and integrate new and expanded operations. These men, in cooperation with the many qualified members of the new organization, have been responsible for blending Roadway Industries, Inc., with the rest of our corporate family. They have done so rapidly, smoothly and efficiently. Equally important, they have the capacity to do so again in the future.

FINANCIAL HIGHLIGHTS

Corporate sales volume was approximately doubled and earnings more than doubled as compared with the previous fiscal year despite two divisional strikes and somewhat unsettled business conditions.

Consolidated net sales amounted to $57,000,000 compared with $28,000,000 the prior year. It should be noted that net sales of Roadway Industries, Inc., are included only for the eight months from March 1, 1962.

Consolidated net income after taxes rose to $1,000,000, equal to $2.00 per share on 835,000 shares outstanding on October 31, 1962, as compared with $826,000, or $1.00 per share on 768,000 shares the previous year.

Stockholders' equity at the end of the current fiscal year increased to $13,000,000 or $15.00 per share on the 835,000 shares now outstanding as against $10,000,000 a year ago, or $13.00 per share on the 768,000 shares outstanding at that time. Net current assets and other balance sheet items similarly reflect the sound financial position of your corporation.

DIVIDENDS—WORKING CAPITAL

Cash dividends have now been paid by Roadway Industries Corporation for the past twenty-eight consecutive years. During the period under review, such dividends amounted to $.50 per share plus 2% in stock.

Additional working capital was required as a result of the acquisition of Roadway Industries, Inc., and the corresponding substantial increase in corporate sales volume. Your directors believed it would be prudent, therefore, to temporarily reduce cash dividends and took such action during the fiscal year. They are confident that future earnings and dividends will fulfill stockholders' faith in Roadway Industries Corporation. Long-term financing was also arranged with the Reliable Insurance Company, a portion of the proceeds being used to retire a previous obligation to the same institution.

LABOR RELATIONS

The favorable labor climate enjoyed by your corporation is the result of the mutual recognition by management and the representatives of the various labor groups who produce your company's products and of our joint responsibilities to deal fairly and openly with each other. Despite two divisional strikes reported earlier in the fiscal year, noninflationary three-year agreements, establishing mutually satisfactory terms and conditions, have been negotiated with labor unions that represent more than two thirds of Roadway Industries employees. These agreements and the progressive, intelligent attitude displayed by both sides should enable the corporation to operate profitably and without interruptions because of labor disputes.

ROADWAY INDUSTRIES SALES FINANCIAL CORPORATION

Your Company's wholly owned finance subsidiary, Roadway Industries Sales Financial Corporation, continued its growth and increased its importance to operations and earnings. Active for fewer than four years, this division earned $215,000 during the current fiscal year, notwithstanding substantial nonrecurring costs for initiating operations in the mobile homes field and establishing an allowance for credit losses.

Accounts of Roadway Industries Sales Financial Corporation are not consolidated in the financial statements of the corporation. This subsidiary is carried on Roadway Industries Corporation's balance sheet as an investment.

CHANGES IN DIRECTORS AND EXECUTIVES

Retirement because of illness of Mr. R. F. Fay as a member of the Board of Directors is confirmed with regret. Mr. Fay is well known in the automotive industry and served your company in various capacities for more than twenty-five years, many of them as Chairman of the Board, a post he held until 1959.

Mr. J. J. Lee was elected a Director by the Board in March, 1962. Mr. Lee is Vice-Chairman of the Board of Directors and Chairman of the Executive Committee, I. Weisman, Inc.; Chairman of the Board, E-S Investors, Inc.; and a Director and Chairman of the Executive Committee, National Bank of Commerce (Danesville).

Mr. H. Nezih was elected a Director by the Board in August, 1962, to fill the vacancy created by Mr. Frank's retirement. Mr. Nezih is a partner in the firm of Nezih & Co., New York Certified Public Accountants and a Director of Coe, Inc.; Pugh, Inc.; Anne Rose Vending Corp.; and Benedick Co., Inc.

Mr. S. Doe was elected Treasurer of Roadway Industries Corporation in June, 1962. Mr. Doe was formerly a Comptroller with Tank Motor Company and a Vice-President of Shank Brothers, Inc.

Mr. H. R. Roe was elected President of the Corporation's Roadway Industries, Inc., subsidiary in July, 1962. Mr. Roe was formerly a Senior Partner in the management consulting firm of P. Rubens.

GENERAL REMARKS

We would be remiss if we did not recognize and acknowledge the importance of our loyal and aggressive dealer organizations and the increasing efficiency of all our sales, manufacturing and administrative departments. We are confident that you can anticipate the earnest continuing efforts of management, labor and other company personnel to carry on your company's business and affairs in a manner consistent with the policies that have proven successful up to the present time.

Although your corporation is engaged in seasonal industries, the need for our products continues in good times and bad. Although future annual sales volumes and profits will, no doubt, reflect changing business conditions, our increasing demands for most of the products produced or built by your company are expected to sustain satisfactory levels of operation and earnings.

We are proud of our progress in all four of the fields in which Roadway Industries Corporation now operates. We intend to maintain and continue our progress, growth and development.

Your management looks ahead with caution, but also with vigorous and justified optimism.

By Order of the Board of Directors

E. F. B.
President
January 10, 197–

news for release

For Immediate Release

VERSATILE PROFESSIONAL-STYLE HOME MEAT GRINDER
FEATURES THREE ATTACHMENTS

An electric meat grinder, the first adaptation of a butcher's meat grinder for home use, and the only one to feature three versatile attachments, is manufactured by the Ex Manufacturing Co. of Elm City, a leading designer and producer of quality electrical appliances.

Manufacturers also of the original liquefier-blender, the Ex Manufacturing Co. has developed its meat grinder base with a motor powerful enough to be used with three other functional attachments frequently required by the homemaker. A nine-chip size ice crusher head, an electric can opener attachment, and a sausage stuffer tube can all be purchased separately and fitted into the single all-in-one food-center base.

Meat Grinder

Designed to give the homemaker fast and professional results, the Ex electric meat grinder makes grinding and chopping jobs effortless. Coarse or fine, the compact powerhouse grinds both the hardest foods and the softest. It handles smoothly all cuts of raw or cooked meat. Hard or soft cheese, vegetables for salads or thick soups, fish for appetizer spreads and leftovers for delicious hash or croquettes can all be handled effortlessly. The grinder even turns out a delicate dusting of nuts for pastry toppings. Most outstanding is the fact that the unit grinds without crushing and

(more)

bruising food and will not string raw meat or squeeze out the natural juices.

The base is designed to be used on counter or table top without clamping down, to occupy a minimum of space, and is shaped to accommodate a mixing bowl or cooking utensil directly beneath the grinding wheels. Made of baked white refrigerator enamel, the motor housing is rustproof and easy to clean. The steel grinding unit self-locks into place, making it simple to insert or remove. An extra-large feeding platform allows the machine to operate as fast as it can be fed.

Price: $49.95.

Ice Crusher

This power ice crusher is perfect for fruit cups, sea food cocktails, fresh vegetable or relish trays, cocktails, ice cream freezers and for chilling glassware.

Interchangeable with the meat grinder head, the power ice crusher unit self-locks into the base of the grinder and provides a choice of nine different chip sizes. Ice sizes from shaved to chopped are made merely by changing the selector lever, even while the machine is in operation.

Durable hardened steel blades mean that the unit can be immersed in water for washing without fear of rust.

Price: $12.92.

Can Opener

Also slotted to fit into the motor base, this electric can opener tackles any cans from small frozen-juice size to large bulky gallon cans. Most odd-shaped, dented or damaged or sardine or Polish ham cans are no problem.

Price: $9.95.

(more)

Sausage Stuffer Tube

The sausage stuffer tube fits quickly and easily on to the grinder and with a flick of the switch makes and stuffs sausages right at home. Makes sausages from the tender little breakfast variety to juicy succulent larger ones.

Price: $1.50.

# # #

*public relations program for
german wines in the united states*

The objective of the public relations program for German wines in the United States should be to create as wide an interest as possible among those accustomed to drinking wine with their meals, and to intrigue as far as possible the nonwine-drinking population by the sensational taste qualities of German wines. Because this has been attempted unsuccessfully so often, we are of the opinion that only a well-planned consistent campaign can accomplish results. Converts to the pleasures of German wines can only be made by providing the opportunity for tasting them. For this reason the foregoing campaign concentrates on stimulating a pronounced increase in demand in a very short time. Habits of taste are known to be contagious. Therefore, we place great emphasis on the broad approach—that is, using techniques that have the strongest impact on the American consciousness: daily articles in the press and full coverage in magazines and opportunities for seeing the wine served at tables in restaurants that have a good clientele.

Fortunately, for German vintners, the more sophisticated elements in America who do drink wine with their meals call for them by name and take great pride in doing so. The ritual of examining a label and tasting a wine is an impressive ceremony in which the American host loves to indulge. Americans have long accepted this ritual as a part of the French rather than the European tradition, and for this reason the French wines are better known and enjoy a higher preference. To overcome this handicap for German wines should be the first objective of a public relations campaign.

The campaign should be modest but very intensive, aimed at the upper-middle- and high-income bracket Americans. It is very rare in the public relations business when one can combine a limited budget with the most effective means of conducting a campaign. In the case of German wines this very rare combination of circumstances does prevail.

1   Therefore, we recommend the insertion of feature articles describing the virtues of German wines on the editorial pages of publications such as THE NEW YORKER, ESQUIRE, VOGUE, HARPERS BAZAAR, TOWN AND COUNTRY, CUE, BETTER HOMES AND GARDENS, GOURMET, THE NEW YORK TIMES, CHICAGO TRIBUNE, ST. LOUIS POST DISPATCH, SAN FRANCISCO CHRONICLE, LOS ANGELES TIMES, NEW ORLEANS TIMES-PICAYUNE, ATLANTA CONSTITUTION, MIAMI HERALD, and other leading periodicals.

2   Because Americans are notable for favoring mixed drinks, we plan to do the research that will result in the development of

a popular mixed drink that can be ordered at a bar, the base of which will be ordinary Rhine wine. By intensive publicity, this Rhine drink, appropriately named, can easily become the channel by which high popularity for German wines can be achieved.

3 Because the arbiters of dining habits in the United States are the wine stewards or head waiters in the better restaurants and hotels, we recommend that two well-planned mailings should be sent to this list. The first mailing should be merely a letter enclosing a questionnaire that would obtain in detail their patrons' preferences and habits regarding wines. The incentive for filing these questionnaires with us would be contained in our offer to mention their names, along with the restaurant in which they are employed, in our publicity material. The second mailing should contain a brochure, preferably in color, on German wines for table use. Practitioners, Inc. would prepare this brochure in a manner so that it could be used in conjunction with a menu, or it might be designed so that a daily menu could be inserted.

4 We recommend a very modest advertising campaign that we now estimate would require about a $50,000 budget. This sum would be spent mainly on paid space for modestly sized but eyecatching ads in some of the publications mentioned here.

5 A great effort would be made to obtain the cooperation of society editors and gossip columnists in the press and magazines to express, as frequently as possible, the choice of German wines by discriminating people.

6 Make a concentrated effort to secure the cooperation of noncompetitive advertisers to show German wines being served as part of the sophisticated atmosphere surrounding the people who use the products being advertised. (Examples are ads for fine furniture, automobiles, resorts, restaurants and airlines.)

7 Conduct a series of German wine parties for the press, prominent restaurateurs and hotel managers. The purpose of these parties, of which there would not be more than four during the first six-month period, would be merely to cause talk. However, the more subtle purpose would be to identify German wines with America's most exclusive restaurants and clubs.

8 In Television scenes using a prominent restaurant such as the COLONY, "21" or QUO VADIS as background, we will arrange for German wines to be an important prop on the tables.

9 All trade journals such as BEVERAGE BULLETIN, BEVERAGE JOURNAL and BEVERAGE INDUSTRY NEWS should be supplied with an editorial kit containing the full story of German wines, along with pictures and biographies of personalities connected with the making and distribution of German wines. This could be done in cooperation with the existing distributors in the United States.

The cost of the plan outlined here including the $50,000 budget for advertising would be $75,000 (seventy-five thousand dollars). There would be an additional cost of approximately $5,000 (five thousand dollars) for printing, mailing, photography and entertainment. The parties described here are not included in this budget, but cost should be nominal—about $500 for each. This amount could be paid to Practitioners, Inc. in four quarterly installments, and it would be agreed that the contract can be mutually canceled at the termination of any quarterly period.

It is our considered judgment that the present condition of the fine wine market in the United States invites the introduction of an aggressive campaign for German brands. We think this program conducted vigorously should very quickly result in substantially increased sales.

*a public relations program for
an appliance corporation*

APPLIANCE CORPORATION

Without sifting through the morass of recent Appliance Corporation history (we do not believe this will ever be necessary), the public relations problem presented is to reverse surface and deep-seated negative feelings toward Appliance Corporation now held by dealers and consumers and to substitute for it a public relations base of confidence for Appliance Corporation products. It is our belief that this can be done quickly, economically and without reorganizational pain.

It must be done simultaneously on three levels: corporate, product and dealer. In all three cases the approaches must be original, imaginative and easy to digest. The campaign must be designed to reflect the unfailing integrity of the company, the excellence of its products and the unwavering loyalty toward its loyal dealers.

In this connection, we recommend kicking off the campaign with an institutional ad titled Loyalty, in which the copy would stress the close bond that exists between the household appliance industry and the daily routine of American life, and that the management and operation of the American household without dependable appliances are unthinkable. The theme of this ad would be the exploration of the abstract, lofty cliché, "the American standard of living" in the practical terms of household appliances. It would go on to show how the work of Appliance Corporation is daily making new strides toward offering this standard to all. We also believe that this initial ad, properly merchandised, would mobilize dealer sentiment nationally.

Appliance Corporation dealers relationships need strengthening. We would place great emphasis on the trade press and in the commercial sections of the general press. We recommend the institution of regular mailings to the dealer family, preferably signed by the president of the company. These regular messages should have a newsletter quality and should embrace comment on general business conditions, forecasts and tips on how to expand the appliance idea, and most of all, seek to create an environment of paternalism for the dealer—a short bridge between the dealer and the president of Appliance Corporation.

With due respect for the long and honorable commercial history of Appliance Corporation, we would at this juncture recommend approaching the trade press with a spirit of newness. We would like to give the impression that with this campaign we are revealing, with the enthusiasm that newness engenders, new products, new dealer policies, new selling aids, and new vigor in advertising and public relations. To implement this plan, we would initiate a series of press conferences for the trade and commercial press at which dealer policy would be outlined. In some cases we would invite dealer participation in the press conferences for inclusion of the retail viewpoint toward Appliance Corporation's program.

We recommend that a series of citywide promotions be inaugurated in which the Practitioners, Inc. staff would exploit Appliance Corporation products on the floor of selected dealers in much the same fashion as a movie opening is handled. This should be done over a six-month period in a separately supervised campaign to be known as "Know Your Appliance Corporation Dealer." The device used in this campaign would be the enlistment of the individual communities, women's club memberships and school home economics departments so that maximum concentration within the community would be mobilized for attention on Appliance Corporation leadership. This would result in a consumer press, as well as a trade press—that is, in a consumer press locally, and a trade press nationally.

Because Appliance Corporation integrity can be demonstrated only through the personalities who stand behind the product, we would assure a thorough publicity campaign on the voices who speak for Appliance Corporation. We would attempt to bring these personalities very close to the dealer, not only through the trade press but also by a series of well-planned regional meetings, attractive enough in their programming to assure maximum dealer participation.

ABOUT THE PRACTITIONERS, INC. COMPANY

Practitioneis, Inc. does not believe in long and frequently unprofitable investigative or survey approaches. We believe that a client seeking public relations as an aid to merchandising and increased sales needs servicing now, not after a protracted study that usually produces a text, the contents of which the client is already profoundly aware. That does not mean Practitioners, Inc. ignores the consideration of market analyses, but it firmly holds to the belief that surveys are of more profit to the client when they are the product of work in progress than as an abstract prelude merely consuming time before work commences. Therefore, the only initiatory stage Practitioners, Inc. would require before launching the Appliance Corporation campaign would be a series of short conferences between Practitioners, Inc. personnel and Appliance Corporation executives directly concerned with public relations.

the foreign agents registration act of 1938

AS AMENDED
Department of Justice
United States Government Printing Office
Washington: 1966

AN ACT

To amend the Foreign Agents Registration Act of 1938, as amended.

Be it enacted by the Senate and House of Representatives of the United States of America in Congress assembled, That section 1 of the Foreign Agents Registration Act of 1938, as amended, is amended as follows:

Foreign Agents Registration Act of 1938, amendments.
56 Stat. 249.
22 USC 611.
"Foreign principal."

(1) Subsection (b) is amended to read as follows:

"(b) The term 'foreign principal' includes—

"(1) a government of a foreign country and a foreign political party;

"(2) a person outside of the United States, unless it is established that such person is an individual and a citizen of and domiciled within the United States, or that such person is not an individual and is organized under or created by the laws of the United States or of any State or other place subject to the jurisdiction of the United States and has its principal place of business within the United States; and

"(3) a partnership, association, corporation, organization, or other combination of persons organized under the laws of or having its principal place of business in a foreign country."

(2) Subsection (c) is amended to read as follows:

"Agent of a foreign principal."

"(c) Except as provided in subsection (d) hereof, the term 'agent of a foreign principal' means—

"(1) any person who acts as an agent, representative, employee, or servant, or any person who acts in any other capacity at the order, request, or under the direction or control, of a foreign principal or of a person any of whose activities are directly or indirectly supervised, directed, controlled, financed, or subsidized in whole or in major part by a foreign principal, and who directly or through any other person—

"(i) engages within the United States in political activities for or in the interests of such foreign principal;

"(ii) acts within the United States as a public relations counsel, publicity agent, information-service employee or political consultant for or in the interests of such foreign principal;

"(iii) within the United States solicits, collects, disburses, or dispenses contributions, loans, money, or other things of value for or in the interest of such foreign principal; or

"(iv) within the United States represents the interests of such foreign principal before any agency or official of the Government of the United States; and

"(2) any person who agrees, consents, assumes or purports to act as, or who is or holds himself out to be, whether or not pursuant to contractual relationship, an agent of a foreign principal as defined in clause (1) of this subsection."

(3) Subsection (d) is amended by striking out "clause (1), (2), or (4) of".

(4) Subsection (g) is amended by inserting before the words "matter pertaining to" the words "public relations" and before the semicolon at the end thereof the words "of such principal".

(5) Such section is further amended by substituting a semicolon for the period at the end of subsection (n) and adding the following new subsections:

"Political activities."

"(o) The term 'political activities' means the dissemination of political propaganda and any other activity which the person engaging therein believes will, or which he intends to, prevail upon, indoctrinate, convert, induce, persuade, or in any other way influence any agency or official of the Government of the United States or any section of the public within the United States with reference to formulating, adopting, or changing the domestic or foreign policies of the United States or with reference to the political or public interests, policies, or relations of a government of a foreign country or a foreign political party;

"Political consultant."

"(p) The term 'political consultant' means any person who engages in informing or advising any other person with reference to the domestic or foreign policies of the United States or the political or public interest, policies, or relations of a foreign country or of a foreign political party;

Post, p. 246.

"(q) For the purpose of section (3)(d) hereof, activities in furtherance of the bona fide commercial, industrial or financial interests of a domestic person engaged in substantial commercial, industrial or financial operations in the United States shall not be deemed to serve predominantly a foreign interest because such activities also benefit the interests of a foreign person engaged in bona fide trade or commerce which is owned or controlled by, or which owns or controls, such domestic person: *Provided,* That (i) such foreign person is not, and such activities are not directly or indirectly supervised, directed, controlled, financed or subsidized in whole or in substantial part by, a government of a foreign country or a foreign political party, (ii) the identity of such foreign person is disclosed to the agency or official of the United States with whom such activities are conducted, and (iii) whenever such foreign person owns or controls such domestic person, such activities are substantially in furtherance of the bona fide commercial, industrial or financial interests of such domestic person."

Registration statement.

SEC. 2. Section 2 of such Act is amended as follows:

(1) Subsection (a) is amended by striking out the second,

64 Stat. 400.
22 USC 612.

third, and fourth sentences and inserting in lieu thereof the following: "Except as hereinafter provided, every person who becomes an agent of a foreign principal shall, within ten days thereafter, file with the Attorney General, in duplicate, a registration statement, under oath on a form prescribed by the Attorney General. The obligation of an agent of a foreign principal to file a registration statement shall, after the tenth day of his becoming such agent, continue from day to day, and termination of such status shall not relieve such agent from his obligation to file a registration statement for the period during which he was an agent of a foreign principal."

56 Stat. 252.

(2) Subsection (a)(3) is amended by striking out the comma following the word "each" where it first appears, and the following: "unless, and to the extent, this requirement is waived in writing by the Attorney General"; and by inserting before the semicolon at the end of the subsection a comma and the following: "or by any other foreign principal".

(3) Subsection (a)(4) is amended by inserting before the semicolon at the end thereof a comma and the following: "including a detailed statement of any such activity which is a political activity".

(4) Subsection (a)(6) is amended by inserting before the semicolon at the end thereof a comma and the following: "including a detailed statement of any such activity which is a political activity".

Name, etc., of contributors.

(5) Subsection (a)(7) is amended to read as follows:

"(7) The name, business, and residence addresses, and if an individual, the nationality, of any person other than a foreign principal for whom the registrant is acting, assuming or purporting to act or has agreed to act under such circumstances as require his registration hereunder; the extent to which each such person is supervised, directed, owned, controlled, financed, or subsidized, in whole or in part, by any government of a foreign country or foreign political party or by any other foreign principal; and the nature and amount of contributions, income, money, or thing of value, if any, that the registrant has received during the preceding sixty days from each such person in connection with any of the activities referred to in clause (6) of this subsection, either as compensation or for disbursement or otherwise, and the form and time of each such payment and from whom received;".

Statement; political contributions.
56 Stat. 252.
22 USC 612.

(6) Subsection (a)(8) is amended to read as follows:

"(8) A detailed statement of the money and other things of value spent or disposed of by the registrant during the preceeding sixty days in furtherance of or in connection with activities which require his registration hereunder and which have been undertaken by him either as an agent of a foreign principal or for himself or any other person or in connection with any activities relating to his becoming an agent of such principal, and a detailed statement of any contributions of money or other things of value made by him during the preceding sixty days (other than contributions the making of which is prohibited under the terms of section 613 of title 18, United States Code) in connection with an election to any political office or in connection with any primary election, convention, or caucus held to select candidates for any political office;"

Post, p. 248.

(7) Such section is further amended by adding at the end thereof a new subsection as follows:

Exemptions.

"(f) The Attorney General may, by regulation, provide for the exemption—

"(1) from registration, or from the requirement of furnishing any of the information required by this section, of any person who is listed as a partner, officer, director, or employee in the registration statement filed by an agent of a foreign principal under this Act, and

"(2) from the requirement of furnishing any of the information required by this section of any agent of a foreign principal, where by reason of the nature of the functions or activities of such person the Attorney General, having due regard for the national security and the public interest, determines that such registration, or the furnishing of such information, as the case may be, is not necessary to carry out the purposes of this Act."

75 Stat. 784.
22 USC 613.

SEC. 3. (a) Section 3(d) of such Act is amended to read as follows:

"(d) Any person engaging or agreeing to engage only (1) in private and nonpolitical activities in furtherance of the bona fide trade or commerce of such foreign principal; or (2) in other activities not serving predominantly a foreign interest; or (3) in the soliciting or collecting of funds and contributions within the United States to be used only for medical aid and assistance, or for food and clothing to relieve human suffering, if such solicitation or collection of funds and contributions is in accordance with and subject to the provisions of the Act of November 4, 1939, as amended (54 Stat. 4), and such rules and regulations as may be prescribed thereunder;".

22 USC 441-457.

(b) Section 3 of such Act is further amended by substituting a semicolon for the period at the end of subsection (f) and adding a new subsection as follows:

"(g) Any person qualified to practice law, insofar as he engages or agrees to engage in the legal representation of a disclosed foreign principal before any court of law or any agency of the Government of the United States: *Provided,* That for the purposes of this subsection legal representation does not include attempts to influence or persuade agency personnel or officials other than in the course of established agency proceedings, whether formal or informal."

Filing and labeling political propaganda. 22 USC 614.

SEC. 4. Section 4 of such Act is amended as follows:

(1) Subsection (a) is amended by inserting after the words "political propaganda" the words "for or in the interests of such foreign principal"; and by striking out the words "sent to the Librarian of Congress two copies thereof and file with the Attorney General one copy thereof" and inserting in lieu thereof the words "file with the Attorney General two copies thereof".

(2) Subsection (b) is amended by inserting after the words "political propaganda" where they first appear the words "for or in the interests of such foreign principal"; by inserting after the words "setting forth" the words "the relationship or connection between the person transmitting the political propaganda or causing it to be transmitted and such propaganda;"; and by striking out the words "each of his foreign principals" and inserting in lieu thereof "such foreign principal".

(3) Subsection (c) is amended by striking out the words "sent to the Librarian of Congress" and inserting in lieu thereof the words "filed with the Attorney General".

(4) Such section is further amended by adding at the end thereof the following new subsections:

"(e) It shall be unlawful for any person within the United States who is an agent of a foreign principal required to register under the provisions of this Act to transmit, convey, or otherwise furnish to any agency or official of the Government (including a Member or committee of either House of Congress) for or in the interests of such foreign principal any political propaganda or to request from any such agency or official for or in the interests of such foreign principal any information or advice with respect to any matter pertaining to the political or public interests, policies or relations of a foreign country or of a political party or pertaining to the foreign or domestic policies of the United States unless the propaganda or the request is prefaced or accompanied by a true and accurate statement to the effect that such person is registered as an agent of such foreign principal under this Act.

"(f) Whenever any agent of a foreign principal required to register under this Act appears before any committee of Congress to testify for or in the interests of such foreign principal, he shall, at the time of such appearance, furnish the committee with a copy of his most recent registration statement filed with the Department of Justice as an agent of such foreign principal for inclusion in the records of the committee as part of his testimony."

56 Stat. 256.
22 USC 615.

SEC. 5. Section 5 of such Act is amended by inserting after "the provisions of this Act," where they first appear the words "in accordance with such business and accounting practices,".

22 USC 616.

SEC. 6. Section 6 of such Act is amended by inserting the letter "(a)" after the section number and by adding at the end thereof the following new subsections:

Records and information. Transmittal by Attorney General.

"(b) The Attorney General shall, promptly upon receipt, transmit one copy of every registration statement filed hereunder and one copy of every amendment or supplement thereto, and one copy of every item of political propaganda filed hereunder, to the Secretary of State for such comment and use as the Secretary of State may determine to be appropriate from the point of view of the foreign relations of the United States. Failure of the Attorney General so to transmit such copy shall not be a bar to prosecution under this Act.

"(c) The Attorney General is authorized to furnish to departments and agencies in the executive branch and committees of the Congress such information obtained by him in the administration of this Act, including the names of registrants under this Act, copies of registration statements, or parts thereof, copies of political propaganda, or other documents or information filed under this Act, as may be appropriate in the light of the purposes of this Act."

Enforcement and penalties. 56 Stat. 257. 22 USC 618.

SEC. 7. Section 8 of such Act is amended as follows:

(1) Subsection (a) is amended by adding before the period at the end of paragraph (2) a comma and the following: "except that in the case of a violation of subsection (b), (e), or (f) of section 4 or of subsection (g) or (h) of this section the punishment shall be a fine of not more than $5,000 or imprisonment for not more than six months, or both".

(2) Such section is further amended by adding at the end thereof the following new subsections:

Injunctive remedy. Jurisdiction of district court.

"(f) Whenever in the judgment of the Attorney General any person is engaged in or about to engage in any acts which constitute or will constitute a violation of any provision of this Act, or regulations issued thereunder, or whenever any agent of a foreign principal fails to comply with any of the provisions of this Act or the regulations issued thereunder, or otherwise is in violation of the Act, the Attorney General may make application to the appropriate United States district court for an order enjoining such acts or enjoining such person from continuing to act as an agent of such foreign principal, or for an order requiring compliance with any appropriate provision of the Act or regulation thereunder. The district court shall have jurisdiction and authority to issue a temporary or permanent injunction, restraining order or such other order which it may deem proper. The proceedings shall be made a preferred cause and shall be expedited in every way.

"(g) If the Attorney General determines that a registration statement does not comply with the requirements of this Act or the regulations issued thereunder, he shall so notify the registrant in writing, specifying in what respects the statement is deficient. It shall be unlawful for any person to act as an agent of a foreign principal at any time ten days or more after receipt of such notification without filing an amended registration statement in full compliance with the requirements of this Act and the regulations issued thereunder.

"(h) It shall be unlawful for any agent of a foreign principal required to register under this Act to be a party to any contract, agreement, or understanding, either express or implied, with such foreign principal pursuant to which the amount or payment of the compensation, fee, or other remuneration of such agent is contingent in whole or in part upon the success of any political activities carried on by such agent."

SEC. 8. (a) Chapter 29 of title 18, United States Code, is amended by adding at the end thereof a new section as follows:

"§ 613. Contributions by agents of foreign principals

"Whoever, being an agent of a foreign principal, directly or through any other person, either for or on behalf of such foreign principal or otherwise in his capacity as agent of such foreign principal, knowingly makes any contribution of money or other thing of value, or promises expressly or impliedly to make any such contribution, in connection with an election to any political office or in connection with any primary election, convention, or caucus held to select candidates for any political office; or

"Whoever knowingly solicits, accepts, or receives any such contribution from any such agent of a foreign principal or from such foreign principal—

"Shall be fined not more than $5,000 or imprisoned not more than five years or both.

"As used in this section—

"(1) The term 'foreign principal' has the same meaning as when used in the Foreign Agents Registration Act of 1938, as amended, except that such term does not include any person who is a citizen of the United States.

"(2) The term 'agent of a foreign principal' means any person who acts as an agent, representative, employee, or servant, or any person who acts in any other capacity at the order, request, or under the direction or control, of a foreign principal or of a person any substantial portion of whose activities are directly or indirectly supervised, directed, or controlled by a foreign principal."

62 Stat. 690;
76 Stat. 1119.

(b) Chapter 11 of title 18, United States Code, is amended by adding at the end thereof a new section as follows:

"§ 219. Officers and employees acting as agents of foreign principals

"Whoever, being an officer or employee of the United States in the executive, legislative, or judicial branch of the Government or in any agency of the United States, including the District of Columbia, is or acts as an agent of a foreign principal required to register under the Foreign Agents Registration Act of 1938, as amended, shall be fined not more than $10,000 or imprisoned for not more than two years, or both.

Exemption.

"Nothing in this section shall apply to the employment of any agent of a foreign principal as a special Government employee in any case in which the head of the employing agency certifies that such employment is required in the national interest. A copy of any certification under this paragraph shall be forwarded by the head of such agency to the Attorney General who shall cause the same to be filed with the registration statement and other documents filed by such agent, and made available for public inspection in accordance with section 6 of the Foreign Agents Registration Act of 1938, as amended."

(c)(1) The sectional analysis at the beginning of chapter 29 of title 18, United States Code, is amended by adding at the end thereof the following new item:

"613. Contributions by agents of foreign principals."

(2) The sectional analysis at the beginning of chapter 11 of title 18, United States Code, is amended by adding at the end thereof the following new item:

"219. Officers and employees acting as agents of foreign principals."

Effective date.

SEC. 9. This Act shall take effect ninety days after the date of its enactment.

Approved July 4, 1966.

LEGISLATIVE HISTORY:
HOUSE REPORTS: No. 1470 (Comm. on the Judiciary) and No. 1632 (Comm. of Conference).
SENATE REPORT No. 143 (Comm. on Foreign Relations).
CONGRESSIONAL RECORD:
  Vol. 111 (1965): Apr. 5, considered and passed Senate.
  Vol. 112 (1966): May 16, considered and passed House, amended.
                   June 21, House and Senate agreed to conference report.

prospectus for a foreign tourism account

PRACTITIONERS, INC.
Public Relations

His Excellency
The Minister of Press, Broadcasting & Tourism of Atlantis
Atlantia, Atlantis

Your Excellency:

It is with great pleasure that we enclose our proposal for the promotion of tourism to Atlantis, in accordance with the invitation extended through the Director of your Information Office in New York City.

The program we have outlined for Atlantis is one that we consider would have maximum effectiveness without waste. It is based on the consideration that, even where ample funds are available, no government should invest in its public relations activities one penny more than is necessary to do the job properly.

We note that the Government of Atlantis plans to spread its program for the promotion of tourism over a five-year period. Therefore, if our suggested program meets with the Ministry's approval, our company would be prepared to sign a five-year contract.

However, and because of its confidence in its ability to produce more than satisfactory results, Practitioners, Inc. would also be willing to accept at the outset a one-year contract. This would be automatically renewable from year to year, unless canceled by written notice by either party ninety days before the expiration of any annual term.

Our fee for the complete program would be $150,000 per year. This amount would be payable in quarterly installments, in advance.

The fee mentioned here would include the salaries and full-time services of at least three executives who are properly qualified in the field of international public relations, who have an excellent knowledge of the needs and problems of Atlantis, and who would be assigned exclusively to the Atlantis Government account.

Naturally, this would be in addition to the assistance that the Atlantis account would receive from our company's other departments, which specialize in news and magazine copywriting, art, publications, financial publicity, annual reports, merchandising, packaging, industrial design, market research, market conditioning, motivational research, political polling, advertising counseling, photography and direct mail.

In addition, the fee would include each of these services and costs:

The writing of all news releases

The writing of articles for magazines

The writing and layout of booklets and pamphlets

Arrangements for the participation of Atlantis in major commercial fairs

Arrangements for cultural exhibitions on behalf of Atlantis

The making of arrangements for speeches, lectures and press conferences

The scheduling of films on Atlantis to be shown on TV

Arrangements for the appearance of officials of the Atlantis Government on important radio and television programs

All charges for local air or train travel in the United States

All cable, telephone and telegraph charges

All charges for the distribution of photographs, including the printing of photos in required quantities

All domestic and foreign postage charges

All mimeographing and collating and inserting

Complete and continuous contacts with

Newspaper and magazine writers

Newspaper and magazine editors

Radio writers and commentators

Television writers and commentators

Radio and television program producers

Movie, radio and television newsreel writers

Wire services and news syndicates

The furnishing of newspaper and magazine clippings on all public relations news dealing with tourism to Atlantis

The planning, implementation and supervision by our company of any public relations program for Atlantis would be carried out in full consultation with, and under the policy guidance of, the Atlantis Government or its designated official agency or representative.

In conclusion, Practitioners, Inc. would like to underline the honor and profound satisfaction that it would derive from being of constructive service to Atlantis, which has been such a firm and gallant ally of the United States, and such an unswerving supporter of peaceful efforts for a better world.

Respectfully submitted,

President
Practitioners, Inc.

ABC/de

A PUBLIC RELATIONS PROGRAM FOR ATLANTIS

covering tourism and economic, cultural and political campaigns *

* As mentioned in the text, assignments for campaigns covering a complete range of activities including tourism, and economic, cultural and political affairs are rarely given to a single agency. However, for the sake of brevity, these separate areas of activity are included in this one sample prospectus.

FOREWORD

A well-planned program for the promotion of tourism to Atlantis should not be confined solely to emphasizing the scenic, archaeological and historic treasures, or the increasing tourism facilities, offered by that beautiful country.

In order to bring Atlantis to the forefront of as great a measure of American awareness as possible, it would be advisable to provide also for three additional areas of action: economic, cultural and political.

This is because the desire to visit a country does not stem only from the need to spend a vacation amid pleasant surroundings during the peak June–September travel season. There are countless Americans who travel every week of the year on business; and there are equally large numbers of potential visitors who are deeply interested in the cultural, educational and political institutions of different countries. Obviously, it would be to the great economic advantage of Atlantis to attract also these other categories of travelers who can help to keep the nation's tourist facilities running on a year-round basis instead of a part-time one.

Therefore, the purpose of this memorandum is to indicate the broad programs and some of the specific procedures that would be utilized by Practitioners, Inc. in these four major divisions of public relations activities—subject, of course, to the priorities to be indicated by the Government of Atlantis.

TOURISM

Each year since the close of the Second World War has witnessed a dramatic increase in American travel abroad. In 19— this number will exceed three million, the largest in history. This increase is impressive not only for the number of tourists but also for the length of the average stay in Europe and for the amount of dollars spent for merchandise and services in the countries visited. This figure was more than $1 billion in 19— and up 10% the following year.

This profitable flow of traffic to Europe will continue to be accelerated substantially by the addition of income groups whose restricted resources formerly have prevented them from extensive travel. Today, vast credit by large American banks has been allocated toward financing low-income travel on an installment basis.

The advent of the jet assures a further increase in the gross revenues of host countries from the travel industry. In 19—, 75% of transportation requests for Europe were for coach air travel, and international airlines scheduled flights for more than 150,000 passengers per week between June and September. It would be the aim of this proposal for the promotion of tourism to attract a sizeable portion of this flow to Atlantis.

The three countries enjoying the greatest advantages from American tourism are England, France and Italy. For these countries tourism represents a substantial proportion of the national income and is indeed supporting industries within their national economies.

Most Americans visiting Europe attempt to include as many countries as time, convenience and funds will permit; and they often plan their side trips from the point of first destination, which is most frequently London, Paris, Rome or Frankfurt.

Atlantis has the advantage of being on the itineraries of flights from each of these European centers.

The desire to go to Europe might stem from childhood. The desire to see the three or four principal capitals of Europe probably stems from familiarity gained through following current events; but the plan for the tour of Europe itself is implanted in the individual's mind by the competitive public relations efforts of the more interesting locations in Europe. These facts have been ascertained time and again by extensive surveys and public opinion polls, many of which have been conducted by our own company. Even the United States will spend more than $3 million in 19— for tourism promotion centered in nine foreign cities.

1 The objective of the present proposal is to implant in the average traveler's mind a keen desire to visit Atlantis because it would enrich his life's experiences to absorb the ageless environment of this beautiful land.

2 Although Atlantis has always been known to the archaeologist

228

and to the scholar, it would be our purpose to broaden an awareness of Atlantis and the desire to visit it among the huge itinerant population of American tourists who will be going to Europe for the first time with only vague plans in mind for their actual tours.

3 In addition, there is the repeat traveler who makes up one third of the Europe-bound tourists, and who seeks new areas to visit.

4 It is estimated that more than 500,000 students will travel abroad this year. To this substantial figure must be added the teachers and professors, the only group that has a summer vacation that permits them to travel for three months.

5 Our method in changing the average American concept of Atlantis would be to point up factors that are not sufficiently well known, such as ideal climate, hospitable people, good accommodations at reasonable rates, scenic beauty and historic, religious and architectural treasures.

We would concentrate also on such over-all areas as the beautiful and extensive coastline of Atlantis, which has all the scenic beauty and semitropical charm of the Riviera and the Caribbean without the supercharged expensive environment found in those places.

Because a substantial number of medium-income tourists are inclined to follow the so-called fashionable set, it will also be our design to have a reasonable proportion of our stories mention the availability of luxury hotels, night clubs and deluxe restaurants; as well as the opportunity for sailing, water skiing and island hopping by charter boat and plane.

6 Practitioners, Inc. will also seek to emphasize the gay, carefree mood of Atlantis, its natural unspoiled charm and the reciprocal deep admiration and affection that its population has for Americans. This type of publicity would be aimed at the tourists whose objective is fun, and who are mainly attracted by color and gaiety.

7 This constant stream of tourists now travels the northern route: London, Brussels, Stockholm, Helsinki, Leningrad and Moscow. With proper promotion, it could easily be diverted to the southern route, which would be infinitely more picturesque. Great capital could be made of a stopover in Atlantis.

Practitioners, Inc. would solicit the cooperation of major airlines and steamship lines to popularize this second route; and we believe it could be a sufficient source of tourism revenue to initiate a campaign on this aspect alone.

8 There is also an economic benefit to Atlantis from attracting the American businessman. These now travel abroad in larger numbers than ever before; and there is a continuing rise particularly in the percentage who go to the European Common

Market countries (France, Germany, Holland, Italy, Belgium and Luxembourg). The present political stability of Atlantis and the attractive inducements offered to foreign private investors and to technical know-how are calculated to bring a growing number of businessmen-travelers, if presented to their attention through appropriate channels.

9 But the United States is a country of more than 204.6 million people, with 1748 daily newspapers, 302 national magazines, more than 7813 radio and television stations, 1500 radio and television commentators, thousands of political writers, some 339 wire services and news syndicates. No one medium is sufficient by itself to inform, and keep informed, all the people.

Therefore, it is essential to supply information to the writers and other molders of public opinion in the press, radio and television, and to keep this flow constant enough for it to serve as a source for research, ideas and facts.

These objectives can be achieved through the following program:

1 **A Tourism Survey of Atlantis**
The research department of Practitioners, Inc. will send qualified and experienced personnel to tour each area in Atlantis to be indicated by the Ministry.

This crew will do a complete tourism research report on Atlantis: its cities of tourist interest; sites of unusual attraction; historical, religious and archaeological locations; existing and planned hotels and motels and other tourist accommodations; transportation facilities; beach resorts and water sports; home industries and agriculture; liqueurs and wines; famous national foods; arts and crafts; and other aspects of national life of conceivable interest to tourists.

2 **Newspapers and Magazines**
The writing staff of Practitioners, Inc. will then use the complete data collected on these various tourist attractions to write feature articles, news articles and picture stories, all of which would be aimed at formulating the tourist's decision in favor of Atlantis according to his or her special interest.

During the first year of operation, Practitioners, Inc. would make every effort to place these various articles in the newspapers and magazines most avidly read by the huge annual tourist population. Special concentration would be made in large cities, in the press and in tourist agencies located in those centers.

Wherever possible without extraordinary expenditures, our company would arrange with some of the magazines to send their own writers and photographers to Atlantis to cover tourism and other stories of exceptional importance. By "exceptional importance," we mean exceptional stories that would carry color photography, cover stories, and the like.

Special concentration would include in particular those newspapers and magazines that are read not only in their own localities but also on a nationwide basis.

3 News Syndicates and Wire Services

The same tourism data, collected and evaluated by our special crew, would be used to supply specially written stories and feature articles for national distribution by the travel and other departments of the news syndicates and wire services.

4 Radio and Television

Television programs for which the scripts require foreign settings would be contacted with the purpose of convincing the producers that Atlantis would make an ideal setting.

Radio commentators who speak on travel would be supplied with scripts on Atlantis for broadcast use.

Material on Atlantis would be supplied also to the nonnetwork-affiliated local radio and television stations in cities throughout the United States.

Practitioners, Inc. maintains a rigid policy of never bartering for free editorial space or mention by the promise of paid advertising in press, radio or television outlets.

We would also like to say for the purpose of the record that, in this proposed campaign, this policy will be strictly adhered to in every case.

5 Travel Agencies

In many respects, the travel agent might be considered most influential in the determination of a tourist's final itinerary.

For this reason, our company would plan a special campaign to orientate the principal tourist agencies operating in America with a "Visit Atlantis" program.

To accomplish this, the following plan, which has proved successful, would be used:

a. A personal letter would be sent to the head of each travel agency explaining the purpose of our campaign and how they can profit by cooperating with it.

b. Existing or newly designed display posters would be distributed, both for window and counter use, the cost of which might be shared, or may be wholly paid for, by transportation lines: air, rail, or steamship companies servicing travel to Atlantis.

c. A series of small, intimate cocktail parties would be arranged for groups of travel agents operating in the cities in which we are most interested, to make personal contacts and to outline the advantages of recommending an Atlantis holiday to their clients.

It would be additionally attractive for some of these parties to have Government representatives from Atlantis as guests of honor.

d. Each time that an important piece of publicity is developed by Practitioners, Inc. in a newspaper or magazine, the most important travel agencies would receive photo-offset copies for display purposes.

e. We would also recommend the insertion of a few trade advertisements to speak directly to travel agencies in their own trade press.

6 Folders and Brochures

The Atlantis Information Office in New York already has a series of attractive folders and brochures on many of the tourism attractions of Atlantis, as well as a well-planned volume of facts, figures and lists for use by travel agents. A comprehensive program for the much wider and more effective distribution of such materials would be formulated by Practitioners, Inc.

Based on the results of the tourism survey to be done by our organization in Atlantis, our company would also write and design such additional basic brochures as may be necessary for the proper implementation of this program.

7 Window Displays

Practitioners, Inc. would design and promote the use of attractive tourism window displays for use by travel agencies and department stores throughout the United States.

8 Lectures

Lectures to influential travel groups and other audiences, as well as on radio and television programs, would be arranged for speakers to be approved by the Atlantis authorities.

9 Films

It would be against our recommendation for the Atlantis Government to allocate at this point substantial funds with which to make new films. This would not, however, exclude a motion picture program.

a. Practitioners, Inc. would exert every effort to induce the newsreel companies to send crews to Atlantis to make their own films.

b. Our company would also use its experience and resources to get popular and influential programs on the different television networks (whose programs are shown on a total of nearly 664 television stations with audiences running into the scores of millions each night) to send crews to Atlantis to film their own documentaries of a tourism and cultural nature.

c. There are several famous professional lecturers who pay the entire production cost of the films with which they illustrate their lectures. The cost to the Atlantis Government need not exceed that of the round-trip air fare and the facility of providing an interpreter-guide to conduct the lecturer to the points of greatest tourist interest.

In return for such a modest outlay, it would also be possible to purchase from the lecturer, at a cost of copies of the film footage alone, a sufficient footage from which to produce new films under the entire control of the Atlantis authorities.

d. Above all, our company's efforts would be concentrated on arranging for the big commercial producers to make their own theater-type movies on location in Atlantis. In this connection, the tourism benefit of films such as "Never on Sunday" and "Three Coins in the Fountain" hardly needs to be stressed.

e. Therefore, when Atlantis wants a new film, our company can arrange for this to be produced by the organizations concerned. The Government itself would need only to extend the usual courtesy facilities and official cooperation.

f. Finally, should the Atlantis Government at any time dispose of extra funds for the production of new films of its own, Practitioners, Inc. is ready and able to get such a film or films produced by any of the best producing companies in the United States or elsewhere. We would guarantee that, for comparable quality, such films would be produced at lower cost (because we can get them done at cost) and more quickly.

10 Other Media

Practitioners, Inc. will tie in with other travel advertising programs initiated by international airlines, steamship lines, hotels, European railroads and others, so that the "Visit Atlantis" theme can be introduced into advertising not paid for by the Atlantis Government in this campaign.

This can be done by convincing the primary advertiser that the addition of the "Visit Atlantis" slogan would enhance the value of his advertisement and attract additional readership for, and acceptance of, his promotion.

It is the considered opinion of Practitioners, Inc. that this tourism portion of the over-all program is more than adequate, not only for its obvious economy, but also for its effectiveness. We have used similar programs, with highly gratifying and profitable results for the client, in the promotion of other resort areas.

ECONOMIC

As already mentioned under item (8) of the preceding section of this proposal, great benefit can be derived from attracting the American businessman to Atlantis.

Aside from visits on an individual basis, Atlantis could expect to reap considerable tourism revenue from the holding of commercial, industrial and financial conventions. As an example, one major foreign city for which our company is the consultant for public relations has been host to 600 international conventions, attended by 400,000 persons.

There is also the important prospect of directing to the attention of American businessmen the many advantages that Atlantis offers as a door for America in regard to industrial and commercial possibilities for the entire Middle Eastern market. The favorable terms offered to foreign private capital, and the fact that Atlantis is free of controversial considerations that now restrain American corporations from locating their plants or distribution centers in other Near Eastern countries, can be turned into an asset of considerable proportions.

Therefore, the economic aspect of our proposed program of public relations for the promotion of tourism would embrace a planned sequence of projects and approaches aimed specifically at the American leadership in the fields of finance, investment, industry and commerce.

1   Here, too, thoroughly documented material would be prepared to give the relevant economic facts, including information about the resources and industrial-commercial potentials, and emphasizing the stability provided by the Government of Atlantis. This compilation of data, part of a continuous updated reference series, would be supplied to important American institutions such as banking and investment companies, local Chambers of Commerce, trade associations, and its very considerable financial and trade press.

2   This data would be supplemented by a steady stream of up-to-the-minute stories concerning developments and progress in the economic field. And each of these steps would be calculated to project, for the specific benefit of the traveling American businessmen, the concept of a stable Government with a thriving community possessed of still greater potential— a reliable country for foreign investment.

3   As new business developments occur in Atlantis, which mean substance and reality to Americans, they would be thoroughly publicized in story and pictures through all the media in which they properly have a place.

4   Corresponding to our parallel plan in the strictly tourist field,

234

we would undertake to organize a series of congenial formal and informal personal meetings to enable leading personalities in the financial and economic development of Atlantis to meet with, and become close to, their counterparts in the business community of the United States.

5   We would undertake to organize and supervise a series of group sessions with bankers, financiers, industrialists and the heads of commercial establishments.

These smaller and more informal meetings would be introductory to the important public appearances of competent spokesmen of the economy of Atlantis before appropriate business associations and organizations in the United States.

6   The informal meetings, the roundtable conversations and the more formal addresses would in each case be given full press coverage through all of the resources of Practitioners, Inc., when desired.

7   Where appropriate, these functions would be accompanied by the showing of charts, slides or other visual material prepared specifically by our company for the occasion. This would add visual impact in regard to the economic progress made in Atlantis to the spoken impact of the meetings and addresses.

8   It is also our plan, whenever and wherever an economic project of truly exceptional importance is developed in Atlantis, to arrange for representatives of the important business publications in the United States to visit the project and to report on it through interviews, news stories and photographic feature stories.

9   It has become standard practice for some of the outstanding publications in the United States such as THE NEW YORK TIMES, the WASHINGTON POST and the CHICAGO TRIBUNE to publish, on one or more occasions in the course of the year, special international supplements.

These, experience has demonstrated, have become a guide to the alert American businessman in regard to business opportunities abroad. They have equally become a guide for those contemplating industrial and commercial investments in foreign countries.

Practitioners, Inc. would seek to assure a more-than-proportional coverage for Atlantis in these supplements and in others that might emerge as this program is carried out.

10   It is an integral part of our tourism public relations program to assume full responsibility also for the promotion of such economically valuable relationships as have been mentioned here: to do the required planning, contacting, implementation and writing in the closest cooperation and under the policy guidance of the Atlantis authorities.

The wider public knowledge that is to be anticipated from the efforts outlined here would make its own strong impact not only on the American business community but also on other segments of the American public in terms of our mutual economic interests.

CULTURAL

A series of significant developments in the United States in recent years has accentuated the importance of the cultural interests of the American people. These have revealed a substantial informational segment that is responsive to cultural developments in other countries and disposed to cooperate with them.

This is a field that merits extensive cultivation from the viewpoint of promoting tourism to Atlantis, because those Americans who are drawn into its orbit exert a disproportionately high influence within their local communities and on the country as a whole. Therefore, the itineraries of their travels abroad are closely studied and duplicated by tens of thousands of Americans each year.

Accordingly, Practitioners, Inc. would include in its tourism public relations program for the Atlantis Government a carefully organized plan to enlist these cultural forces, the schools and universities and their publications, and the related institutions in the world of art, music, literature and antiquarian interests.

Our company would undertake to prepare material designed to attract this widespread and influential segment of the American public.

This would be done by the following procedures:

1 The exchange of academic and cultural personalities.
2 Arrangements for cultural exhibitions.
3 Arrangements for visits to the United States by such colorful groups as award-winning folklore dancers from Atlantis.
4 Arrangements for appearances by distinguished men of letters and artists on American platforms.

Also, and even more important, these activities will be publicized in every possible media that can be found to have an interest in them.

Finally, there are numerous academic and cultural institutions and art and antiquities in Atlantis. They deserve to be better known. It would be the purpose of our company to see that they become better known as part of the cultural segment of our tourism program designed to cultivate a knowledge and admiration of them and a respect for the nation and the people that have produced them.

POLITICAL

In such a time as the present when the political and economic fates of different nations are increasingly interdependent one on the other, there is a keen curiosity among all Americans for more information on the allies of the United States—and particularly on allies such as Atlantis, whose unswerving dependability has never been in question.

This situation gives the Government of Atlantis a rare opportunity to implement, within its program for tourism promotion, certain measures that will help to establish a long-term favorable public opinion in this country.

1 There is a need for a widespread, intelligent dissemination of basic information to all the opinion-forming media and other agencies in the United States.

2 This could include the answers to such questions as how Atlantis has always carried out its treaty obligations (particularly with regard to the United States, NATO and the United Nations) and what its broad projects are for its international political and economic policies, with respect to the well-being of its people.

3 Every major item in the information to be disseminated would be the basis for publicity efforts on the part of Practitioners, Inc. to clarify the objectives of the Atlantis Government, with due emphasis on foreign policy, internal policy, governmental stability and the country's suitability for foreign investments and, of course, for an influx of tourists.

On the basis of past experience, such releases should receive from modest to front-page coverage, depending on news value and timing.

4 Because much of American public interest revolves around personalities who can be named and identified, special efforts would be made to familiarize the American reader with personalities heading up the Atlantis Government and others responsible for its policies.

5 Augmenting this basic source material, we would undertake the writing and distribution of a press kit of brief material designed to give the newspaper editor and researcher a permanent reference file on Atlantis' Government, its institutions and its people.

This kit could include the following:

a. A map of Atlantis.

b. A document describing the present Government of Atlantis.

c. A series of biographies of members of the Government and of its important representatives in foreign countries, along with photographs.

d. A compilation of significant data on population, agricultural and economic-industrial statistics, educational information and other background data indispensable in the use of news and editorial comment on Atlantis.

6 Practitioners, Inc. would undertake to ensure a thorough distribution of this press kit to every important section of the American press; to other media such as radio and television; and to all important public affairs organizations and libraries.

7 If desired, news releases would be issued containing a series of policy statements by responsible Government personalities.

8 Our company further recommends and contemplates arrangements whereby at least four major American columnists, whose articles are syndicated throughout the country, would visit Atlantis and write on their observations following personal interviews with the political, economic and cultural leadership of the country. These visits would be spaced to get a continuity of coverage over the first year.

From our experience, the cost of such trips would, in the main, be absorbed by the syndicate employing these political commentators; although there may be some supplementary expenses such as nominal hotel bills, provision for the use of a car or an interpreter-guide.

It would be desirable that these visits be arranged informally rather than by official invitation—a procedure that can be followed most advantageously through our agency as intermediary.

9 Still another recommended procedure for the high-level enlightenment of American leadership would be the preparation of important articles on the Government of Atlantis and its policies for appearance in such publications as the FOREIGN AFFAIRS QUARTERLY and other organs of influential American public affairs organizations.

10 Furthermore, Practitioners, Inc. would undertake to arrange television and radio appearances on behalf of personalities from Atlantis that the Government felt it would be desirable to bring to the attention of the American people.

The programs chosen would be restricted to those having a dignified format of presentation and a history of important dignitaries' appearances on them.

11 A high priority in this program would be to add to the official arrangements for visits by leading ministers or other dignitaries by adding to their list of meetings with Administration heads in Washington still other meetings with civic and industrial leaders as well as the press.

12 Such visits would also become the occasion for arrangements for these distinguished representatives of the Government of Atlantis to appear and give addresses at important functions in this country, some expressly organized for this purpose.

13 Auxiliary to this series of personal contacts, an intensive public relations effort would be made by our company for a series of conferences with the editors and publishers of America's most important publications.

Such background conferences, designed to brief these important leaders of public opinion, could be initiated and carried out by our company, because the absence of diplomatic intermediaries is essential if such conferences are to be conducted in an atmosphere devoid of protocol and without the risk of direct or indirect quotations that might normally be attributed to officials of the Government of Atlantis.

14 Each of these recommendations would have the planning, counsel, negotiation, supervision and implementation of our company in cooperation with, and under the policy guidance of, the official agencies and representatives of the Government of Atlantis.

securities and exchange commission statement of policy

as amended November 5, 1957

The Securities and Exchange Commission with the assistance of the National Association of Securities Dealers, Inc., in 1950 reviewed samples of advertising and supplemental sales literature used in the sale of investment company shares, much of which was not filed with this Commission. This review revealed the existence of many practices in connection with the use, form and content of certain advertising and sales literature which, in the opinion of the Commission, might violate statutory standards, including provisions of the Securities Act of 1933 and the Investment Company Act of 1940.

The Commission, therefore, has issued the following Statement of Policy so that issuers, underwriters and dealers may understand certain of the types of advertising and sales literature which the Commission considers may be violative of the statutory standards.

It should be emphasized that the following Statement of Policy, as amended, does not attempt to cover all possible abuses, and that literature which complies with this Statement may not be used if it is in fact misleading. Conversely, nothing in this Statement of Policy is intended to prevent the use of factual statements, fairly presented, concerning fundamental investment policies and objectives, investment restrictions or other characteristics of a particular investment company.

"Sales literature" as used hereafter shall be deemed to include any communication (whether in writing, by radio or by television) used by an issuer, underwriter, or dealer to induce the purchase of shares of an investment company. Reports of issuers to the extent they are transmitted to shareholders and do not contain an express offer are not deemed to be "sales literature" within the meaning of this definition but shall conform to this Statement of Policy. Communications between issuers, underwriters and dealers are included in this definition of "sales literature" only if such communications are passed on either orally or in writing or are shown to prospective investors or are designed to be employed in either written or oral form in the sale of securities.

For the purpose of interpreting this Statement of Policy, a piece of sales literature shall be deemed materially misleading by reason of an implication, as contemplated herein, if such sales literature (1) includes an untrue statement of a material fact or (2) omits to state a material fact necessary in order to make a statement made, in the light of the circumstances of its use, not misleading.

It will be considered materially misleading hereafter for sales literature—

Rates of Return

    (a) To represent or imply a percentage return on an investment in the shares of an investment company unless based upon—

        (1) Dividends from net investment income paid during a fiscal year related to the average monthly offering price for

such fiscal year, provided that if any year prior to the most recent fiscal year is selected for this purpose, the rate of return for all subsequent fiscal years, similarly calculated, shall also be stated; or

(2) Dividends paid from net investment income during the twelve months ending not earlier than the close of the calendar month immediately preceding the date of publication related to an offering price current at said date of publication;

in either case the basis of the calculation shall be shown and adjustment made for capital gains distributions and any other factor necessary to make the presentation not misleading. "Net investment income" as used above shall include net accrued undivided earnings included in the price of capital shares issued and repurchased and shall be as required to be included in the issuer's prospectus. Every such statement of return shall be accompanied by a statement to the effect that such return is based upon dividends paid in the period covered and is not a representation of future results. Either in the same text, or by reference in the same text to an historical table elsewhere in the same piece of literature, there must be shown the per-share asset value at the beginning and end of the period, or the increase or decrease (stated in percentage) in asset value.

Show Asset Value Change (appears in left margin)

Capital vs. Income (appears in left margin)

(b) (1) To combine into any one amount distributions from net investment income and distributions from any other source.

(b) (2) To represent or imply an assurance that an investor will receive a stable, continuous, dependable, or liberal return or that he will receive any specified rate or rates of return.

Explain Risks (appears in left margin)

(c) To represent or imply an assurance that an investor's capital will increase or that purchase of investment company shares involves a preservation of original capital and a protection against loss in value. To discuss accumulation of capital, preservation of capital, accumulation of an estate, protection against loss of purchasing power, diversification of investments, financial independence or profit possibilities without pointing out or explaining the market risks inherently involved in the investment.

Government Regulation (appears in left margin)

(d) To make any reference to registration or regulation of any investment company under Federal or state authority without explaining that this does not involve supervision of management or investment practices or policies.

Custodial Services (appears in left margin)

(e) To represent or imply that services of banking institutions as custodian of securities, transfer agent, or dividend disbursing agent, provide protection for investors against possible depreciation of assets or that such institutions maintain any supervisory function over management in such matters as purchase and sale of portfolio securities or payment of dividends or provide any trusteeship protection, or to fail to state the extent of the limited role of the custodian whenever the advantages of custodial services are discussed.

Redemption

(f) To state or discuss the redemption features of investment company shares without explaining in such statement that the value of the shares on redemption may be more or less than the investor's cost, depending upon the market value of the portfolio securities at the time of redemption.

Comparisons Generally

(g) (1) To represent or imply that shares of an investment company are similar to or as safe as government bonds, insurance annuities, savings accounts or life insurance, or have the fixed income, principal, or any other features of a debt security.

(2) To represent or imply that the management of an investment company is under the same type of investment restrictions or is operated under limitations similar to or has fiduciary obligations such as those imposed by governmental authorities on savings banks and insurance companies, except to the extent that it is so restricted or limited by its statement of policy on file with this Commission.

Comparisons With Market Index or Other Security

(h) To use any comparison of an investment company security with any other security or medium of investment or any security index or average without pointing out—

(1) that the particular security or index or average and period were selected; and,

(2) that the results disclosed should be considered in the light of the company's investment policy and objectives, the characteristics and quality of the company's investments, and the period selected; and,

(3) the material differences or similarities between the subjects of the comparisons; and,

(4) what the comparison is designed to show; and

(5) anything else that may be necessary to make the comparison fair.

New Capital

(i) To represent or imply that investment companies in general are direct sources of new capital to industry or that a particular investment company is such a source unless the extent to which such investments are made is disclosed.

Performance Charts and Tables

(j) To use any chart or table which is inaccurate in factual detail or tends to create a false or misleading impression as to any material aspect of the investment company's past performance or of an assumed investment of any investor in the investment company, or appears to represent that the investment company's past performance or investor experience will be repeated in the future. Charts or tables which conform to the

"Approved Charts and Tables," described below and illustrated in the Appendix, will not be regarded by the Commission as materially false and misleading in the absence of facts or circumstances which make such charts or tables or their use in fact false and misleading in a particular use. Persons using other charts and tables must assume responsibility that they are not materially false or misleading. Any such chart or table may be submitted to the Commission for its views in advance of its use.

(1) Approved charts should conform with the following:

(i) The text, graphic detail and arrangement of any such chart should be substantially as shown on sample Charts A, B, C, and D in the Appendix, whichever is applicable.

Drawn to Scale

(ii) Each chart should be drawn to scale which should be shown on the side of the chart and the same scale should be used for all segments of the chart. Appropriate shading or coloring should be added to distinguish between the different elements of the chart.

(iii) Charts A and B may not be used to show the reinvestment of dividend income.

(iv) The caption of sample chart B may, if desired, be changed to read as follows:

Record of   Fund in Terms of Net Asset Value per Share, and Illustration of an Assumed Investment in One Share with Capital Gains Distributions Accepted in Additional Shares

(v) Chart C should be accompanied in the same piece of literature by Table 1 and Chart D should be so accompanied by Table 2. These tables should be prepared on the same assumption and cover the same period as the related chart, and should appear in a manner and location which permit easy reference from the chart to the corresponding table.

(2) Approved tables should conform with the following:

(i) The text, detail and arrangement of any table illustrating a dividend reinvestment or continuous investment program should be substantially as shown in Tables 1 and 2 in the Appendix, whichever is applicable. Tables prepared in accordance with the requirements for a table prescribed for use in the investment company's prospectus, or tables containing the same information as is shown on Charts A and B, may also be employed. *See Sample Tables 1 and 2 . . . Pages 14 and 15.*

Contractual Plans

(ii) Any table designed to show any other investment program should contain comparable information. (*Contractual plan companies must use Sample Tables 3 and 4 on Pages 18 and 19*)

246

(iii) When Table 1 is used with Chart C or Table 2 is used with Chart D in accordance with subparagraph (1)(v), above, such table need not contain any specific reference to the sales commission. When such table follows immediately after the chart, on the same page as the chart, the caption of the table and any notes thereto which are contained in the chart may be omitted from the table.

(3) Approved charts and tables should conform with the following:

Highest Sales Charge

(i) Charts and tables may be set up on a per share basis, or in amounts other than those shown on the attached samples, provided the charts and tables give effect to the maximum sales commission currently charged. The amounts used in constructing the chart or table should be amounts capable of being invested under the particular program being described. Any chart or table may be accompanied, in the same piece of literature, by a chart or table (which may be in summary form) illustrating investments in large amounts at reduced sales commissions.

(ii) Any chart or table which reflects either the acceptance of capital gains distributions in additional shares or the reinvestment of dividends from investment income should not be captioned or characterized as the record of the fund, except as permitted in subparagraph (1)(iv).

Periods Covered

(iii) The period covered by such chart or table should be the most recent period ending with the latest available fiscal or calendar year and embracing:

A. The life of the company or the life of the issuer of the underlying investment company shares, or,

B. The duration of any plan or contract of the type referred to in Section 27(a) of the Investment Company Act of 1940, or,

C. The immediately preceding 10 years, or,

D. Periods longer than 10 years but less than the life of the company or the duration of such plan or contract, if such additional periods are multiples of five years;

provided that a portion of the current year may be added to the period ended with the last fiscal or calendar year. In no event should such chart or table relate to a period that exceeds the life of the company or the life of the issuer of the underlying shares.

Summary Results

(iv) Charts A, B, C, and D and Tables 1 and 2 may be accompanied in the same piece of literature by summary tables for the same period covered by the chart or table showing the end results which would have been obtained if alternative assumptions had been made as to the acceptance of capital gains distributions in shares or the reinvestment of dividends from investment income or both.

247

Use Same Basis

(v) Charts and tables may be accompanied in the same piece of literature by summary tables prepared on the same basis as the chart or table they accompany as follows:

A. A summary table showing the end results depicted in the chart or table.

Successive Summaries

B. Successive summary tables showing the end results over several periods of equal length, provided that the latest 10-year or longer period as well as every other such period within the total time span covered by the chart or table is included and that the chart or table and the summary tables are presented on the same page or on facing pages.

C. Successive summary tables showing the end results over several periods of unequal length, provided that such unequal periods start with each successive year and end with the last date shown on the chart or table, that every such period of unequal length within the total time span covered by the chart or table is included, and that the chart or table and the summary tables are presented on the same page or on facing pages.

Summary Content

(vi) In depicting the end results in any summary or successive summary tables provided for in (iv) and (v) above, the total of initial and periodic investments, total dividend reinvestment cost, total investment cost, total of capital gains distributions accepted in shares, and ending total asset value shall be shown separately to the extent applicable. The total capital gains distributions accepted in shares may be shown in a footnote. Summary tables need not contain any specific reference to sales commission.

May Need Added Facts

(vii) Any approved chart or table may be prepared on a basis which does not reflect the acceptance of capital gains distributions in shares or the reinvestment of dividends from investment income, or both, provided that no chart or table should reflect the reinvestment of dividends from investment income unless it also reflects the acceptance of capital gains distributions in shares.

(viii) Any chart or table should be preceded or accompanied by a prominent statement of any additional information or explanation of material significance to investors in appraising the figures shown, when necessary in a particular case to provide adequate and accurate disclosure of material facts.

(ix) Other relevant data in addition to that shown on the Approved Charts or Tables, such as the number of shares of stock acquired through assumed investments or the price of the shares so acquired, may be included, if the addition of such data does not result in a false and misleading presentation.

Management Claims

(k) To make any extravagant claims regarding management ability or competency.

(l) To represent or imply that investment companies are operated as, or are similar to, "co-operatives".

(m) To represent or imply that investment company shares generally have been selected by fiduciaries.

Continuous Investment Programs

(n) (1) To use the phrase "dollar averaging" or "averaging the dollar" (although the phrases "dollar cost averaging" or "cost averaging" are not objectionable) in referring to any plan of continuous investment in the shares of an investment company at stated intervals regardless of the price level of the shares.

Cost Averaging and Contractual Plans

(2) To discuss or portray the principles of dollar cost averaging, or cost averaging, or to discuss or portray any Periodic Payment Plan referred to in section 27(a) of the Investment Company Act of 1940, without making clear—

(i) that the investor will incur a loss under such plan if he discontinues the plan when the market value of his accumulated shares is less than his cost; and

(ii) that the investor is investing his funds primarily in securities subject to market fluctuations and that the method involves continuous investment in such shares at regular intervals regardless of price levels; and

(iii) that the investor must take into account his financial ability to continue such plan through periods of low price levels; and

(iv) that such plans do not protect against loss in value in declining markets.

(3) To discuss or portray any other type of continuous investment plan without making clear that such type of investment plan does not assure a profit and does not protect against depreciation in declining markets.

Sales Commissions

(o) To fail to include in any sales literature which does not state the amount or rate of the sales commission (except communications which deal only with routine business matters or which do not purport to discuss or describe any investment company or investment company security) a clear reference to the prospectus or prospectuses for information concerning the sales commission, and other information.

(p) To fail to include in any sales literature which is designed to encourage investors to switch from one investment company to another, or from one class of security of an investment company to another class, the substance of the following statement in a separate paragraph in type as large as that used generally in the body of the piece:

"Switching from the securities of one investment company to another, or from one class of security of an investment company to another, involves a sales charge on each such transaction, for details of which see the prospectus. The prospective purchaser should measure these costs against the claimed advantage of the switch".

Industry
Performance
against
Company
Performance

(q) To represent or imply that the performance of any particular company may be measured by or compared with or related to the performance of a particular industry unless the extent and scope of the portfolio of the particular company is such that its performance will generally approximate that of the industry.

Reprints

(r) To employ material in whole or in part from published articles or documents descriptive of or relating to investment companies unless such material, or the literature including such material, complies with this Statement of Policy and in addition such material is not taken out of context in a manner which alters its intended meaning.

Sample Chart A *Illustration of an assumed investment of $10,000*

With capital gains distributions accepted in additional shares

The chart below covers the period from January 1, 1946 to December 31, 1955. This period was one of generally rising common stock prices. The results shown should not be considered as a representation of the dividend income or capital gain or loss which may be realized from an investment made in the fund today.

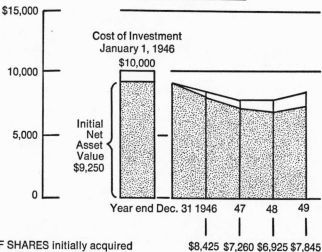

RECORD OF INCOME
Dividends Paid from Investment Income

$272 $334 $334 $352

RECORD OF PRINCIPAL

Cost of Investment
January 1, 1946
$10,000

Initial
Net
Asset
Value
$9,250

Year end Dec. 31 1946   47   48   49

VALUE OF SHARES initially acquired through investment of $10,000	$8,425	$7,260	$6,925	$7,845
VALUE OF SHARES accepted as capital gains distributions (cumulative)	349	905	1,175	1,354
TOTAL VALUE	8,774	8,165	8,100	9,199

Initial net asset value is the amount received by the fund after deducting from the cost of the investment the sales commission as described in the prospectus.

No adjustment has been made for any income taxes payable by stockholders on capital gains distributions accepted in shares. The dollar amounts of capital gains distributions accepted in shares were: 1946 - $334; 1947 - $578; 1948 - $207; 1949 - none; 1950 - $127; 1951 - $215; 1952 - $594; 1953 - $163; 1954 - $128; 1955 - $315; Total $2,661.

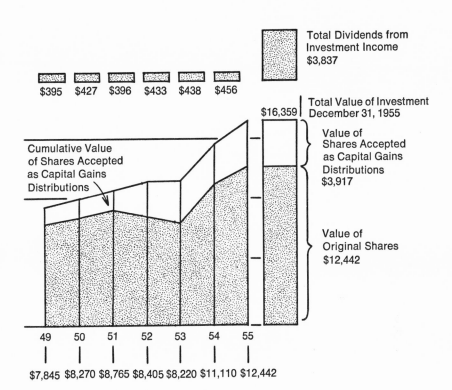

Total Dividends from
Investment Income
$3,837

$395 $427 $396 $433 $438 $456

Total Value of Investment
December 31, 1955
$16,359

Value of
Shares Accepted
as Capital Gains
Distributions
$3,917

Cumulative Value
of Shares Accepted
as Capital Gains
Distributions

Value of
Original Shares
$12,442

49   50   51   52   53   54   55

$7,845 $8,270 $8,765 $8,405 $8,220 $11,110 $12,442

1,354   1,521   1,860   2,840   2,888   3,253   3,917

9,199   9,791   10,625 11,245 11,108 14,363 16,359

Sample Chart B *Illustration of an assumed investment in one share*

With capital gains distributions accepted in additional shares

The chart below covers the period from January 1, 1940 to December 31, 1954. This period was one of generally rising common stock prices. The results shown should not be considered as a representation of the dividend income or capital gain or loss which may be realized from an investment made in the fund today.

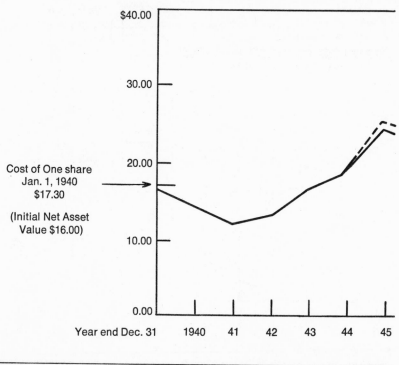

Per share for year ending Dec. 31	'40	'41	'42	'43	'44
Value of share initially acquired	$14.04	$12.18	$13.38	$16.40	$18.94
Value of shares accepted as capital gains distributions (cumulative)	—	—	—	—	—
Total value	$14.04	12.18	13.38	16.40	18.94
Dividends from income	.64	.69	.76	.64	.64

Initial net asset value is the amount received by the fund after deducting from the cost of the investment the sales commission as described in the prospectus.

No adjustment has been made for any income taxes payable by stockholders on capital gains distributions accepted in shares. The dollar amounts of capital gains distributions accepted in shares were: 1940-1944 - none; 1945 - $0.34; 1946 - $0.92; 1947 - $2.58; 1948 - $0.57; 1949 - none; 1950 - $0.35; 1951 - $0.59; 1952 - $1.63; 1953 - $0.45; 1954 - $0.35; Total $7.78.

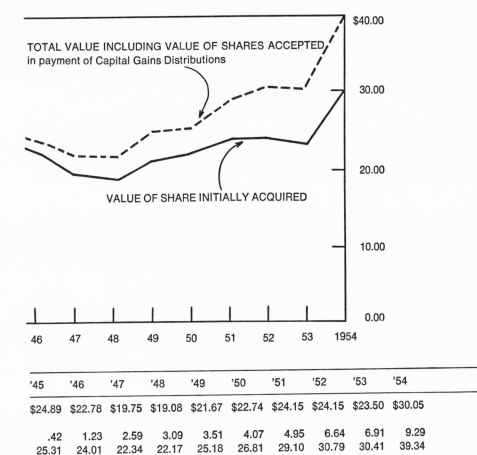

TOTAL VALUE INCLUDING VALUE OF SHARES ACCEPTED
in payment of Capital Gains Distributions

VALUE OF SHARE INITIALLY ACQUIRED

'45	'46	'47	'48	'49	'50	'51	'52	'53	'54	
$24.89	$22.78	$19.75	$19.08	$21.67	$22.74	$24.15	$24.15	$23.50	$30.05	
.42	1.23	2.59	3.09	3.51	4.07	4.95	6.64	6.91	9.29	
25.31	24.01	22.34	22.17	25.18	26.81	29.10	30.79	30.41	39.34	
.71	.75	.91	.91	.96	1.08	1.17	1.08	1.18	1.20	Total 13.32

Sample Chart C *Illustration of an assumed investment of $10,000*

With dividends reinvested and capital gains distributions accepted in shares

The chart below covers the period from January 1, 1946 to December 31, 1955. This period was one of generally rising common stock prices. The results shown should not be considered as a representation of the dividend income or capital gain or loss which may be realized from an investment made in the fund today.

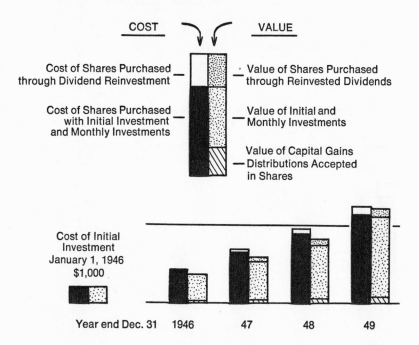

COST   VALUE

Cost of Shares Purchased — through Dividend Reinvestment   · Value of Shares Purchased through Reinvested Dividends

Cost of Shares Purchased — with Initial Investment and Monthly Investments   Value of Initial and — Monthly Investments

Value of Capital Gains — Distributions Accepted in Shares

Cost of Initial Investment January 1, 1946 $1,000

Year end Dec. 31   1946   47   48   49

Initial net asset value is the amount received by the fund after deducting from the cost of the investment the sales commission as described in the prospectus. Income dividends were assumed to have been reinvested in additional shares at the public offering price which includes a sales commission of 7½% as described in the prospectus.

No adjustment has been made for any income taxes payable by shareholders on capital gains distributions and dividends reinvested in shares.

256

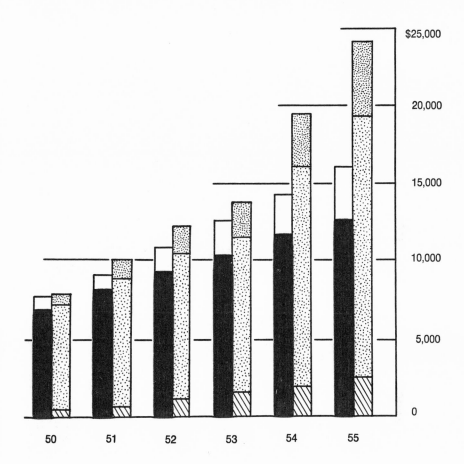

Sample Chart D *Illustration of a continuous investment program*

In terms of an assumed initial investment of $1,000 and subsequent investments of $100 per month with dividends reinvested and capital gains distributions accepted in shares

The chart below covers the period from January 1, 1946 to December 31, 1955. This period was one of generally rising common stock prices. The results shown should not be considered as a representation of the dividend income or capital gain or loss which may be realized from an investment made in the fund today. A program of the type illustrated does not assure a profit or protect against depreciation in declining markets.

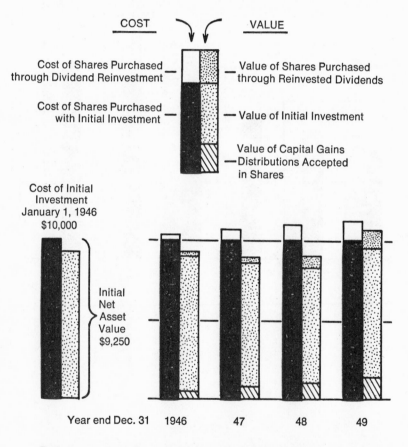

Total cost for each year represents the initial investment of $1,000 plus the cumulative total of monthly investments of $100 per month plus the cumulative amount of income dividends reinvested. The cost for all shares so purchased includes sales commissions of 7½% as described in the prospectus.

No adjustment has been made for any income taxes payable by shareholders on capital gains distributions and dividends reinvested in shares.

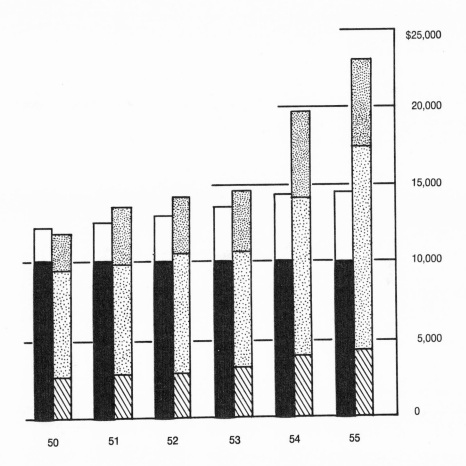

	$25,000
	20,000
	15,000
	10,000
	5,000
	0

50   51   52   53   54   55

Sample Table 1 *Illustration of an assumed investment of $10,000*

With dividends reinvested and capital gains distributions accepted in shares

The table below covers the period from January 1, 1946 to December 31, 1955. This period was one of generally rising common stock prices. The results shown should not be considered as a representation of the dividend income or capital gain or loss which may be realized from an investment made in the fund today.

Year ended Dec. 31	1946	1947	1948
Amount of dividends from investment income reinvested annually	$ 275	$ 349	$ 361
Cumulative cost of shares purchased through investment of income dividends	275	624	985
Total cost, including reinvested dividends	$10,275	$10,624	$10,985
Value of shares:			
a. Initially Acquired	$ 8,434	$ 7,268	$ 6,962
b. Accepted as Capital Gains Distributions (cumulative)	320	860	1,090
Sub-total	$ 8,754	$ 8,128	$ 8,052
c. Purchased Through Reinvestment of Income (cumulative)	$ 260	$ 580	$ 925
Total value	$ 9,014	$ 8,708	$ 8,977

The total cost figure represents the initial cost of $10,000 plus the cumulative amount of income dividends reinvested, and includes sales commissions of 7½%, as described in the prospectus, on all shares so purchased. The dollar amounts of capital gains distributions accepted in shares were: 1946 - $334; 1947 - $594; 1948 - $220; 1949 - none; 1950 - $1,148; 1951 - $147; 1952 - $258; 1953 - $210; 1954 - $171; 1955 - $436; Total - $3,518.

No adjustment has been made for any income taxes payable by shareholders on capital gains distributions and dividends reinvested in shares.

1949	1950	1951	1952	1953	1954	1955
$ 397	$ 463	$ 791	$ 227	$ 565	$ 594	$ 637
1,382	1,845	2,636	2,863	3,428	4,022	4,659
$11,382	$11,845	$12,636	$12,863	$13,428	$14,022	$14,659
$ 8,120	$ 7,240	$ 7,189	$ 7,699	$ 7,391	$ 9,871	$11,473
1,120	2,400	2,600	2,890	3,220	4,170	4,350
$ 9,240	$ 9,640	$ 9,789	$10,589	$10,611	$14,041	$15,823
$ 1,370	$ 2,100	$ 3,450	$ 3,910	$ 4,250	$ 5,800	$ 7,400
$10,610	$11,740	$13,239	$14,499	$14,861	$19,841	$23,223

Sample Table 2 *Illustration of a continuous investment program*

In terms of an assumed initial investment of $1,000 and subsequent investments of $100 per month with dividends reinvested and capital gains distributions accepted in shares

The table below covers the period from January 1, 1946 to December 31, 1955. This period was one of generally rising common stock prices. The results shown should not be considered as a representation of the dividend income or capital gain or loss which may be realized from an investment made in the fund today. A program of the type illustrated does not assure a profit or protect against depreciation in declining markets.

Year ended Dec. 31	1946	1947	1948
Amount of dividends from investment income reinvested annually	$ 38	$ 89	$ 139
Cumulative cost of shares purchased through investment of income dividends	$ 38	$ 127	$ 266
Total of initial and monthly investments	2,100	3,300	4,500
Total cost, including reinvested dividends	$ 2,138	$ 3,427	$ 4,766
Value of shares:			
a. Acquired Through Initial and Monthly Investments	$ 1,816	$ 2,659	$ 3,706
b. Accepted as Capital Gains Distributions (cumulative)	25	147	198
Sub-total	$ 1,841	$ 2,806	$ 3,904
c. Purchased Through Reinvestment of Income (cumulative)	30	108	225
Total value	$ 1,871	$ 2,914	$ 4,129

The total cost figures represent the initial investment of $1,000 plus the cumulative total of monthly investments of $100 per month plus the cumulative amount of income dividends reinvested, and include sales commissions on all shares so purchased of 7½%, as described in the prospectus. The dollar amounts of capital gains distributions accepted in shares were: 1946 - $33; 1947 - $129; 1948 - $76; 1949 - none; 1950 - $86; 1951- $178; 1952 - $575; 1953 - $181; 1954 - $161; 1955 - $436; Total $1,855.

No adjustment has been made for any income taxes payable by shareholders on capital gains distributions and dividends reinvested in shares.

1949	1950	1951	1952	1953	1954	1955
$ 201	$ 286	$ 372	$ 403	$ 501	$ 572	$ 649
$ 467	$ 753	$ 1,125	$ 1,528	$ 2,029	$ 2,601	$ 3,250
5,700	6,900	8,100	9,300	10,500	11,700	12,900
$ 6,167	$ 7,653	$ 9,225	$10,828	$12,529	$14,301	$16,150
$ 5,506	$ 6,863	$ 8,404	$ 9,432	$10,113	$14,237	$16,941
218	340	548	1,152	1,430	2,005	2,592
$ 5,724	$ 7,203	$ 8,952	$10,584	$11,543	$16,242	$19,533
425	790	1,237	1,753	2,272	3,511	4,790
$ 6,149	$ 7,993	$10,189	$12,337	$13,815	$19,753	$24,323

CONTRACTUAL PLAN TABLES

Under Section (j) of the Statement of Policy, hypothetical tables used by contractual plan company underwriters in supplemental sales literature must conform to Sample Tables 3 and 4 on the following pages.

Use Highest Sales Charge

These tables are prepared on the basis of an assumed investment of $10 monthly. This is to meet the requirement that such tables must be prepared on the basis of assumed investments involving the smallest permissible monthly payment and carrying the largest sales charge. Anyone wishing to do so may also include in sales literature containing tables such as these, additional tables or summaries based on larger monthly payments and carrying smaller sales charges; but no such additional tables or summaries may be used except when published in the same literature that contains tables on the basis of the largest sales charge.

Summary Option

The sample tables contain summary results. Such summaries are not required. They are included in the samples simply to make clear that, at the minimum, any such summaries must include at least the following: total payments, total dividends reinvested, total investment cost, total capital gains reinvested, and total liquidating value.

Where a particular type of contractual plan does not wholly fit the details of the samples, such tables may be adapted to be applicable to the particular plan being shown. However, the overall format and text of the tables must be followed as closely as possible.

Sample Table 3　Illustration of a twenty year contractual plan for investment in _____

This illustration is in terms of an assumed investment of $10 per month (minimum monthly payment plan) for ten years, with dividends reinvested and capital gains distributions accepted in shares, followed by an additional ten years during which dividends from investment income and distributions from capital gains on accumulated shares continue to be received in shares.

The period covered, from January 1, 1938 to December 31, 1957, was one of generally rising common stock prices. The results shown should not be considered as a representation of the dividend income or capital gain or loss which may be realized from an investment made in the fund today. A program of the type illustrated does not assure a profit or protect against depreciation in declining markets.

Accumulation period (1st through 10 years)

Year end	Monthly payments Annually	Monthly payments Cumulative	Annual div'd. income reinvested	Total cumulative cost (a)	Deductions Sales charge	Deductions Custodian fee	Balance invested after deductions Annually	Balance invested after deductions Cumulative	Annual capital gains dists. reinvested	Value of accumulated shares	Total shares accumulated
1938	$130.00*	$130.00	$1.44	$131.44	$65.00*	$3.25*	$61.87	$61.87	$1.08	$43.40	6.9
1939	120.00	250.00	5.12	256.56	4.80	3.00	117.32	179.19	1.16	179.17	25.6
1940	120.00	370.00	6.93	383.49	4.80	3.00	119.13	298.32	9.76	320.97	44.5
1941	120.00	490.00	13.39	516.88	4.80	3.00	125.59	423.91	9.03	439.68	64.6
1942	120.00	610.00	25.38	662.76	4.80	3.00	138.08	561.99	6.74	529.49	86.3
1943	120.00	730.00	31.58	814.34	4.80	3.00	143.78	705.77	10.87	743.62	111.1
1944	120.00	850.00	38.69	973.03	4.80	3.00	150.89	856.66	23.43	1,047.76	133.4
1945	120.00	970.00	42.19	1,135.22	4.80	3.00	154.39	1,011.05	41.51	1,373.90	156.6
1946	120.00	1,090.00	43.32	1,298.54	4.80	3.00	155.62	1,166.57	84.21	1,817.35	181.5
1947	110.00	1,200.00	45.89	1,454.43	4.40	2.75	148.74	1,315.31	79.87	1,872.27	205.0
			$254.43		$107.80	$30.00			$267.66		

(a) Reflects the cumulative total of monthly payments, plus the cumulative amount of income dividends reinvested.

*Under the terms of this plan, out of the initial payment of $20, $10 is deducted as a sales charge, with $5 being deducted as a sales charge from each of the next 11 payments. Additional deductions include $.50 from the initial payment, and $.25 from each of the next 11 payments for custodian fees, with $1.32 also being deducted, from the initial payment only, for Federal issuance tax. Total deductions from the first 12 payments equal $69.57, or 53.5% of the total of the first 12 monthly payments. If all of the first 10 years' payments are made, total sales charge and other deductions amount to 11.5% of the total agreed payments.

266

Retained investment period (11th through 20th years—distributions accepted in shares)

Year ended	Annual div'd. income reinvested	Total cumulative cost (b)	Deductions Sales charge	Deductions Custodian fee	Balance invested after deductions Annually	Balance invested after deductions Cumulative	Annual capital gains dists. reinvested	Value of accumulated shares	Total shares accumulated
1948	$ 60.53	$1,514.96	—	$ 2.40	$ 58.13	$1,373.44	$ 44.04	$1,805.10	216.9
1949	71.70	1,586.66	—	2.40	69.30	1,442.74	39.04	1,872.10	229.9
1950	91.25	1,677.91	—	2.40	88.85	1,531.59	26.19	2,178.45	243.4
1951	98.94	1,776.85	—	2.40	96.54	1,629.13	37.70	2,452.40	257.8
1952	104.91	1,881.76	—	2.40	102.51	1,730.64	66.38	2,752.56	274.9
1953	111.78	1,993.54	—	2.40	109.38	1,840.02	70.61	3,052.82	292.4
1954	118.70	2,112.24	—	2.40	116.30	1,956.32	69.27	3,107.43	311.0
1955	129.30	2,241.54	—	2.40	126.90	2,083.22	100.60	4,064.16	330.4
1956	145.51	2,387.05	—	2.40	143.11	2,226.33	148.69	4,692.64	352.5
1957	158.78	2,545.83	—	2.40	156.38	2,382.71	162.41	4,894.43	376.7
	$1,091.40			$24.00			$765.00		

(b) Based on total cumulative cost at beginning of 1948 of $1,454.53, plus income dividends reinvested for the period 1948-1957. No allowance has been made for any income taxes payable by planholders on capital gains distributions and dividends reinvested in shares for the 20-year period.

Summary

		Shares
Total Payments	$1,200.00	141
Income Dividends Reinvested	1,345.83	135
		276
Total Investment Cost	$2,545.83	
Capital Gains Distributions Reinvested	$1,032.00	100
Total Liquidating Value (Dec. 31, 1957)	$4,894.43	376

267

Sample Table 4   Illustration of a twenty year contractual plan for investment in

This illustration is in terms of an assumed investment of $10 per month (minimum monthly payment plan) for ten years, with dividends reinvested and capital gains distributions accepted in shares, followed by an additional ten years during which dividends from investment income and distributions from capital gains on accumulated shares are received in cash.

The period covered, from January 1, 1938 to December 31, 1957, was one of generally rising common stock prices. The results shown should not be considered as a representation of the dividend income or capital gain or loss which may be realized from an investment made in the fund today. A program of the type illustrated does not assure a profit or protect against depreciation in declining markets.

Accumulation period (1st through 10th years)

Year end	Monthly payments Annually	Monthly payments Cumulative	Annual div'd income reinvested	Total cumulative cost (a)	Deductions Sales charge	Deductions Custodian fee	Balance invested after deductions Annually	Balance invested after deductions Cumulative	Annual capital gains dists. reinvested	Value of accumulated shares	Total shares accumulated
1938*	$130.00*	$130.00	$1.44	$131.44	$65.00*	$3.25*	$61.87	$61.87	$1.08	$43.40	6.9
1939	120.00	250.00	5.12	256.56	4.80	3.00	117.32	179.19	1.16	179.17	25.6
1940	120.00	370.00	6.93	383.49	4.80	3.00	119.13	298.32	9.76	320.97	44.5
1941	120.00	490.00	13.39	516.88	4.80	3.00	125.59	423.91	9.03	439.68	64.6
1942	120.00	610.00	25.38	662.76	4.80	3.00	138.08	561.99	6.74	529.49	86.3
1943	120.00	730.00	31.58	814.34	4.80	3.00	143.78	705.77	10.87	743.62	111.1
1944	120.00	850.00	38.69	973.03	4.80	3.00	150.89	856.66	23.43	1,047.76	133.4
1945	120.00	970.00	42.19	1,135.22	4.80	3.00	154.39	1,011.05	41.51	1,373.90	156.6
1946	120.00	1,090.00	43.32	1,298.54	4.80	3.00	155.62	1,166.57	84.21	1,817.35	181.5
1947	110.00	1,200.00	45.89	1,454.43	4.40	2.75	148.74	1,315.31	79.87	1,872.27	205.0
			$254.43		$107.80	$30.00			$267.66		

(a) Reflects the cumulative total of monthly payments, plus the cumulative amount of income dividends reinvested.

*Under the terms of this plan, out of the initial payment of $20, $10 is deducted as a sales charge, with $5 being deducted as a sales charge from each of the next 11 payments. Additional deductions include $.50 from the initial payment, and $.25 from each of the next 11 payments for custodian fees, with $1.32 also being deducted, from the initial payment only, for Federal issuance tax. Total deductions from the first 12 payments equal $69.57, or 53.5% of the total of the first 12 monthly payments. If all of the first 10 years' payments are made, total sales charge and other deductions amount to 11.5% of the total agreed payments.

No allowance has been made for any income taxes payable by planholders on capital gains distributions and dividends reinvested in shares during the first 10 years.

Retained investment period (11th through 20th years—distributions received in cash)

Year ended	Total cumulative cost	Dividends from investment income	Deductions Sales charge	Deductions Custodian fee	Net dividends from investment income received in cash	Capital gains received in cash	Value of accumulated shares	Total shares held
1948	$1,454.43	$ 59.47	—	$ 2.40	$ 57.07	$ 43.06	$1,706.16	205.0
1949	1,454.43	66.63	—	2.40	64.25	35.89	1,669.25	205.0
1950	1,454.43	79.98	—	2.40	77.58	22.56	1,835.35	205.0
1951	1,454.43	82.03	—	2.40	79.63	30.76	1,950.19	205.0
1952	1,454.43	82.03	—	2.40	79.63	51.26	2,052.73	205.0
1953	1,454.43	82.03	—	2.40	79.63	51.26	2,140.90	205.0
1954	1,454.43	82.03	—	2.40	79.63	47.16	2,048.63	205.0
1955	1,454.43	84.08	—	2.40	81.68	64.60	2,522.33	205.0
1956	1,454.43	89.20	—	2.40	86.80	90.23	2,729.45	205.0
1957	1,454.43	91.25	—	2.40	88.85	92.28	2,663.83	205.0
		$798.75		$24.00	$774.75	$529.06		

Summary

		Shares
Total Payments	$1,200.00	141
Income Dividends Reinvested	254.43	32
Total Investment Cost	$1,454.43	173
Capital Gains Distributions Reinvested	$ 267.66	32
Total Liquidating Value (Dec. 31, 1947)	$1,872.27	205

Accidents
  public relations concerning, 52
Account executive, 113–114
  functions of, 113
  qualifications for, 114
  selection of, 113
Account solicitation
  ethics in, 127
Account supervisor, 113–114
  see also Account executive
Accuracy, 87
Acquisition of new business, 105–110
Advertising
  agencies, 84
  budget, 45
  choice between, and public relations, 4
  claims, 120–121
  definition, 3
  during strikes, 40
  for fashion, 60
  for foreign clients, 115
  guide rules, 121
  on radio, 26
  as related to commercial public relations, 45, 47
  on television, 121
  for tourism, 57, 83–85
Agency
  advertising, 84
  governmental, 3
    polls for, 123
    scrutiny by, 119
    strength, 109

  tourism, 87
  travel, 83–84
American Stock Exchange, 34
Amusement business, 95
Announcement of an important news event, 21
  pertinent case exercises, 143, 144
Annual report
  contents, 34, 35
  example, 183–186 (Appendix B)
  for health and welfare institutions, 76
  need for, 34, 35
  pictures, use in, 112
Appearance, of account executive, 114
Appetite, prodigious, of radio and television, 25
Approach
  to editors, 84
  to prospective clients, 108–109
Associated Press (AP), 22
ASTA (American Society of Travel Agents), 83
Attitude, public, 68
Audience, film, 95–96

Banker, 53
Banks, 30, 53
  pertinent case exercise, 176
  run on, 54
"Blue Sky" laws, 29
Brainwashing, 126
Broadcasting medium, dependence of public on, 25

index

Building an image, 119–120
Business
    amusement, 95
    entertainment, 95
    European, 114–117
    favorable public concept of, 2
    new, 105–110
    old, 105
Business community, 24
    attitude towards public relations, 126
Business Week, 24
By-line column, 22

Campaign
    advertising, for foreign tourism, 83–85
    fund raising, 73–78
    mailing, 77
    public relations, 2
    public relations for foreign tourism, 83–85
    publicity, 49, 61
    television, 97–101
Candidates, 97–101
Captions for photographs, 19
Case exercises, 133–180 (Appendix A)
Causes, mass-motivated, 125
Cerebral Palsy Association, 67
Charges, consultative, 124–125
Charity, 65
Circulation, magazine, 23
Claims, advertising, 120–121
Client
    evaluation, 122–123
    getting, 105–109
    holding, 109–110
    industrial, 38–40
    losing, 112–113
    political, 98–100
    prospective, 122–123
    rejection, 122–123
    reports, 109–110
    responsibility, 51
Client-practitioner relationship, 107, 125–126
Columbia University, 19
Commercial public relations, 2–3, 45–61
    budget, 45
    compared with advertising, 45
    definition, 45
Commercials, television, 96
Commission agreement, 123
Communications
    ethical level of, 20
    growth of systems, 1
    technique, 107
Community Chest, 68–69
Company ownership, 30
Competition, 112
Conference, press, 21–22
    see also Press conference
Confidence of public in media, 107
Considerations, ethical with client, 125
Consultative charges, 124–125
Consumer, 24, 30, 45, 48, 120, 121
Consumer goods, 120
Consumer press, 31, 32, 38, 47
    use of photographs in, 48
Convention, sales, 50–51
Copy, 85, 119
Corporate character, how to establish, 38
Corporate giving, 66, 68–70
Corporate reputation, 127
Coverage
    editorial, 8
    press in financial public relations, 35
    range, 17
    television, 97, 100
Credibility, 127
Credulity, 95, 101–102, 121

Daily newspapers, 48
    use for fashion publicity, 60
    use for travel publicity, 84–85
Deadline for feature acceptance, 20
Defamation, 122
Demand, seasonal, 46
Departments of newspapers, 17–18
Dinners, fund-raising, 77
Diplomacy, 81
Discretion
    editorial, 119
    in handling governmental accounts, 93
Displays, 47
Documentary, 40–41

Donor
   corporate, 69–70
      pertinent case exercise, 162–163
   individual, 66, 68, 71–73

Economic literature, 92
Editor
   explanatory note to, 17
   feature, 20
   gifts to, 48–49
   placing a story with, 17
Editor & Publisher Year Book, 22
Educational institutions, 68
Elections, television use in, 97–101
Embassy literature, 91–92
Embassy newsletter, 91–92
Entertainment, business, 95
Enticement, client, 127
Environment
   commercial, 120–121
   ethical, of business, 120
Esquire, 57
Ethical level of communications, 20
Ethics, 119–128
   gifts, 48–49
   junkets, 57
   pertinent case exercises, 179, 180
European business, 114–117
European Common Market, 8, 116, 117
European travel, 59
Evaluation of prospective client, 122–123
Excitement level, 110
Exclusivity, 20
Exercises, pertinent cases, 4–5, 26–27, 41–42, 61–62, 78–79, 93–94, 104, 117, 128, 133–180 (Appendix A)
Experience, 114
Exploitation of radio and television, 25–26
Exporting public relations, 114–117

Fact sheet, 31, 49
"Fair return", 51
Familiarity with newspapers, 7
Fashion publicity, 59–61
   pertinent case exercise, 169–170
Feature editor, 20

Features
   definition of, 20
   how to write, 20
   story potential, 31
   structure of, 20
Federal Communications Commission, 101
Fees, formula for, 124–125
Film audience, 95–96
Films, industrial, 40–41
Financial community, 2, 30, 31
Financial newspaper, 24
Financial press, 31, 32
Financial public relations, 2, 29–41
   definition, 29
   pertinent case exercises, 145, 148
Financial statement, 76
Foreign Agents Registration Act, 85–86, 211–218 (Appendix F)
Foreign dignitaries, 89–91
Foreign information program, 86–89
Foreign tourism account, prospectus for, 221–240 (Appendix G)
Formula for fees, 124–125
Fortune, 24
Foundations
   history of, 70
   solicitation to, 71
Free-lance photographers, 23
Free-lance writers, 23
Freudian therapy, 125
Function of public relations, 107
Fund-raising, 3, 65–78
   campaign, 124
   dinners, 77
   letters, 76–77
   literature, 76
   pertinent case exercises, 156–157, 160–161
   volunteers for, 66, 78
Funds, private sources of, 66

Gifts to editors, 48–49
Give-aways, 77
Government information office, 126
Governmental agency, 3
   polling for, 123
   scrutiny by, 119

index

Governmental public relations, 2–3, 81–93
 pertinent case exercises, 166–167
Grammatical errors, avoidance of, 19

Harper's Bazaar, 60
Health institutions, 68
Holiday, 57
Human credulity, 95, 101–102, 121
Human interest, 20, 23, 87

Identity for fund-raising cause, 75
Image
 concept of, 119
 creation of, 119
 pertinent case exercise, 146–147
 of practitioner, 126–128
Impact
 of magazines, 23
 of television, 97
Importing a product, 115–116
 pertinent case exercise, 140–141
Individual consumer, 121
Individual television station, 97
Industrial client, 38–40
Industrial films, 40–41
Industrial psychology, 126
Industrial public relations, 2, 29–41
 definition, 29
 pertinent case exercises, 136–137, 138–
  139, 177–178
Infiltration of radio and television by pub-
 lic relations practitioner, 25
Information office, government, 82, 126
Institutional public relations, 2–3, 65–78
Institutions
 educational, 68
 health, 68
 religious, 73
 welfare, 68
Insurance company, 54
Interest, human, 20, 23, 87
Interim report, 34
Investing community, 29, 33
Invitation to press party, 22

Journal, trade, 24
Junkets, 57

Label, product, 47
Labor relations, 39–40, 126
 pertinent case exercise, 149
Land development, 55
 pertinent case exercise, 152–153
Lead, 17
Legislative problem, 123
Letter
 to foreign prospect, 115
 fund-raising, 76–77
 to prospective client, 109
Level of excitement, 110
Life, 23, 57
Listed corporation, 33–34
Literacy, 7
Literature
 economic, 92
 embassy, 91–92
 fund-raising, 76–77
 travel, 59, 85
Lobbying, 123

Magazines, 23–24
 consumer, 23
 departments, 23
 difference from newspapers, 23
 function, 23–24
 impact, 23
 and television, 103
 trade, 24
Mailing campaign, for fund raising, 77
Manufacturer, 120
Mass conditioning, 1
Mass-motivated causes, 125
Mass selling, 120
Media, 26
 magazines, 23–24
 newspapers, 7–16
 pertinent case exercise, 168
 radio, 25–26
 selection of, 26
 television, 25–26, 95–103
Merchandising, 48
Message, sales, 3
Motion pictures, 95
Motivation for contributions, 72
Mutual funds, 36–37

National Press Club, 89
Nation's Business, 24
Networks, television, 97, 100
New business
  acquisition of, 105–110
  solicitation for, 105–110
New issue, publicity for, 31–33
New product, 112
  pertinent case exercises, 135, 144
New York Stock Exchange, 34
New York Times, 32
News release
  see release
News, spot, 8
News story, planting or placing, 20–22
News syndicate, 22
  functions, 22
  how to service, 22
News, television, 97
Newsletter, embassy, 91–92
Newspaper departments, 48, 57, 60, 84
Newspaper editor, 17
  see also editor
Newspapers
  categories of, 8
  daily, 7
    "A" list, 9–12
    "B" list, 13–16
    departments, 17–18
    honesty of, 7
    as a medium, 26
    regional, 7
    Sunday, 55
    weekly, 8
Newsweek, 23
Non-profit organizations, 3

Objectivity, 106–107
Overseas Press Club, 89

Paid space, 3
Paid time, 3
Paine, Thomas, 1–2
Party, press, 49, 21–22
  see also Press party
Personality
  corporate, 33, 38, 39

industrial, 38, 39
one's own, 1
Philanthropy, 65, 68–69
Photo desk, 21
Photographs
  in fashion publicity, 60–61
  in product publicity, 48
  in real estate publicity, 55
  in travel publicity, 84
Photography
  during strikes, 40
  industrial, 39
Pictures
  accompanying releases, 19
  in annual reports, 112
  new product, 112
Placement, 20–21, 22, 90
  in product publicity, 47
  seasonal, 46, 57
Plant tours for security analysts, 35
Planting a story, 20–21, 22, 90
  see placement
Playboy, 57
Point of sale, 47
Policy, 81, 106
  formulation of, in communications, 2
  practitioner part in making, 107
Policy level, practitioner on, 125
Political client, 98–100
  pertinent case exercise, 173–174
Politics, television role in, 97–101
Polls, 123–124
  use of, for radio and television, 123
Practitioner, 47
  conservatism becoming to, 127
  image, 126–128
  public concept of, 126
  role of, 7–26
    in commercial public relations, 45–61
    during strikes, 39–40
    in financial public relations, 31, 33
    at sales conventions, 50–51
    at stockholders' meetings, 37
Practitioner-client relationship, 125
Presentation
  examples, 195–197, 201–208, 225–240
    (Appendixes D, E and G)

index

Presentation *(cont.)*
  to foundation, 71
  to prospective client, 108–109
Press
  appraisal of, 8
  consumer, 31, 32, 38
  daily, importance of, 47
  financial, 31
  trade, 24, 31
Press bureau, 82
Press conference
  advance release, 21–22
  for foreign dignitaries, 89–90
  notification, 21
  organization of, 21–22
  pertinent case exercise, 142
  time, 22
Press kit, 22
Press party, 21–22, 49
  atmosphere, 22
  invitations, 22
  organizations, 22
  pertinent case exercise, 143
  press kit for, 22
  product introduction at, 21
  seating, 22
Press release
  see release
Press, trade, 24
Private ownership, 30
Problem
  client's, 105–106, 108
  legislative, 123
Product, 45–49
  foreign, 115–116
  new, 48
  pertinent case exercises, 154, 175
  press party introduction, 21
Product publicity, 45–49
  in consumer press, 47
  on radio and television, 47
Program, public relations
  for an appliance account, 201–208 (Appendix E)
  for a wine account, 195–197 (Appendix D)
Proofreading, 19

Propaganda, 81
Prospect, 108
  foreign, 115
  solicitation of, 105–110, 114–117
    ethics in, 127
Prospective client
  see prospect
Prospectus, 107
  for foreign tourism account, example, 221–240 (Appendix G)
    covering letter, 221–223
    cultural aspect, 237
    economic aspect, 234–236
    political aspect, 238–240
Proxy battle, 37
Psychology, as effecting one's personality, 1
Psychology, industrial, 126
Public, 26
Public awareness, 97, 103
Public ownership, 30
Public relations
  advertising, relationship to, 3–4
  commercial, 45–61
  definition of, 1–2
  effect on general population, 1
  financial, 1–2, 29–41
  function, 107
  governmental, 2–3, 81–93
  industrial, 1–2, 29–41
  institutional, 2–3, 65–78
  introduction to, 1
  methods, 1
  objective of, 2
  practitioner, role of, 7–26
  tools, 1
Public relations campaign
  categories, 2–3
    commercial, 3
    financial, 2
    governmental, 3
    industrial, 2
    institutional, 3
  definition, 2
Publicity
  basic currency of, 7
  business of, 2

dominant role of, 3
in financial public relations, 36
for foreign clients, 90, 93
in fund raising, 74
technique, 2
Publicity campaign, 49
Publicly-owned companies, 30
Publishing, effect of television on, 97, 103

Qualifications for public relations account executive, 114

Radio
effect on advertising, 25–26
effect on public relations, 25–26
use in product publicity, 47
Radio and television use, for foreign clients, 90, 93
Reader's Digest, 23, 32
Reading
newspapers for client prospects, 109
requirements for practitioner, 88–89, 114
supplemental, 5, 27, 42–43, 62–63, 79, 94, 104, 117, 128
Real estate publicity, 55–56
Reality, 121
Red Cross, 66, 73
Relationship, client-practitioner, 125–126
Release, 17, 20
accompanying note to editor, 19
best publication potential, 18
example, 189–191 (Appendix C)
how to write, 19
ideal, 17
most successful, 17
necessity for proofreading, 19
for press conference, 21
source, status, validity made clear, 17
use in daily press, 19
what to avoid in writing, 19, 20
who to send to, 18
Religious institutions, 73
Report
annual, 34, 35
in fund-raising, 76
to client, 109–110

interim, 34, 35
to stockholders, 34, 35
Reputation, corporate, 127
Responsibility
civic, 127
client, 51
editor, 17
practitioner, 120–121
for releases, 112

Sales convention, 50–51
entertainment, 50
pertinent case exercises, 133–139
releases for, 51
role of practitioner, 50–51
speakers, 50
Sales message, 3
Sales personnel, 49
Saturday Evening Post, 103
Seasonal demand, 46
Seasonal placement
merchandising connection, 46
for tourism, 57
SEC
see Securities Exchange Commission
SEC Statement of Policy, 243–269 (Appendix H)
Securities Exchange Commission, 29–32
regulations act, 30
statement of policy, 30, 243–269 (Appendix H)
Security analyst, 35, 37
Sensationalism, 19
Service and utility companies, 51–52
Solicitation
ethics of, 127
for new business, 105–110
for overseas business, 114–117
Solicitation of funds
from corporations, 68–71
from foundations, 71
from individuals, 71–72
methods of, 73–78
Source of release material, 17
Spokesman, 112
Spot news, 8
Staff for public relations account, 113–114

index

Statement
  annual, 34–35
  interim, 34–35
  see also Report
Statement, financial, 76
Stockholder, 29, 30
  mailing, 34
  meeting, 37–38
  report, 34–35
Story
  handling, 17, 20
  planting or placing, 20–21
Strikes
  public relations during, 39–40
Sunday newspapers
  for real estate publicity, 55
  for travel publicity, 84–85
Supplement
  advertising, 85
  travel, 84–85
Supplemental reading, 5, 27, 42–43, 62–63,
    79, 94, 104, 117, 128
Syndicated columns, 8
  fashion, 60
Syntax, 19

Television
  addictive patterns of, 96
  campaign, 98–99
  candidates on, 97–101
  commercials, 96
  educational values of, 96
  impact of, 25–26
  individual stations, 97
  and magazines, 103
  networks, 97, 100
  news, 97
  pertinent case exercise, 171–172
  positive aspects of, 96
  role in politics, 97–101
  use in product publicity, 47
Tie-ins, 58
Time, 23

Tools, public relations, 1
Tourism, 56–59
  agency, 87
  foreign, 82–85
  pertinent case exercises, 150–151, 164–
    165
Trade association, 36
Trade fair, 39
Trade press, 24, 31, 36
  definition, 24
  fashion, 60
  function, 24
  servicing, 24
Travel agency, 83–84
Travel copy, 85
Travel, European, 59
Travel literature, 59, 83–85
Travel section, 84–85
Treasury Act of 1943, 82
Truth, 119, 121

Understanding, 81
United Fund, 74, 75
United Press International (UPI), 22
Urban redevelopment, 55
U.S. News & World Report, 23
USO, 66
Utility and service companies, 51–52
  pertinent case exercise, 155
  stockholders in, 52

Vanity, 73, 112
Variety, 24
Visiting foreign dignitaries, 89–91
Vogue, 60
Volunteers for fund raising, 66, 78

Wall Street Journal, 24
Welfare institutions, 68
Wire service, 17
Women's Wear Daily, 24, 60
Word, 2, 7, 19